American Fiction

Historical and Critical Essays

Daniel Aaron
John Cawelti
Melvin J. Friedman
Joseph Katz
Harrison T. Meserole
Donald Pizer
Milton R. Stern
Ronald Sukenick
Darwin T. Turner
Linda W. Wagner
Viola Hopkins Winner

Edited, with an introduction, by
James Nagel

Northeastern University Press, Boston
Twayne Publishers, Boston

1977

Published by Northeastern University Press and Distributed by
Twayne Publishers, a Division of G.K. Hall and Company.

Library of Congress Catalog Number: 77-088848
ISBN 0-8057-9006-3

Contents

In Memory of
Ruth Sullivan

Introduction

In anticipating the national Bicentennial celebration in the United States, and in contemplating the appropriate observance of this event on the campus of Northeastern University, the academic community, led by President Kenneth G. Ryder, came to the support of a proposal to host a program devoted to the study of American fiction. Residing in a city which served for more than two centuries as the literary center of America, and as sponsoring institution for the scholarly journal *Studies in American Fiction*, the university seemed an appropriate host for a serious discussion of the history of American fiction and the contributions it has made to the national culture. As a result, under the direction of the editorial board of *Studies in American Fiction*, the university invited eleven scholars, all at the forefront of their specializations, to deliver formal papers and participate in the continuing dialogue which constituted "American Fiction: A Bicentennial Symposium," which was held in Boston on October 15-16, 1976. This volume is the commemorative record of that symposium.

The essays here printed represent, with only minor alterations, the papers presented at this program; the concluding section, "A Conversation in Boston," is an attempt to record a small portion of the informal discussion which continued for two days. In accord with the spirit of an historical observance, the papers and discussions retained a consistently broad focus, presenting assessments and observations rather than hermeneutic analysis. Within this perspective, the essays as a group cover the spectrum of the development of fiction in America from the "fictive points" of early colonial narratives to the "post-contemporary" nature of surfiction and other movements in the 1970s. In addition, there are four discussions of somewhat more specialized subjects within this historical framework: the use of history and myth by American Black writers, the occasional novels by writers primarily involved in other vocations, the interplay between fictive and pictorial art forms in America, and a consideration of the concepts of fame and celebrity in the lives and works of important American writers.

The first essay, "Some Notes on Early American Fiction: Kelroy Was There," is by Harrison T. Meserole, Professor of English and Chairman of the American Studies Program at Pennsylvania State University. Professor Meserole's work in early American literature is sufficiently well-known among serious students of literature to preclude extended comment. His edition of *Seventeenth-Century American Poetry* has been the standard volume in that period since its publication in 1968. His four volume anthology published the following year, *American Literature: Tradition and Innovation*, which he edited with Brom Weber and Walter Sutton, has become an important anthology providing reliable texts of significant literary works. His most recent book, the third edition of *A Guide to English & American Literature*, on which he collaborated with F. W. Bateson, has already taken its place as a major source of information on standard editions and critical resources for major authors. His service for nearly a decade as editor of the indispensible *MLA International Bibliography*, and his continuing work as editor of *Seventeenth-Century News* and on the editorial board of *Studies in American Fiction*, combine with his own scholarly investigations to produce a memorable assessment of the study of early American fiction. His call for more comprehensive study of American magazines before 1850, which would retrieve such delightful tales as William Dunlop's "It Might Have Been Better! It Might Have Been Worse," for a study of early nineteenth-century gift books and annuals, and, perhaps most importantly, for a reassessment of the early American novel, may well provide the impetus for a rejuvenation of scholarly activity in those areas. His own discussion of *Kelroy: A Novel*, by that "lady of Pennsylvania," Rebecca Rush, provides a rich demonstration of the important historical contributions to be gained by such investigation.

Milton R. Stern is similarly provocative in his essay "American Values and Romantic Fiction." Professor Stern, recently named the first Distinguished Alumni Professor at the University of Connecticut in recognition of his teaching and research, is a familiar figure in American literary scholarship. In *The Fine Hammered Steel of Herman Melville* (1957), which explores the theme of the idealized quest, and subsequently in *The Golden Moment: The Novels of F. Scott Fitzgerald* (1970), which examines the "uses of history, the American identity, the moral reconstruction of the American past," the penetrating intelligence and broad cultural implications which mark his present essay were abundantly evident. In "American Values and Romantic Fiction," Stern challenges the assumption that the thrust of Romantic literature derives solely from Emersonian millennialism and posits a counter thesis which emphasizes an ideological unity among the major writers of the period based on a far more conservative philosophy than the current critical record would admit. His essay has implications which range beyond the Romantic period, and which require exploration in depth of the political concepts in American literature, and he is at work on a full study which will expand the concerns of this essay into a critical and historical book.

In "Eroticism in American Literary Realism," Joseph Katz examines what has long been accepted as a theoretical paradox in Realistic fiction, that writers who attempted to present life with fidelity to actuality had ignored an essential element of common human experience: sexuality. Basing his analysis on Edwin H. Cady's assessment in "The Howells Nobody Knows" that sexual concerns are more prevalent in Realism than has previously been acknowledged, Professor Katz goes on to assert that "sex is approached honestly, openly, and directly from the beginnings of realism in American literature" and to document this fact in the fiction of John W. DeForest, Stephen Crane, Theodore Dreiser, Harold Frederic, Frank Norris, and other seminal writers. Katz's demonstration that not only is erotic love a continuing subject in serious fiction of the period but that it is handled with balance and a great deal of artistic control makes an important contribution to the understanding of the aesthetic of Realism as well as its handling of delicate subjects. Students of American fiction will, of course, be familiar with Katz's innumerable contributions to his field, especially his editorship of the *Stephen Crane Newsletter* and such volumes as *The Portable Stephen Crane*, *Stephen Crane in the West and Mexico*, and *Stephen Crane: Centenary Essays*. As Professor of English at the University of South Carolina, where he also serves as the editor of *Proof: Yearbook of American Bibliographical and Textual Studies*, Joseph Katz is continuing his work in this area. He is now engaged on a new biography of Frank Norris and on the *Centenary Edition of the Works of Frank Norris*, to be published by J. Faust.

No one who begins a serious study of American literature can be long innocent of the work of Donald Pizer, Pierce Butler Professor of English at Newcomb College of Tulane University. In over fifty articles in the major scholarly journals, and in such central books as *Hamlin Garland's Early Work and Career* (1960), *Realism and Naturalism in Nineteenth-Century American Literature* (1966), and *The Novels of Frank Norris* (1966), Professor Pizer has established his credentials as one of the leading American scholars of literary Naturalism. His essay in this volume, "American Literary Naturalism: The Example of Dreiser," is most closely related to his recent book *The Novels of Theodore Dreiser: A Critical Study* (1976), which explores the relationship of the sources and compositional history of Dreiser's novels to their artistry and themes. His concern for the aesthetic skill of American Naturalism in this book is reflected in his provocative essay, in which he attempts to modify the traditional view that works within the Naturalistic mode may contain interesting philosophical assumptions but are regretable examples of fictional art. Pizer finds an implicit antagonism to Naturalism as emerging from its deterministic philosophy, from the association of the movement in the 1930s with the Communist party, and from an "increasingly refined view of the aesthetic complexity of fiction." By using Dreiser as an example against which to assess the validity of these antagonistic assumptions, Pizer finds Naturalism to be one of Dreiser's strengths as a novelist and *Jennie Gerhardt* and *An American Tragedy* to be both artistically and philosophically satisfying manifestations of Naturalistic art which exhibit traditional humanistic values as well as the contemporary doctrine of determinism.

Linda W. Wagner's approach in "Tension and Technique: The Years of Greatness" is personal and comprehensive. In looking back on modern writers from 1912 to 1940, she explores the "exuberance, innovation, temerity, the compulsion to create a new consciousness, in modes and patterns that were equally new" which dominate the period, especially as manifested in a sense of nationalism and artistic freedom. On looking at the writers of the period, particularly Ernest Hemingway, F. Scott Fitzgerald, William Faulkner, John Steinbeck, John Dos Passos, Gertrude Stein, and Nathaniel West, she is struck by the immense talent of the period and by its aesthetic depth. Professor Wagner, who teaches in the English Department at Michigan State University, has long been a leading figure in the poetry of the modernist period. Her most recent books, however, have dealt with American fiction, especially *William Faulkner: Four Decades of Criticism* (1973), *Ernest Hemingway: Five Decades of Criticism* (1974), and *Hemingway and Faulkner: Inventors/Masters* (1976). She is currently at work on a study of John Dos Passos, on a book on Amy Lowell, and on a series of essays on Gertrude Stein.

Melvin J. Friedman began work on "Dislocations of Setting and Word: Notes on American Fiction Since 1950" while lecturing on a Fulbright at the University of Antwerp. After an extended lecture tour through France, Germany, Belgium, Portugal, and Israel, he resumed his position as Professor of Comparative Literature at the University of Wisconsin at Milwaukee. His service as editor of both *Comparative Literature Studies* and *Wisconsin Studies in Contemporary Literature*, and research for such books as *The Vision Obscured: Perceptions of Some Twentieth-Century Catholic Novelists* (1970), *The Added Dimension: The Art and Mind of Flannery O'Connor* (1966), and *William Styron* (1974), as well as his extensive exploration of modern French literature, place him in a position to survey and evaluate the directions of contemporary American fiction. Professor Friedman goes beyond a catalogue of books and events to strike at some of the central philosophical and artistic questions of the last two decades. In surveying the contributions of John Hawkes and William Styron he raises the issue of the definition of the novel. In discussing Saul Bellow (for whom he predicted a Nobel Prize for Literature several months prior to the actual award) and Norman Mailer, he posits some distinctions between their brand of modernism and the subsequent development of postmodernism and surfiction. Ranging through recent developments in the novel with impressive catholicity, he analyses and describes such categories as the academic novel, the Jewish novel, and the Southern novel and goes on to deal with the most recent "literary disruptions" which challenge traditional forms and techniques and yet give a new sense of life and optimism to the novel in America.

Ronald Sukenick, Professor of English and Director of the Creative Writing Program at the University of Colorado, is uniquely qualified to assess the present state of the art of American fiction and to offer some observations on the ways in which that art is being perceived. After the appearance of his controversial but widely praised book on Wallace Stevens in 1967, Professor Sukenick devoted his energies to fiction, publishing *Up* in 1968 and *The Death of the Novel and Other Stories* the following year. His novel *Out*, which appeared in 1973, was noted by the *New York Times Book Review* as one of the best novels of the year. His most recent work, *98.6*, was published in May of 1976 by the Fiction Collective. He is currently working on a series of short stories as well as on a critical study of the theory of fiction. In his essay "Fiction in the Seventies: Ten Digressions on Ten Digressions" Professor Sukenick challenges the critical record of recent American fiction, finding fallacies both in the standard responses to contemporary fiction and in the categories which have been constructed to organize disparate works into coherent units. In the process he offers a definition of fiction, of fictive discourse, as an organic form which is neither mimetic nor hermetic, which has no reference beyond itself, and which requires that criticism endeavor to "defamiliarize the novel, to de-define fiction, as fiction simultaneously creates and decreates itself."

Darwin T. Turner's "Black Fiction: History and Myth" presents the view that until the past decade Afro-American novelists have not fully utilized historical or mythic materials from their culture to improve the image of Black Americans by re-interpreting the past. However, given this creative reluctance, modern scholars have similarly been negligent in not fully exploring those important historical novels which were written and which offer a view of American history which runs counter to the prevailing doctrine. Beginning with Paul Lawrence Dunbar's *The Fanatics* in 1901, Professor Turner reviews by decade the most important historical novels by Black Americans, including works by

Arna Bontemps, Zora Neale Hurston, Frank Yerby, W. E. B. DuBois, Margaret Walker, Ernest Gaines, and Ishmael Reed. He concludes that Black writers, in an atmosphere of ethnic pride and interest in their heritage, have rediscovered the historical novel and have made it into one of the most important contemporary art forms. Professor Turner's observations, presented in October of 1976, have proved prophetic with the enormous success and popularity of Alex Haley's *Roots* as both a novel and television series. As Professor of English and Head of the Afro-American Studies program at the University of Iowa, Darwin Turner has made important contributions to the study of Black literature in America, especially in his books *In a Minor Chord: Three Writers of the Harlem Renaissance, Images of the Negro in America*, and *Black American Literature: Essays, Poetry, Fiction, Drama*. Beyond his scholarship, he has given his counsel to numerous professional groups, serving as President of the College Language Association, as Chairman of the National Council of Teachers of English Committee on the Literature of Minority Groups, and as a member of the Executive Committee of the MLA Ethnic Studies Division. Early in 1977 he participated in the second International Festival of Black and African Arts in Lagos, Nigeria. His current work includes a critical edition of Jean Toomer's *Cane* as well as a volume of Toomer's uncollected works.

Daniel Aaron is Professor of English and Chairman of the Committee on Higher Degrees in the History of American Civilization at Harvard University. He taught at Smith College for many years before returning to Harvard, where his teaching career began. He has also been a visiting professor at the University of Helsinki, Warsaw University, and the University of Sussex as well as serving as a Guggenheim Fellow and as a Fellow at the Center for Behaviorial Studies at Stanford University. His books include *Men of Good Hope: A Story of American Progressives* (1950), the widely acclaimed *Writers on the Left: Episodes in American Literary Communism* (1961), *Emerson: A Modern Anthology*, done with Alfred Kazin, and, most recently, *The Unwritten War: American Writers and the Civil War* (1973), a comprehensive study of the complex and elusive nature of the Civil War as a subject for literature. His essay "The Occasional Novel: American Fiction and the Man of Letters" explores one of the "interstices of literary history," the single novel by men of letters which makes an important ideological contribution but which is often regarded as being outside the flow of American literary history. After a systematic definition of the "occasional novel," with its topical focus and persistent authorial voice, Professor Aaron goes on to discuss in detail several of the most important examples of the genre in American fiction, including Henry Adams' *Democracy*, James Gibbon Huneker's *Painted Veils*, Edmund

Wilson's *I Thought of Daisy*, Kenneth Burke's *Towards a Better Life*, George Santayana's *The Last Puritan*, and Lionel Trilling's *The Middle of the Journey*.

After her influential book *Henry James and the Visual Arts*, Viola Hopkins Winner was widely recognized as a leading scholar of the interactions of the pictorial and verbal arts in America. Most recently Professor of English at Sweet Briar College, Professor Winner has taught at Adelphi College, Hunter College of the City University of New York, and the University of Virginia. Her current research is a book-length study of the British caricaturist Richard Doyle and his literary associates. In her essay "The American Pictorial Vision: Objects and Ideas in Hawthorne, James, and Hemingway," Professor Winner explores the tendency in American fiction for treating epistemological and philosophical themes in terms of visual states. Looking closely at *Islands in the Stream, The House of Seven Gables, The Ambassadors*, among other works, she discovers a propensity for spatial rather than temporal ordering in the American novel and for aesthetic values closely associated with continental and American painting.

As a past President of the Popular Culture Association, John G. Cawelti, Professor of English and Humanities at the University of Chicago, appropriately addresses himself to an attempt to assess those "popular" elements of American literature which influence and effect its cumulative developments. His books on various dimensions of this subject include *Apostles of the Self-Made Man* (1965), a study of the idea of success in America, *The Six-Gun Mystique* (1970), an analysis of the western and its significance in American culture, *Focus on Bonnie and Clyde* (1973), an interpretation of the popular film, and, most recently, *Adventure, Mystery, and Romance* (1976), which develops a theory of popular literature formulas. In "The Writer as Celebrity: Some Aspects of American Literature as Popular Culture" he explores the complex nature of the popular reception of American literature and the ways in which public response has influenced its development. Distinguishing between celebrity, a temporary interest in a writer which goes beyond his literary accomplishments, and fame, the continuing visibility of a writer through the permanent significance of his work, Professor Cawelti explores in these terms the careers of such writers as James Fenimore Cooper, Henry James, Ernest Hemingway, and Norman Mailer.

The concluding section of this volume, "A Conversation in Boston," is an attempt to represent and preserve some of the attendant dialogue occasioned by these eleven papers during the Symposium. It is in many ways inadequate: for reasons of space limitations, it reproduces only a small portion of several hours of comments, questions, and exchanges; it does not adequately reflect the persistent tone of scholarly civility which permeated the atmosphere of the program; and, perhaps most importantly, it does not begin to suggest the ambience of professional energy and stimulation which steadily grew throughout the two days. However, even in its present form, it does record something of the substance and range of the continuing dialogue among the speakers and members of the audience. As an American fiction program, there was a sustained concern for constructing some determination of what is uniquely "American" in American fiction, for its history, origins, and influences, and for its central aesthetic forms, subjects, and role in American culture. The discussion also indicates something of the pervading sense of the Symposium that the papers presented were not ideas in stasis but organic concepts which grew and changed as the program continued through its historical progression. In the comments which followed the readings there was continued development of several topics: the earliest stirrings of fictive instincts in America, the viability of the concept of such movements as Realism and Naturalism, the role of the scholar in literary history, the dominance of the concerns of publishing houses in the publication and availability of important works of American literature. In all its shortcomings, this discussion is offered, as is this volume, as a record of "American Fiction: A Bicentennial Symposium" and as an attempt to preserve a moment of reflection on the literature of the United States on the occasion of its Bicentennial.

This volume and, indeed, the Symposium itself, would not have been possible were it not for the enthusiastic support of Kenneth G. Ryder, President of Northeastern University, who provided a grant which funded both the program and the publication of its papers. Provost Harry T. Allan was generous in offering the assistance of his offices, as were many other members of the university community, especially Paul F. Cowan, whose gracious arrangements and hospitality brightened an already pleasant occasion. William A. Frohlich, Director of Northeastern University Press, and the University Press staff, gave willingly of their time and energy in the preparation of this volume. Many of the English Department graduate students, including Laura Dunn, Lolly Ockerstrom, Donald Flynn, Alan Gifford, and Kitty Meijer, contributed essential support to the program, as did Catherine Ezell, Editorial Assistant for *Studies in American Fiction*, and Mary Elizabeth Leu, journal work-study student. Finally, the Symposium could not have flourished without the efforts of the members of the Department of English, especially Wallace Coyle, Candace K. Brook, Jane Nelson, Robert B. Parker, Stanley Trachtenberg, and Guy L. Rotella, to whom belong no small portion of the existence and satisfaction of this volume.

James Nagel

SOME NOTES ON EARLY AMERICAN FICTION: KELROY WAS THERE

Harrison T. Meserole
Pennsylvania State University

Even before July 4, 1776, the date we are celebrating this year with such *élan* and *éclat*, American fiction had begun to be written and published, followed shortly thereafter by the first American criticism of American fiction. I use both terms—*fiction* and *criticism*—in the full knowledge that to many historians of American literature the phrase "early American fiction and criticism" engenders images not of aesthetics or ideas but instead of something akin to a kitchen midden. Nonetheless, I am convinced that in this Bicentennial year, we stand at a challenging point in our study of eighteenth- and early nineteenth-century fiction and criticism written by earnest, assiduous men and women with astoundingly prolific, if sometimes inept, propensities.

What I intend, therefore, is to propose three directions our studies of early American fiction may take to meet this challenge. Much remains to be done, despite the now impressive number of books and essays on Charles Brockden Brown and a few other early novelists, and despite—perhaps, indeed, because of—Henri Petter's compendious, and I should add, indispensable book published just six years ago.

One thing we must do is explore more fully the contents of our literary and general magazines published before 1850. In this connection, scholars of my generation and, let us hope, some others too, will have made the small linguistic transformation necessary to reveal the mild pun in my title, for those who do take up this gage and begin systematic scanning of these early periodicals will find that Kilroy has been there before you. In this context Kilroy is, of course, *not* the ubiquitous and mysterious and elusive creation of World War II American GI's but is rather a courteously conceived pseudonym for some scholars who have read these early magazines for specific purposes and who have mined real gold: my esteemed friend and colleague, the indefatigable Burton Pollin, who has, I am ready to wager, looked at every page of every American magazine and newspaper (and probably every French and British one as well) published after 1825 in his continuing search for material by and on Edgar Allan Poe; Lewis Leary, and in the field of journalism, Philip Marsh, who have done the same for

Philip Freneau; Ralph Aderman for James Kirke Paulding; and some years ago, Nelson F. Adkins, who searched many an unturned page for Fitz-Greene Halleck; and Kendall Taft, who exhumed among other materials the writings of the early nineteenth-century American drama critic and essayist William Cox, till then (1947) forgotten and now, unfortunately in my opinion, forgotten again. This is by no means an exhaustive list. I mean these six scholars' names to represent four times that number who have enriched the literary history of the United States in part as a result of their study of our early periodicals.

For the most part, too, their work was done without the assistance of indexes or bibliographies. Indeed, Nelson Adkins found that he had to begin such an index to permit him to pursue the work he set out to do. But today such is not the case. I had better say, by next year such will not be the case, for those of us who work in American literature of the late eighteenth and early nineteenth centuries are about to be presented with a major work of reference entitled *An Annotated Bibliography of American Literary Magazines 1741-1850*. Prepared by Professor Jayne K. Kribbs of Temple University, and to be published next year by G. K. Hall of Boston, this long-needed study will name, describe, locate, and provide publication data on every important magazine published during this period of 110 years. More, it will index the names of all authors of pieces published in these magazines; and perhaps most important, it will index the titles of the more than 5,000 stories, tales, sketches, poems, essays, and plays printed in these magazines.

With such a key to our early periodicals, the task of searching them will be relatively simple. Of course we must still look closely at every bit of fiction Kribbs's index leads to, for the habit editors of these early publications had of lifting prose and poetry from English magazines of the period without acknowledgement or attribution continues to make identification and verification necessary preliminary steps. But the material is there waiting for the assiduous and imaginative scholar, perhaps most challengingly for the doctoral candidate searching for a thesis topic in literary history. Perhaps he will not be so fortunate as to uncover a story as important as Charles Brockden Brown's "A Lesson on Concealment; or, Memoirs of Mary Selwyn," only recently brought to light, though Kribbs's index contains a number of references to writings by Brown which must be tracked down and examined. Selection, too, will be important. The verse of the blind poet of New York City, James Nack, which crowded the "Apollo's Corner" and similar magazine "departments" in the early nineteenth century, will be advisedly left in the obscurity in which it has slumbered for a century and a half. The redoubtable Mrs. Emma Embury's prose sketches, which jostled Nack's verse for column space at the same time, may be permitted to occupy the same bed without fear of untoward result.

But we must retrieve from its forgotten niche in one of the longest-lived magazines of the early nineteenth century a delightful tale by William Dunlap, a tale that could well take its place beside Washington Irving's "Stout Gentleman" or "The Art of Book-Making" as a well-conceived, charmingly written, and compact fiction. Dunlap's tale, entitled "It Might Have Been Better! It Might Have Been Worse," reminds one of the myriad Gothic stories that filled the pages of many of our early periodicals. For his subject Dunlap chose one of the best-known mystery plots—the account of two close friends who take an oath that whoever is first to die will return from the grave to impart to his friend "that knowledge of the eternal mystery he so thirsts for." Dunlap's two friends are Peter Prince, bachelor farmer, and John Horner, neighborly married man. Prince dies, and Horner, in a severe melancholy, takes to his bed:

> Suddenly he heard his name pronounced solemnly, and *thrice* "John Horner" was repeated! The curtains were drawn aside, and there stood Peter, in flowing robes, unlike his former guise, and much changed even in countenance, but still *it was Peter Prince!* Horner gazed upon his former friend, and tried to ask for the important communication, but he could only say,
> "Speak!"
> He then saw the vision bend toward the floor, and, rising, pronounce the mysterious words,
> "It might have been better—it might have been worse!"
> Horner started up in bed, exclaiming, "Stay! tell me more!" but the vision was gone. . . .

From classical times to the present this plot has fascinated writers and readers, regardless of the denouement, which has varied from a) the deceased returns but is unable to speak; b) the deceased returns—at the moment of his friend's death; c) the deceased does not return, thus leaving his friend to wonder, and, like the real life situation of Houdini, to persist in the belief that he *will* return; and numerous other variations—all ghostly and Gothic. But Dunlap's impatience with the Gothic was well known, an impatience expressed in clear terms when he wrote the biography of his friend Charles Brockden Brown in 1815.[1] It is not surprising, therefore, to note that Dunlap chose to end his story differently:

> . . . and he saw his wife, standing, with a bowl in her hand.
> "As I live, I saw him!" exclaimed the sick man.
> "Saw who?" asked Mrs. Horner.

"Peter Prince!"

"Nonsense."

"As plain as I see you! He stood just where you are!"

"Well, what did he say?" said the dame.

"He called thrice, 'John Horner! John Horner! John Horner!' He bowed low, and, rising, said, 'It might have been better—it might have been worse!'

"Ha! ha! ha!" almost shouted his wife. "I called you three times before I could make you open your eyes; and, finding that I had knocked over the tin, I stooped for the bowl, and exclaimed, on seeing that it was not broken, 'It might have been better—it might have been worse.' "

John Horner was cured.[2]

As a second project, we must re-examine those numerous literary annuals and gift books which enjoyed a brief but significant time in the early nineteenth-century limelight. We know, of course, that the Irvings and Paulding wrote for them, as did many of the lesser New York literati; so did Nathaniel P. Willis and George Pope Morris and Samuel Woodworth and, later, Hawthorne and Longfellow and Holmes. But there are kernels yet to be gleaned. Tucked away in one of these annuals, so far unexamined, are, for example, another anecdote involving spontaneous combustion; an account of the seventeenth-century English dwarf, Jeffrey Hudson; a piece on the superstitions of New England; and side by side, a retelling of the Flying Dutchman legend and the full text of William Austin's "Peter Rugg, the Missing Man."[3]

Yet our most challenging task, in my judgment, is a reassessment of the early American novel. A quick survey of the scholarship suggests that we are well provided for in two of the four principal *desiderata* for work in the field. In bibliography, Lyle Wright's *American Fiction 1774-1850* (rev. ed. 1969) with the addenda contributed by Wright himself and by other scholars gives us what we need. In literary history, Henri Petter's recent book, *The Early American Novel* (1971), more than adequately surveys the entire field and supplies useful lists of titles and plot synopses of a selected group of early novels. Here, too, we may still read with profit earlier histories by Lillie D. Loshe (1907), Arthur Hobson Quinn (1936), and the first three—perhaps the first four—chapters of Alexander Cowie's *Rise of the American Novel* (1948). But in the other two requirements, we are sorely lacking. Have you tried to find texts for teaching a course in early American fiction? For Brown, yes: *Wieland* and *Edgar Huntly* and *Arthur Mervyn* are available with stimulating introductions by reliable scholars. Brackenridge's *Modern Chivalry*, yes. William Hill Brown's *Power of Sympathy*, yes. Even that bit of curiosa, Freneau's *Father Bombo's Pilgrimage*, has recently been brought into print, and of course there are a few others to eke out a small list. Yet even for James Fenimore Cooper we have no more than eight titles available.

One reason for this scarcity of texts is that of demand: publishers will not invest in an edition for which they cannot see a market. I suggest another reason, however. Our critical assessments of early American fiction, understandably concerned primarily with Brockden Brown, Brackenridge, Tyler, and one or two others, have not focused on those novels which so far are generally known only by their appearance in a list of titles. Perhaps we have been put off by one of Alexander Cowie's memorable one-liners: Enos Hitchcock's *Memoirs of the Bloomsgrove Family* (1790) is the "very cambric tea of American fiction" (p. 17); "it is hard to see how any Maine maiden or swain could be improved by being exposed to the mesh of intrigue and emotionalism that constitutes [Mrs. Sally Wood's] *Julia and the Illuminated Baron*" (1800) (p. 23). Perhaps we have not been able to read certain early novels, some of which are extant in unique copies, requiring a travel grant if we are to get to them. And for some of these novels we shall find, often enough, that once read they may be returned uncommented upon to the shelves of rare book collections. In this connection, Alexander Cowie did not deter me. I have read the Hitchcock *Memoirs*—and Cowie has it dead to rights.

But just as often, I am convinced, we shall find one that has been undeservedly overlooked and that once examined can well convince a publisher to make a modern text available—to join the company of, say, William Williams's *Mr. Penrose: The Journal of Penrose, Seaman* or George Lippard's *The Quaker City; or, The Monks of Monk Hall*. My candidate is *Kelroy: A Novel*, "By a Lady of Pennsylvania," published in Philadelphia in 1812.

Kelroy has not gone unnoticed. Samuel Allibone wrote a brief note on the book and its author in his *Critical Dictionary of English Literature and British and American Authors* . . . (Philadelphia, 1858-71), Lillie D. Loshe gave it 75 words in her *Early American Novel* (1907), and A. H. Quinn matched that in his *American Fiction* (1936). Only Henri Petter has provided more than brief notice of the book, and I am indebted to his five-page discussion that introduced me to a most interesting and rewarding experience.

The author of *Kelroy* was Rebecca Rush, daughter of Jacob Rush, an eminent Philadelphia jurist, and niece of Benjamin Rush, the renowned physician and essayist. We know little else about her, but quite clearly that is because no one has looked into the Rush papers, where she is referred to as Becky, or probed the quite complete resources of the Philadelphia libraries. We do know that she was an imaginative literary artist, able to sustain and control a narrative for 300

closely printed pages, and with a gift all too rare in these nascent years of
American fiiction—that of creating lively, and lifelike, conversation. In
Kelroy, too, she created an intriguing gallery of characters, among
whom three are principal.

Edward Kelroy, the titular hero, is a poet: pale of complexion,
sensitive and delicate of person and personality, and with a melancholy
demeanor emphasized by his predilection for dressing all in black. Of a
temperament particularly responsive to music, Kelroy is invited to a
soirée at the Hammonds' home, at which, "as it [was] considered an
unpardonable piece of neglect not to ask every lady to play who has ever
tried to learn, the ladies were handed to the piano one after another . . ."
(p. 38). Kelroy suffers increasingly until seventeen-year-old Emily
Hammond "performed in a style of superiority which rivetted the
attention of all present" (p. 39) a song in the style of Thomas Moore's
Irish Melodies:

> To distant climes forbid to rove,
> And doomed to linger here,
> Alas! how shall I cease to love,
> Whilst sooth'd by scenes so dear? —
> Each wood-crown'd hill, and lowly plain,
> Where happy oft I've met her,
> Memorials sweet to me remain—
> I never shall forget her.
>
> Though far from me her wishes stray,
> My soul, to her so true,
> In silent anguish each sad day,
> Its sorrows shall renew.
> With many a bitter sigh, this heart
> Through life shall still regret her;
> Shall droop, the victim of her art—
> But never shall forget her (p. 39).

Sung in Emily's "remarkably soft and plaintive voice," the song has an
immediate effect on Kelroy. He is so touched by its beauty that he leaves
the salon in a "high wrought state," and falls deeply in love with the
singer—and she with him. But the song is also prophetic. Its lyrics speak
not only of love but of anguish, and anguish is the proper word to
describe the atmosphere in which the novel ends.

Kelroy is an imperfectly conceived character who, though absent
from the action for more than half the novel, makes his presence felt
throughout, not only because of his attachment to young Emily and close
friendship with Walsingham but also because he has so aroused Mrs.
Hammond's hatred that no day can pass without her vilifying him. He is,
of course, blameless in the tragedy that ensues, but he has his flaws. He

condescends to those whose perceptions do not match his own, he does not hesitate to reveal his impatience with those who speak too loudly or guffaw at social gatherings, and on one occasion he treats his fiancée with distrust and suspicion. He is clearly more than a stereotype, but just as clearly, Rebecca Rush has not fully succeeded in her characterization.

Young Emily Hammond is like many another heroine in early American fiction. She is beautiful, virtuous, with "quick feelings and keen perceptions so happily blended with sweetness and equanimity of temper . . . she preserved towards all who approached her a gentleness, and amenity which soon rendered her the idol of her acquaintance" (pp. 6-7). At the beginning of her eighteenth year her heart has so far been untouched by love; but along comes Kelroy, who declares his devotion with predictable results. *Predictable* is the word. Emily is completely so, and thus cannot engage the reader to a point of genuine involvement. She is so noble, so naive, so trusting that she cannot withstand even the minor buffetings of society. Her sister Lucy, shallow and calculating and thoroughly thick-skinned, is obviously drawn to stand in contrast to the sensitive Emily, but neither this device of characterization nor the occasionally effective conversation that Miss Rush composed for her can bring Emily Hammond to life.

It is in the realization of Mrs. Hammond, widowed mother of young Emily and her older (by one year) sister Lucy, that Rebecca Rush achieves genuine distinction, for in the person of Mrs. Hammond, Rush has drawn what may well be the most memorable female villain in American literature.

Married rather later than usual and widowed at thirty, with total assets of £6,000 and a house in Philadelphia, Mrs. Hammond directs all her resources and energies into finding suitable husbands, men of wealth and station, for her two daughters. Early on, she is successful. Lucy is won by Mr. Walsingham, who has an independent fortune and vague connections with a family listed in Burke's *Peerage*. But the success has been costly. Convinced that maintaining the appearance of wealth and social leadership is the only means to her desired end, Mrs. Hammond "was ready to fancy herself an absolute princess surrounded by her subjects":

> Nobody's parties were half so crowded, or so fashionable as Mrs. Hammond's; nobody was half so elegant, or so fashionable as her daughters; and by some well timed innuendoes . . . she circulated as belief that their fortunes would be as immense, as their claims to admiration were indisputable (p. 13).

With the £6,000 now reduced to a few hundred, and having run up heavy overdue bills with Philadelphia merchants and shopkeepers, Mrs.

Hammond is forced to borrow $900 from Walsingham—a trifling sum, she tells him, to tide her over until she is able to convert some vaguely described assets into cash.

With Lucy's future secure, Mrs. Hammond's problem is now the attachment between Emily and Kelroy, which she strongly disapproves of because Kelroy is nearly penniless. Emily is convinced that Kelroy's lack of cash is not important, not only because Edward is planning a voyage to India[4] to make his fortune but also because she herself believes she will come into money left her by her father when she marries, a fiction Mrs. Hammond has encouraged in her daughter. Believing that she can still coerce Emily into a more advantageous marriage, Mrs. Hammond attempts to block any private meeting of the lovers, and introduces Marney, a newly rich social boor, as a rival to Kelroy in the hope that Emily will obey her wishes as the dutiful daughter she is. But the plan fails, for with the help of a servant devoted to Emily, the lovers meet during one of Mrs. Hammond's rare absences from her home, and exchange promises.

Mrs. Hammond does not give up. She continues to make things difficult for Emily and Kelroy until Walsingham, who has discovered in casual conversation with the Hammonds' greengrocer that Mrs. Hammond is heavily in debt, uses the $900 she owes him to blackmail Mrs. Hammond into agreeing to the lovers' engagement. The wedding is planned for a year hence, after Kelroy returns from India.

Lucy and Walsingham sail for England, and after Kelroy departs, Emily takes to walking alone or in company with her bosom friend Helen Cathcart along the steep banks of the Schuylkill which borders the Hammond property. In a scene clearly reminiscent of Charles Brockden Brown's *Wieland*, one day the two girls hear sounds of troubled voices and discover at the foot of a cliff two men standing over a black man lying unconscious. Emily goes for help, and the servant is taken to the Hammond house where the doctor orders that he cannot be moved until he has recovered.

Emily finds the servant's master, Dunlevy, a very pleasant young man, and when Mrs. Hammond learns that he is wealthy and of impeccable family, she plots to bring Dunlevy and Emily together. To eliminate Kelroy, Mrs. Hammond has Marney forge a letter from Kelroy to Emily telling her he has found someone else and releasing her from her engagement, and she intercepts genuine letters from Kelroy to Emily. Crushed by what she believes to be Kelroy's perfidy, Emily finally marries Dunlevy, and Mrs. Hammond's triumph seems complete. With two wealthy sons-in-law she anticipates no further money problems and returns to playing cards for money and buying lottery tickets—gambling habits which had drained her husband's resources while he was alive and part of the small estate she had inherited from him. A careless servant causes a fire, however, and the Hammond house is burned to the ground. Only a few things are saved, among them a small case containing some of Mrs. Hammond's keepsakes, including a lottery ticket which turns out to be the $50,000 winner. Elated, Mrs. Hammond pays all her debts, buys a new house, and returns to her life of social pretense and elaborate party-giving. Advancing age and the high life are too much for her, however, and she falls victim to a stroke. Partly paralyzed, unable to speak, Mrs. Hammond expires.

To help settle her mother's affairs, Emily searches for her father's will and in the process accidentally trips a hidden spring in a desk, revealing a small packet of papers containing evidence of Mrs. Hammond's treachery, copies of Marney's forgeries, and the real letters from Kelroy to Emily that Mrs. Hammond had intercepted. The shock is too much for Emily, who falls into a swoon, succeeded by a fever and a lingering decay. Within days she dies, but on her deathbed entrusts to Helen Cathcart all the incriminating papers, from which, however, she has removed Marney's name. Three years elapse. Dunlevy recovers from the sorrow of Emily's death and marries Helen. Kelroy returns; Helen gives him the packet Emily had left and tells him the whole story. Distraught, Kelroy boards a ship for Leghorn which goes down with no survivors.

Rebecca Rush's comic characters and situations provide effective relief from the scenes of anguish and tragedy. Aging Dr. Blake, who pays court to every lady he meets under middle age, stirs up near altercations at tea parties and musical evenings by spilling coffee on dowagers, criticizing furniture and paintings, and declaiming nonsense arguments in stentorian tones.

> "Great people!" said he, holding up his hands, "grand quality!— tip-top gentry to be sure!—I'll be hang'd if I hav'n't been at a husking-frollick in the country where they behav'd better!—I drop a spoonful of coffee on one ugly thing, "you're a Hottentot," says she.— I stand behind another old witch, and ask her a civil question, and she snaps my head off!—Oh! if these are your tea-drinkings, the mischief may take 'em for me!"
>
> "Poh! nonsense man!" said Charles; "you must have done something amiss?"
>
> "I didn't though!—they both began at me for nothing!—as for that last one," pointing to Mrs. Hammond, "she looked so plaguey fierce, that I never even answered her. Oh, she's a clinker!—the devil himself wouldn't get the odd word from her, for a wager."

"Suppose you challenge her?" said Charles.

"Challenge her? why you don't think she'd fight?"

"If she is as angry as you appear to be, nothing short of a battle can settle the matter!"— (pp. 91-92).

They then went to the side-board, where different refreshments were placed, and [Blake] began helping himself, and eating as he stood. . . . The doctor began a whimsical disquisition on the opposite qualities of every different article he swallowed, which lasted till he could contain nothing more. Having demolished five ice creams, three jellies, and a pound or two of cake, and drank above a quart of lemonade, he said "it was poor washy stuff, enough to freeze a fellow's insides!" (p. 92).

Rush is equally deft when she moves fully into slapstick comedy. Chapter XIV describes the visit the Hammonds and Cathcarts make to the Gurnets, a newly rich family consisting of husband Job, who has made his money in a "wholesale huckstery" and as a salt merchant; Nancy, his wife, a former serving maid; and their three girls, who, after three years at finishing school, have learned to write their names, do a bit of needlework, and play (if that is the word) the piano. But the girls know what they want: "Miss Nancy . . . fastened herself upon Dunlevy, whom she teased with her unmeaning prate almost into a fever; whilst Miss Catharine, sat on the other side of the room watching Charles and whenever he happened to look at her, signified her approbation with a grin" (pp. 241-42). Catharine is easily persuaded to play the piano and sing; her sister Eleanor slips out of the room and returns with a little dog. She "pinched both its ears until it sent forth such a horrible outcry as entirely overcame the little remaining self-command of the company, and the shrill voice of Miss Catharine was drowned in a peal of universal laughter" (p. 246).

Then everything goes wrong, hilariously. A syllabub in process is lost when a black servant drops the punch bowl. In chasing the servant to cane him for his carelessness, Job Gurnet trips and falls headlong, in his best clothes, into a puddle behind the barn—which has more in it than water. Mrs. Gurnet screams:

"The *laws a marcy*! was ever *sitch* a sight upon *arth*?—why your breeches are ruined!—and your new Sunday waistcoat all over nothing but mud!—I wonder how you could fall into that stinking truck?—"

"The next time I fall," returned [Job]," I'll get you to choose the place—I did it because I could not help it, Mrs. Fool" (p. 252).

Good as they are—and it must be remembered that genuinely effective comic writing is rare in this early period, with perhaps only Royall Tyler and Hugh Henry Brackenridge having achieved marked success therein—the comic scenes in *Kelroy* are few, and they are brief.

The dominant mode is tragic, and at the center from beginning to end is the powerful figure of Mrs. Hammond. Hers is a consuming ego that must try to control all: people, situations, events, even destiny. Her efforts to do what she considers best for her two daughters appear laudable at first, but we soon learn that the success she achieves with Lucy's match is more important to her than Lucy. That Mrs. Cathcart has some social standing, and that Mrs. Hammond can manipulate her as she wishes are the principal reasons she maintains a relationship with that colorless woman. She is alternately protective of and cruel to Emily, and when Walsingham forces her to accept Kelroy's engagement to Emily, her anger at being defeated makes her all the more receptive to the plan of forgery that the equally amoral Marney proposes in return for a chance to marry Emily and, as he innocently assumes, gain control of the girl's patrimony.

Yet Mrs. Hammond is in some ways ignorant of the ways of the world. She regularly accepts appearance as reality, misreads Walsingham's politeness and generosity as weaknesses of character, cannot understand Kelroy's casual attitude toward material wealth, and regards Emily's deep love for the young poet as youthful naiveté, or worse, filial intransigence. Though she worships money and possessions, she buys without thought and is often taken advantage of by furniture dealers or real estate salesmen more mendacious than she.

The complexity of Mrs. Hammond's character is suggested near the end of the novel. Confined to her bed, partly paralyzed, not able to speak coherently, and aware that she is dying, she struggles several times to say something to Emily, but all she can manage are incomprehensible sounds. What was she trying to communicate? A plea that Emily forgive her? The location of the hidden packet of letters? An explanation that Kelroy had not deserted Emily as the forged letter stated? Rush leaves it ambiguous, as indeed she should have.

Kelroy contains strong social criticism, occasionally voiced by the author herself in her role as omniscient narrator, but more often dramatized by one of Rush's favorite techniques: contrast. Bold strokes distinguish Mrs. Hammond and Lucy from Emily and Helen Cathcart. Subtler lines are used to limn the picture of the sensitive man and woman, and the moral man and woman, in a society that embraces a different set of values, and the uneasiness their presence causes in that society. Such criticism places *Kelroy* well within the company of other American novels of the time, all of which sought to instruct as well as to entertain. But Rebecca Rush's moralizing is never bathetic. Her style is crisp and economical, never inflated into the gorgeously adjectived prose of the Della Cruscans. Her narrative is controlled and moves at a steady pace throughout. Her characters are lifelike, and for the most part, exceptionally well drawn—particularly the character of Mrs. Hammond, who will become, once *Kelroy* is more widely known, one of the memorable characters in American fiction.

As I have suggested, we may leave some of our early novels to rest undisturbed in their obscurity. The Reverend Enos Hitchcock's *Memoirs of the Bloomsgrove Family* belongs in that darkness, as does Sarah Savage's *The Vain Cottager; or the History of Lucy Franklin* (1807). But Gilbert Imlay's *The Emigrants* (1793) deserves a full reassessment despite some efulgent passages involving Venus, Morpheus, Somnus, and Aurora, as do Jeremy Belknap's *The Foresters* (1787-88) and perhaps a dozen others of the period. The challenge is there. Let us take it up.

Notes

[1]See, however, Paul Allen, *The Late Charles Brockden Brown*, ed. with an introd. by Robert E. Hemenway and Joseph Katz (Columbia, S.C.: J. Faust & Co., 1976).

[2]*New-York Mirror* (31 January 1835), p. 241.

[3]*The Marvellous and Entertaining Repository*, 4 vols. (Boston: Baker and Alexander, 1827)

[4]In one of only three or four slips of the pen, Henri Petter has Kelroy voyaging to China in his *Early American Novel* (Columbus: Ohio State Univ. Press, 1971), p. 437.

AMERICAN VALUES AND ROMANTIC FICTION

Milton R. Stern
University of Connecticut

One generally assumes that the driving impulse of American Romantic literature is the energy of Emersonian millennialism. In large measure this is true, especially for the earlier productions of Thoreau, Whitman, and Emerson himself. However, by suggesting some relationships between three of the commonplaces of twentieth-century criticism and scholarship, I wish to propose that the center of energy in American Romantic fiction is not so much American millennialism as it is a creative set of recoils, or antagonisms, or tensions between the radicalism of millennial assumptions and a conservative, experiential response.[1]

The first of our commonplaces is the nature of the literary marketplace available to the fiction writer during the Romantic period— let us date that period roughly from William Ellery Channing's appointment to the Deanship of Harvard's Divinity School in 1815 to the Civil War. The second commonplace is the complex of definitions that distinguish the romance from the novel, the tale from the sketch. And the third is the millennialistic separatism of American psychology implicit in the assumptions underlying the Declaration of Independence and the Monroe Doctrine and flowering in the assertion of Transcendentalist principles made by Emerson in his publication of *Nature* in 1836—a flowering that was to pollinate our great, national, Romantic, literary anthesis. Utilizing these simple materials of what is common ground for all of us, I propose to weave them together in brief outline with familiar patterns in the work of Cooper, Poe, Hawthorne, and Melville in order to suggest that the concatenation of these elements reveals an unannounced ideological unity among our very disparate major American writers of Romantic fiction, a political substratum of much significance to us in our bicentennial celebration of our nation's fiction.

Ever since Frank Luther Mott's *History of American Magazines, 1850-1865* (Cambridge, 1938), and especially since Fred Lewis Pattee's *The Feminine Fifties* (New York, 1940),[2] literary scholars have been aware of some of the conditions of the popular literary marketplace that led Hawthorne to observe in his famous 1855 letter to his publisher, William Ticknor, that "America is now wholly given over to a d—d mob of scribbling women, and I should have no chance of success while the public taste is occupied with their trash—and should be ashamed of myself if I did succeed." So much attention has been paid to the purple, lush, outrageous, and hilarious sentimentalities of publications with such names as *Godey's Lady's Book, The Token, Pearls of the West, The Bower of Taste,* and *Friendship's Offering,* so much critical attention has been paid to one satirical representation of popular literature, the rhetoric of Melville's *Pierre,* wherein the style and substance of the feminine popular market is characterized in that oft-quoted passage as "a volume bound in rose-leaves, clasped with violets, and by the beaks of humming-birds printed with peach-juice on the leaves of lilies," that we may leave this aspect of the subject without further elucidation.

Less attention has been paid to the gentlemen's magazines. Theodore Greene's recent study[3] indicates that the male side of this sexist literary coin is the perfect obverse of the be-frilled and furbelowed distaff side. The models of success in American magazines up through the early Romantic period all delineate a Ciceronian "Idol of Order," a being, who, though willing to be "elevated" by the fictive, the poetic, and the sentimental, left such higher, "spiritual" stuff to the finer clay of ladyhood, and who dedicated himself to the most noble activities of church and state: theology, ecclesiastical polity, arms, business, education, the law, and politics. One tabulation, skewed somewhat toward the clergy because of the samples used, offers the following statistics for the percent of essays about role-models in the gentlemen's magazines up through 1820: politicians (including soldier-statesmen, professor-statesmen, lawyer-statesmen, and business-statesmen) received 25% of the national attention; the military received 23%; the clergy (including clergymen-professors and clergymen-college presidents) received 22%; professor-scholars received 8%; lawyers 7%; physicians 5%; and businessmen 4%. It is not insignificant that women and writers received only 3% each and that in the future, although the percentage for professor-scholars would not rise, and lawyers would increasingly become subsumed under the politician's rubric, the businessman category would rise astronomically, especially during and after the first World War.[4]

As any liberationist arguing against sexism will point out, women's liberation is also man's liberation from the rigidity of molds and roles. Whatever one's political attitudes toward the Equal Rights Amendment, an examination of the Romantic period's editorial policies and reviews makes unmistakable the conclusion that for the most part, both men and women agreed in the maintenance of a cultural priority of values wherein femaleness, poetry, ethereality, fiction, hysteria, sentiment, and sexual passion, however sublimated, provided the general ambience of one amalgam, and maleness, fact, history, and the business of the world provided the general ambience of the other. For instance, Sarah Josepha Hale, for forty years (1837-1877) very much the lady editor of *Godey's Lady's Book* and one of the most influential of all the literary ladies, made priorities plain in an 1828 essay in the *Ladies' Magazine.* If, as she asserts, "the time has come when our American authors should have something besides empty praise from their countrymen," she makes the assertion in a significantly left-handed way: "Our institutions and character demand activity in business," she continued; "the useful should be preferred before the ornamental; practical industry before speculative philosophy; reality before romance. But still, the emanations of genius may be appreciated, and a refined taste cultivated among us."[5]

And a male, Charles Fenno Hoffman, in an 1838 review of Hawthorne's *Twice-Told Tales*, offers a similarly ambiguous compliment to Hawthorne in the diction of a rhetoric recognizably appropriate to ladies' pursuits. Specifying the "types of the soul of Nathaniel Hawthorne" as a "rose bathed and baptized in dew—a star in its first gentle emergence above the horizon," he then goes on to put matters in their proper perspective:

> Minds, like Hawthorne's, seem to be the only ones suited to an American [literary] climate. Quiet and gentle intellect gives itself, in our country, oftener to literature, than intellect of a hardier and more robust kind. Men endowed with vigorous and sturdy faculties are, sooner or later, enticed to try their strength in the boisterous current of politics or the Pactolian stream of merchandize. . . . Thus far, American authors, who have been most triumphant in winning a name, have been of the gentler order. We can point to many Apollos, but Jove has not as yet assumed his thunder, nor hung his blazing shield in the sky. . . . Yet men like Hawthorne are not without their use; nay, they are the writers to smooth and prepare the path for nobler (but not better) variants, by softening and ameliorating the public spirit.[6]

The exhortations, perorations and kudos offered by the popular literary marketplace reflected for our literary artists certain assumptions of our national culture. As early as the 1820s—of course, one can find earlier evidence—one of our cultural commonplaces was the understanding that the real man leaves art to the women and goes off into the virile, jovian necessities of building the visible and material foundations of the new and expanding republic. To announce that one was choosing the vocational identity of a fiction writer was to call down on one what Hawthorne imagined as the reaction of the hardheaded, hardhanded, graybearded men of God and the civil magistracy who were his forebears: the outraged ancestors imagined in the "Custom House" introduction to *The Scarlet Letter* voice their famous exclamation quoted, and justly so, by generations of scholars: " 'What is he?' murmurs one gray shadow of my forefathers to the other. 'A writer of story books! What kind of a business in life,—what mode of glorifying God, or being serviceable to mankind in his day and generation,—may that be? Why the degenerate fellow might as well have been a fiddler!' " The response is merely an early example of a strain in American life that announces its conformist impulses periodically, as was most dramatically witnessed in our own century in the insistence of Wisconsin's late Senator, Joseph McCarthy, on associating modern art, un-Americanism, and homosexuality.

I suggest that the familiar material I sketch here indicates a subtle but strong and profound relationship between literary genres and the risks of personal identity, and in this suggestion I will continue to insist on our scholarly and historical commonplaces as our best materials. We all know about Hawthorne's characterization of Trollope's novels as verisimilitudes that were "just as real as if some giant had hewn a great lump out of the earth, and put it under a glass case, with all its inhabitants going about their daily business, and not suspecting that they were made a show of."[7] For his part, Trollope speculated that "the creations of American literature generally are no doubt more given to the speculative—less given to the realistic—than are those of English literature. On our side of the water we deal more with beef and ale, and less with dreams. . . . But in no American writer is to be found the same predominance of weird imagination as in Hawthorne."[8]

As many commentators have recognized, Hawthorne and Trollope defined the division between the two great fictive modes of the nineteenth century, the romance and the novel. Although the Romantic age itself did not by any means use these generic terms with absolute consistency or specificity in its critical language, nevertheless its *lexicon rhetoricae* operated with enough clarity of intention that in a later age we are justified in constructing the categories we use retrospectively. The novel meant realism to the age, recognizable verisimilitude that dealt with "actual" people within the historical and probable web of their times and circumstances. The novelistic mode could be "trusted:" it fulfilled a didactic function of instruction in the actualities of the visible world. The sketch, often sentimentalized, often not even fictional, was in point and purpose the short baby brother of the novel, much as a small snapshot of life by the wayside is related to a panoramic view of an entire society. The romance, however, was quite something else again, as one anonymous reviewer recognized when he complained about the intrusion of fictional modes upon each other in *The Blithedale Romance*. The reviewer remarked that if Hawthorne "shaded and clouded his incidents somewhat more obscurely, if he removed them farther back or farther off from the region of our actual sight and knowledge, he would be safer in using the *privileges* of the *romancer*. But he gives us such distinct and sharp boundary lines, and deals so boldly with matters and persons, *the truth of whose prose* life repels *the poetry of his fiction*, that we are induced to *confide in him as a chronicler*, rather than *indulge him as a romancer*" [italics mine].[9] The romance, like its short baby sister, the tale, was ostensibly a matter of "feminine" sensibility. It was ethereal, imaginary, and perhaps luxurious—a "poetry" to be "indulged" as a "privilege" of those who have time for what Sarah Josepha Hale had called "a refined taste cultivated among us." But if one indulges the ladies with privileges, one trusts the chronicler as a surveyor of the prosy truths of actualities.

When I say that the tale was to the romance as the sketch was to the novel, I hope I indicate the ways in which the writer of tales and romances involved his personal identity as a man and a citizen in his vocational identity. It was "American" and "manly" to concern oneself with actualities. It was "American" and "manly" to turn to the sketch and the novel. One need not think long about the pragmatic values of American culture or read many reviews or pronouncements from editors in the Romantic period to recognize the political substratum of literary genres that entered into Hawthorne's famous plaint, in the Preface to *The Marble Faun*, that "actualities" are "so terribly insisted upon, as they . . . must needs be, in America." In this light, one comes to see the deep significance for Hawthorne when in "The Custom House" he reduces Salem to the materials of romance in order to manage them within the purposes of his own unique imaginative mode, and then repudiates Salem's common actuality as though it were a dull romance in order that he may assume nationality, as it were, in a world other than that of "unpicturesque prolixity:" "Soon . . . my old native town will loom upon me through the haze of memory, a mist brooding over and around it; as if it were no portion of the real earth, but an overgrown village in cloud-land, with only imaginary inhabitants to people its wooden houses, and walk its homely lanes, and the unpicturesque prolixity of its main street. Henceforth it ceases to be a reality of my life. I am a citizen of somewhere else."

Having identified his Salem with sterile and outgrown terrible insistences upon actualities, Hawthorne has his ironic joke when he dismisses Salem as a romance, but the joke is poignantly on Hawthorne.

When one considers Hawthorne's abiding, conservative, and Flaubertian desire to belong to the common world of daily "unpicturesque prolixity" as a solid and respected burgher, one sees the impossibility of his declaration of independence. He could characterize Melville as a man who could neither believe nor rest comfortably in unbelief because he suffered from a very similar disease himself. Declaring independence from the world of American actualities in favor of citizenship in the "somewhere else" world of the imagination, he yet hungered strenuously for citizenship in both, and he paid homage and allegiance to both. Aware of how his role as writer was inextricably intermeshed in his identity according to gender and patriotism, he never reconciled the conflicting tugs from the polar regions of his creative life. What is more, I suggest that this very tension was at the center of his creative energies, at the center of his themes, and at the center of the impingement of fictive modes upon each other—the queer ways in which the techniques of verisimilitude and fairy-tale, of novel and romance, of immersion in his materials and disclaimer of them, as Henry James noted, disturbingly alternate with each other not only in Hawthorne's fiction, but also in the fiction of Cooper, Poe, and Melville, and last throughout the romantic period and even into the fiction of that post-Romantic realist, Mark Twain.

The third commonplace of our century's retrospective reconstitution of Romanticism is injected into this discussion by an objection that must have occurred to most of you when I said that "it was 'American' and 'manly' to turn to the sketch and the novel." First of all, there was, of course, the sentimentalized, idealized, lady-ized fluff of such sketch productions as N. P. Willis's *Pencillings by the Way*. The sketch could be as removed from the terribly insisted upon actualities as any tale. Second, as an entire continuum of twentieth-century commentators has pointed out (F. O. Matthiessen, Richard Chase, R. W. B. Lewis, and Leo Marx eminent among them) the romance is the unique expression of the American literary imagination. Both objections must be admitted, and I wish here only to indicate how the political implications of literary genres and imaginative modes illuminate the relationship between the two objections and introduce our third commonplace, the millennialism of American Romantic thought.

As Wright Morris suggested in his brilliant essay on Norman Rockwell in *The Territory Ahead*, the *means* of the novelistic need not at all be disconnected from the sentimentalizing purposes of "the ladies'" idealizations. Rockwell, like Willis, and like Hawthorne and Cooper in their "sunny" sketches, gratified a deep American hunger. The contemporary language of the Romantic marketplace generally used the word "sunny" as a term of approbation for cheerful sketches that showed mundane American life as good; the words "morbid" and "gloomy" were reserved for works of the imagination that questioned American assumptions. Since one assumption was that mundane American life in fact *was* good, the gloomy and the morbid were not reflections of actualities, but were merely unpatriotic and disturbing reflections of what the literary marketplace called "subjective" in the artist's imagination.[10] That imagination, when unhealthy, tended toward the tale; when brightly open to the diurnal cheerfulness of common American experience, it tended toward the sketch. What Morris suggests about Rockwell establishes Rockwell as an example of what I am saying about the literature, for he is a twentieth-century continuation in paint of the essential techniques and purposes of the word-sketch of the Romantic period. Verisimilitude is the common ground in consistent and significant ways. The most common representative details, whether of people, places, or things, are deliberately selected and presented through the most realistic techniques so that the viewer responds to the recognizable actualities and says, "That's it! That's it! That's the way things really are!"

Those realistically presented details of verisimilitude are arranged in such a way that they add up to a statement of how good, how beautiful, how humanly warm and rich they are. That is, looking at what we take to be the common, simple details of daily life, we think we are looking at an unretouched photograph of our own American life, whereas we are looking at a consummate example of one kind of art. And because we can say, like Walter Cronkite, "And that's the way it is!" to a portrait of what really is that's-the-way-we-wish-it-were, we come away from this "sunny" and graphic representation of our own homely American life with all the pleasure of revivified and reassured self-esteem. What I am proposing is an irony of American cultural history: the fictive and reportorial sketch in the Romantic period, addressing itself in this idealizing way to "actualities," did two things at once. First it indicated the strength of the subterranean impulsion not at all toward the actualities it was supposed to serve, but, paradoxically, toward the ostensible purposes of Romance. Second, it served not to invite or continue investigation into the meanings of American society, but rather foreclosed discussion by assuming that the meanings, all of goodness, were self-evident and that the cheerful surfaces were also the truth within the depths. Way down deep, it was shallow. Therefore, since the sketch and novel generally were foreclosed and foreclosing genres in America, ironically the artist who wished to really investigate the meaning of American actualities in depth was nudged toward the disguise of allegory and symbolism, the maskings of the Romance in order to exercise what Melville called "the great art of telling the truth." When one considers the thematic function of the serious tales and Romances of the period, and then considers the function of the popular sketch of the period, what becomes apparent is that generally the sketch was the vehicle for sentiment, and the Romance and tale were the vehicle for dissent and questionings. Consciously or otherwise, the literary marketplace sensed the ironic, subterranean reversal and repudiated the dark questionings. In a period of strong cultural nationalism, people simply did not want to hear the echoes of dissent, and nowhere better than in the reviews of the popular marketplace—in which Cooper, Poe, Hawthorne, and Melville all longed to be accepted—was the fact made more clear. The works of Hawthorne that one reviewer would accept and those he would reject were presented in terms and categories that illuminate the subject: " 'The Birth-Mark,' 'Rappaccini's Daughter,' and 'Roger Malvin's Burial,' are the nettles and mushrooms of Mr. Hawthorne's mind, and certainly should not be tied up with a bouquet of flowers for the public. Perhaps we hate these *tales* the more, that they are bound in the same covers with 'The Celestial Railroad,' and 'Drowne's Wooden Image,' the happiest efforts of the author in *sketch writing*."[11]

When we consider the idiosyncratic imaginations of our four major writers of Romantic fiction, together with the millennialistic shibboleths of their society, we find small wonder in the ascendency of the Romance. Those familiar shibboleths of our third commonplace all derive from millennialistic assumptions of vastly varying contexts. The assumptions of the seventeenth-century New England Calvinist differ as night from day from the assumptions of the late eighteenth-century rational, radical American deist. Yet they both have deeply in common the millennialistic self-imagery that was prepared for the New World by centuries of European imagination which transmogrified into the Christian contexts of Paradise regained and the City on the Hill the older Classical contexts of the lost Golden Age. Again, we share as one of our scholarly and critical commonplaces the idea that the physical discovery of America was the reification of the millennial idea of the type of the City of God, the lost Eden, the visible body of Christ. Our seventeenth century specified the plantation religious and our eighteenth century specified Jeffersonian agrarianism and "the republican machine." The assumptions underlying our Declaration of Independence and the Bill of Rights translated the older Puritan providential imagination into radical eighteenth-century visions of America as a special and new redemptive force in history. When Edward Johnson, in his *Wonder-Working*

Providences of Sion's Savior in New England, gleefully considered the meteor and the plague that wiped out Indian populations as a providence visited by Christ upon the land to clear it for His Chosen People, he was celebrating in radical Puritan terms what an otherwise antithetical radical and deistic age would announce in the Monroe Doctrine.

So, too, although the nineteenth century, with its Romantic Transcendentalism, differed as much from either of the two preceding centuries as they did from each other, it, too, replaced culturally exhausted language and concepts in order to forge new ones to express the continuing idea of America as a special symbol. It opened wide the door unlatched by eighteenth-century concepts of primitivism and democracy and cosmic benevolence, resuscitated the existential intensity and symbolic imaginativeness of the Puritan mind, and blended those qualities with the concept of immanence that derived from both the Orient and German idealism, re-creating thereby in Romantic terms, the new-old product of millennial prospects. Whitman's vision of America is nothing if it is not a sense of the ultimate and absolute democracy of unific cosmic love translated into the individualism and political principles of an expanding nation. Where better than in America could be seen the symbols, portents, and promises of a millennial state of being, where, in our insistently individual identities, we merge in the very vocation of God, which is the expanding and eternal process that makes all forms one cosmic identity? When Whitman sees in the disparate forms of minute entities that "a kelson of the creation is love," or when Emerson creates the "Prospects" with which he concludes *Nature*, both extend to the type of the true human consciousness what they had extended to America among nations as the new and visible working of infinite, eternal, divine principles. In their terms and contexts they were millennialistically doing with the idea of America what the eighteenth-century makers and shapers had done before them in their own terms and contexts, what the seventeenth-century makers and shapers had done earlier in theirs, and what the earlier Renaissance and medieval expectant Christian imaginations had done in theirs even before the land was discovered. Even in imagination, "the land was ours before we were the land's."

What I am getting at in this very brief review of very familiar generalizations is that when the assumptions of our self-image, formed in various contexts through many centuries, become concrescent in the popular shibboleths of the first half of the American nineteenth century, our culture arrives at ideological and rhetorical conclusions that demand conformity to the assertion that America, historically different from all

other nations, is in fact God's Country wherein the historical differences
are signs of a difference in state of being, or, as we like to say today, in
"the human condition." In short, the debasement and popularization of
the millennialistic strain of many centuries of self-image is the political
substratum upon which the critical edifices of the literary marketplace
were built, and it is a major perspective through which literary genres
and modes were judged. Our materialistic insistence upon actualities
turns the millennialistic strain into something like this: the visible
actualities and necessities of common life are Reality; the success of
historical process is proved in successful marketplace identity.
American Reality is cheerful, fulfilling, good, and, in all those terms,
expansively and expandingly progressive. In sum what *is* is millennium
realized or in the state of being very rapidly realized, and to question the
unstated assumption that American society and bourgeois values are
perfectibility in process was un-Christian, un-American, and unmanly.
In the generation gap of the 1820s and 1830s, the Lockeian and Scotch
"Common Sense School's" epistemological insistences on Andrews
Norton's polite State Street Unitarianism reflected, in opposition to
Emerson's Transcendentalism, the extent to which the noblest radical
aspects of our millennilism could devolve into brittle and smugly
optimistic socially conservative ideological conformism.

When conservative reviewers, for instance, responded to that strain.
in Hawthorne's work that reveals his deep desire to identify with his
bourgeois society as the world of Reality, they responded in ways whose
ontological and epistemological implications were politically significant
and very recognizable to Emerson's contemporary audience. "It
happens," said one sturdy Whig in a representative review in 1846, "that
we have not only found Conservatism, but a good many other things we
have asked for, in our national literature, expressed through the pages of
Nathaniel Hawthorne." What the "Conservatism" means is nothing other
than that old, familiar, terrible insistence upon actualities, for when the
palpable world, which is taken without question to be the Real world, is
scrutinized as such, what one finds is a very lovely American place
indeed, a natural state that surpasses all the plans and reforms of the
dreamy-eyed idealists. The status quo, things as they are, are quite good
enough:

> It is a favorite expression with regard to Hawthorne [says the
> reviewer, Charles Wilkins Webber] that he *"Idealizes"* everything.
> Now what does this Idealization mean? Is it that he *improves* upon
> Nature? Pshaw! this is a Literary cant. . . . Talk to me of *Idealizing*
> the violet, and you talk nonsense. . . . Hawthorne does not endeavor
> to improve upon the Actual, but with a wise emulation attempts—
> first to reach it, and then to modify it suitably. . . . He is led by his

> fine taste to . . . make you see it in precisely that light in which . . .
> its highest beauty is revealed. . . . We can't get away from the
> physical, and just as our material vision informs the inner life will that
> inner life know Wisdom. When some of our crude Theorists have
> learnt to realize this truth . . . they will have come to the knowledge
> that one Fact of the external life is worth a thousand Dreams, and that
> they need not waste their lives in seeing sights that have no substance,
> and dreaming Dreams that have no reality; for if they will only wake
> up, and look at the real World as it absolutely is, they will find that
> they have a Paradise made to their hand. But there is a still more
> interesting and even wiser exhibition of the Ethical Conservatism of
> [Hawthorne's] mind given in that fine allegory, "Earth's Holocaust."
> Here he represents a saturnalia of the Reformers, [men like Emerson
> and that whole] brawling tribe of Innovators—each of whom
> imagines he has certainly found the Archimedean lever, and is
> heaving at it in the effort to turn the world topsy-turvy.[12]

In order to express the relationship of conservatism to Romantic radicalism in the vocational identities of the major American writers of Romantic fiction, I wish to recall to you the useful categories and definitions supplied long ago by that crusty old Tory, T. E. Hulme, in his seminal essay "Romanticism and Classicism."[13] You will remember that Hulme offers his categories as opposing constellations of assumptions centering on concepts of man, God, society and history. For the Romantic, man is an infinite reservoir of possibility whose essential nature is love and goodness, and whose development is expansively seen as potential merger with the Godhead in consciousness. Man, therefore, is divine, is God, and God, by the same token, is immanent. Consequently, the Romantic imagination and rhetoric tend to be cosmic, vague, and large. History is a progress, in large, whelming, cosmic surges, toward the full development of man's potential identity, and is a constant lesson in the need for the destruction of trammels and restrictions so that on the other side of the ultimate revolution man will achieve that total liberty which will allow him to express the hitherto repressed energy of love and goodness that is his essential nature. Because the state has been a repressive perversion of that nature, the Romantic looks toward the revolutionized future rather than to the past, looks toward a pre-civilized vent and expression of the self, and champions freedom and unrestraint rather than social institutions.

The Classicist, on the other hand, sees man as a limited reservoir whose essential nature is chaotic and potentially bestial. There is a vertiginous gulf between the perfection of God and the mandates from Him on the one hand, and the limited and fallen nature of man on the other. Because of his nature, man must be subject to rules, discipline, and decorum, for a precivilized vent and expression of the self is a release of the beast. History is a continuing illustration of the hypothesis, "*Plus ca*

change, plus c'est la même chose," and the best examples of decorum are
found in the precedents and continuations of institutionalized civilization, from the classical past to the present. Consequently, classicism
tends to be past-facing, and it tends to emphasize subordination of the
self, the importance of institutions, and the knowing of one's place. The
classicist imagination and rhetoric tend to be specific, dry, historical, and
legalistic.

I think we should leave aside Hulme's extrapolations about rhetoric;
if we compare the dictum of the neoclassicist, Dr. Johnson, that it is not
our task to number the streaks in the tulip, with the appeal of the
Romantic, Emerson, for a rhetoric of the milk in the firkin, the meal in
the pan, then Hulme's conclusions about rhetoric become less useful
than the other constituents of his constellations. But when we think of the
conflict between Andrews Norton and Waldo Emerson, of Thoreau's
civil disobedience, and of Whitman's insistence on wearing his hat
indoors or out, on sounding his barbaric yawp, and on his own self as
finer than all churches and bibles, then Hulme's categories become a
very useful point of departure. Moreover, they are clear in their political
implications as a beginning for a distinction between the radical and the
conservative, even in the debased sloganeering of the Viet Nam years
and the assumptions underlying "Love" and "Let It All Hang Out" on the
one hand, and "Love It or Leave It" and "Law and Order" on the other.

Taking Hulme as my point of departure, I refer to *an evaluative
consciousness* of the materials that constitute his constellations as
"philosophical radicalism" and "philosophical conservatism." But,
clearly, when we are talking about the hardened, popular shibboleths of
a culture, we are not at all necessarily talking about a conscious,
evaluative, philosophical awareness of the assumptions underlying the
rhetoric. One of the ways we distinguish between the surfaces of
radicalism and the surfaces of conservatism is the extent to which the
former rebel against established shibboleths and the latter champion
them and wish to return to them when they are threatened. In an
America where the rhetoric of those shibboleths is that of the terribly
insisted upon actualities of Hawthorne's Custom House world, one
defines categories on the ideological surface of things by their relation to
rhetoric like "God's country," "free enterprise," and "private
individualism." The radical tends to dissent from and the conservative
tends to acquiesce in the ideological terminology of the established
order.

Allegiance to or dissent from the rhetoric and shibboleths of the
ideological status quo is what I designate "social conservatism" or

"social radicalism." Often social conservatism or radicalism will have in its proponents' minds a direct and organic relationship to philosophical conservatism or radicalism, but the history of our century has taught us that this is by no means necessarily so. The established society of the supposedly philosophically radical Soviet Union, for instance, is one of the most socially conservative in the world, and similarly, in the United States of the Romantic period we discover the irony of a social conservatism, conformity to the established shibboleths, that defends rhetoric and assumptions that were the distortions of a millennialistic and largely radical set of philosophies. Clearly, I do not have here the time and space I need to pursue the cross-currents and complexities of this simple observation, but what I am leading up to is the proposition that in order to express their *philosophical* conservatism, writers like Poe, Hawthorne, and Melville had to oppose the *social* conservatism which, like Charles Wilkins Webber's, was, ironically, an unconscious expression of millennialistically radical assumptions. The vocational lives of our serious Romantic fictionists were caught in the same irony that enveloped the ostensible and subterranean lives of the sketch and the Romance. To the extent that I have suggested that the *vocational* identity of the writer of sketches and novels was one of conformity to the shibboleths of the literary marketplace, I have suggested that that identity was essentially conservative. And to the same extent, I suggest that the *vocational* identity of the writer of the tale and romance was essentially radical. In short, I propose the intricate irony of what appears to me to be a central fact of American Romantic fiction: in adopting the disguises of romance in order to express their recoil from their society's dearest assumptions, the American writers of serious Romantic fiction adopted a vocationally radical identity in order to express a philosophical conservatism that was at odds with the millennialistic assertions of American social conservatism, and that it is this irony that lies at the center of the tension within the selves of our serious Romantic fictionists, who, like Cooper, Poe, Hawthorne and Melville, yearned to belong to the common life, yearned to belong to the world of popular literary success, and who yet felt psychologically and vocationally alienated from what they yearned for.

My thesis is that whatever the idiosyncratic, creative, psychological centers of our writers' lives were, the common, cultural, creative, center of their lives was what really is a deeply political act: their attempt to mediate between the truth they wanted to tell their society and their society's unexamined assumptions. It was their attempt to mediate between their vocational and social identities, a conflict destructive of self and creative of fiction, and most intricately and dramatically seen in Hawthorne. In fact the generative cultural center of American literary creative vigor from Emerson on is a continuing dynamism of counter-impulsions toward and away from the millennialistic vision of possibilities so characteristic of American society. I think that in large outline, the fiction of the four major writers I have chosen, chosen because they are so major and so disparate, is in each case a complex and profoundly instructive history of the conflict. Another way of stating the proposition is that our greatest fiction writers of the Romantic period were, like Poe, so romantically transcendental that they repudiated the actualities, or, like Cooper, Hawthorne, and Melville, they were philosophically anti-Romantic.

Cooper is more of a problem than any of the others in this group because despite the convention that places him among the Romantic fiction writers, he is, I think, really a man of the eighteenth century. But as our first major user of Romantic materials—precivilizational, savage nature, the noble man of nature, the unschooled hero—for my purposes he remains instructive in his attitudes. For one thing, in Romantic hagiography, the very idea of Natty Bumppo, the loner, the outcast, the wanderer, the man who prefers untrammeled existence in a state of nature to the restrictions of towns and laws, should be conceived within the Romantic canon of heroes, a semi-mythical subject of emulation. But, of course, he was conceived, name and all, as a joke. The center of Cooper's joke was Bumppo's separation from eighteenth-century classicist ideals of law, property, decorum, and established institutions; and the more the original conception of the character in *The Pioneers* (1823) was associated with Romantic attitudes, the more of a grumpy old fool Natty was. It is not insignificant that as Natty becomes a heroic figure in the Leatherstocking Tales, Cooper uses him to express ideals of pre-Jacksonian democracy within the context of conservative ideals. Cooper provides Natty with two constant dramatic functions. One is to have Natty indicate that lessons derived from Nature and Nature's God are experiential proofs of eighteenth-century assertions of rational decorum and property rights. It becomes Natty's function, especially in *The Prairie* (1827), to combat the logical extension of Jacksonian egalitarianism and the extreme extension of the assertion and gratification of the self, all typified in Ishmael Bush and his "wasty ways." Natty functions to maintain the primacy of common sense, of experience, of the terribly insisted-upon actualities, as he does when he opposes Dr. Batt and his generalizations so reminiscent of the theoretics of Charles Wilkins Webber's "brawling tribe of Innovators." In narrative use, Cooper injects Natty into as many scenes of ideological combat as of physical combat.

In flavor and ambience, Jacksonian democracy is closer than the more aristocratic Jeffersonian democracy to the Whitmanian "feel" of Romantic democracy. The "roughs and the beards" that Whitman loved were not to be found in a landscape wherein the minuet is played, but were on the far side of the line separating the metaphor of settlements from the metaphor of wilderness. The eighteenth-century mind, especially the conservative mind, feared the wilderness, as DeCrevecoeur's *Letters* make clear. The death of Adams and Jefferson on July fourth of America's semicentennial year marked a symbolic dividing line between the neo-classic and the Romantic, just as two years later, in 1828, Jackson's accession to the Presidency marked the beginning of what might be called political Romanticism. One would expect a character representative of the Jacksonian ambience to champion Romantic assumptions, but Natty Bumppo, like his creator, is really very much a man of the settlements despite his *locus operandi*, a man of respect for property, propriety, and place. Natty's second consistent function, closely related to the first, is his willing and immediate subordination of his own identity to those which are superior to his in terms of established social hierarchies. The roughs and the beards and the common people of lower caste may have good fates and good characters if they respect established values and know their place, and bad fates and characters if they don't, but the characters of high birth, high breeding, and high conventions invariably are persons of property who all live happily ever after in ways that leave no doubts about Cooper's conservative eighteenth-century allegiances. We all have our favorites, and my choices for the books most central to Cooper's fictive purposes, even more than *The Last of the Mohicans*, are *The Prairie*, *Satanstoe*, and *Home as Found*. Although I cannot demonstrate the proposition here, I suggest that the generating center of the energies of these books is Cooper's invocation of what one might call Jacksonian Romanticism in order to display it as the web of his society's commonly accepted shibboleths, and to fight against it.

It is interesting to note that Cooper's basic unit in the literary genres is the extended sketch, contiguously placed next to others for the creation of the novel rather than the romance. He attempted romance in the interlarding moments of high adventure, but he did not disguise his political perspectives in those interlardings. The novel afforded Cooper no camouflage: in presenting his society in order to repudiate many of its most cherished assumptions, he joined in open warfare a battle which indicated plainly the irony of how the premises of philosophical conservatism in Romantic America would make a man an outcast from the social conservatism of his society. The openness of auctorial views

within the social purposes of Cooper's novels, together with works like
The American Democrat and *A Letter to His Countrymen*, deposed
Cooper from his role as one of his country's most popularly accepted
authors and toppled him from his place in the literary custom house into
a life of endless and contumacious litigation, in which he was accused,
significantly enough, of being anti- and un-American.

As I find a demonstration of my thesis in the commonplaces we
share concerning Cooper, so, too, the same is true of Poe. In *Eureka* Poe
indicates his metaphysical preference for the instant before the big bang
as Supernal Reality. Once God has dispersed himself into the process of
equable irradiation, space, time and matter become not the
Transcendentalists' specifications of God, but a newly created debasement of supernal being, a debasement in which every atom sentiently
aches for return to that spaceless, timeless, immaterial state of perfect
unity, which is supernal beauty. Poe is indeed, as he has often been
called, the true transcendentalist in his conflict with Emerson. His
injunctions in "The Poetic Principle" endorse in aesthetics what *Eureka*
had proposed in ontologics: the division between the Dionaean Eros and
the Uranian Eros is the clear division of allegiances that Poe found easier
to make than did Hawthorne: Poe is entirely the "citizen of somewhere
else," and repudiates exactly that "Reality" that Charles Wilkins Webber
found to be the absolute state of things, and jolly good—in Hawthorne
and in life—at that. I think that in poetry or prose, in Poe's most
interesting work, "The Raven," "Ulalume," *Pym*, "Ligeia," "The Fall of
the House of Usher," the generating force centers in the conflict between
the supernal and the actual, with all the tonalities of the works aiming at
the sense of death, horror, and putrescence in which, as something less
than supernal, space time and matter inevitably sum themselves up. So,
too, for Poe the epistemology points away from history as realized or
realizable millennial goodness, points away from modes of apprehen-
sion and imagination that can deal with the actualities so terribly insisted
upon. Dream, madness, and surreal vision and memory become the
momentary apprehensions of lost Reality, the Supernal. All the
implications of tone, ontology, epistemology, cosmology, and history in
Poe's work reflect a repudiation of the shibboleths of his countrymen
and his literary marketplace. What remains complex in studying Poe is
the matter of biography rather than of identity-allegiances. The same
Poe I am talking about was also one of the most shrewd and professional
magazinists, one of the canniest competitors in the popular marketplace,
which never gave him reason to think that the actualities, especially the
economic ones, are the redemptive realizations of dream and memory. I
would go so far as to say that this biographical dimension of Poe as a

literary figure can be seen not only in the psychological terms for which and by which it has so often been used, but as an experiential intensification of Poe's metaphysical stance against the assumptions of his culture.

But the one who presents the most fascinating intricacies of identity-allegiances is Nathaniel Hawthorne. At once a "citizen of somewhere else" and a Flaubert observing the bourgeoisie on their Sunday promenade and saying of them *"Ils sont dans le vrai,"* Hawthorne almost never could free his fiction from the struggle which was at its center. There is so much to say about Hawthorne in this context that I will content myself with only four out of the countless possibilities of illustration. The first, and it is a prescription I offer to everyone, is this: arrange chronologically all of Hawthorne's prefaces, the "Custom House" pre-eminent among them, and then read them all at one sitting. There is no better introduction to Nathaniel Hawthorne's fiction and the conflict at the center of his imagination, for it is clear that as the dates at the end of the prefaces advance, certain compulsive and subterranean concerns remain, and all out of proportion to need and fact. The root and trunk of them all is the soft lament that he was never taken to the bosom of his nation as a great success in the popular literary marketplace. Growing organically like branches from this trunk are the aesthetics and the psychologics of Hawthorne's demure self-effacement as a man who belongs to the clear, brown, twilight atmosphere, the shadows, ivies, and lichens of "somewhere else" rather than the cheerful noonday custom house square of his "own dear native land" with all its actualities. His inability to merge the two allegiances or to rest with comfortable finality in either one of them accounts for both the creative energies behind the fiction and the destructive doubts behind the fiction's flaws.

For instance, as my second citation, I offer something as minute as one passing auctorial comment in "The Artist of the Beautiful." Of all Hawthorne's fiction, this tale is the only one that swears complete allegiance to "somewhere else" and completely repudiates the world of terrible actualities, with all their "unpicturesque prolixities." Yet at the very moment when Hawthorne dramatizes the vindication and triumph of the artist of the beautiful despite his society, in this tale of all his tales, he creates a fragile, frozen instant of his own characteristic withdrawal from his own presentations. Peter Hovenden as cold materialism, Robert Danforth as main strength, and Annie Hovenden Danforth as courtship and domestic concerns, have all, in their own ways, destroyed the attainment of the ideal beauty. The rather monstrously shrewd baby, child of Robert and Annie, grandchild of Peter, leaves no doubt about the world of his citizenship. But the social values of Hawthorne's marketplace, whether for the ladies or the gentlemen, also leave no doubt about the value of babies and domesticity and mother love, values which sum up Hawthorne's other allegiances. At the crucial moment when the child holds the butterfly, Hawthorne gives us the following: " 'How wise the little monkey looks!' whispered Robert Danforth to his wife. 'I never saw such a look on a child's face,' answered Annie, admiring her own infant, *and with good reason*, far more than the artistic butterfly. 'The darling knows more of the mystery than we do' " [italics mine]. Those four words, "and with good reason," coming when and where they do, are a sign of abdication on Hawthorne's part, a failure of nerve that allows the author to nudge his audience, to stand with them and his imagined ancestors as one who knows that stories and ideals of beauty are not a grown man's *real* Reality. It is a way to disclaim rather than identify with his own creation and to identify instead with his bourgeois audience, a way, as Henry James had seen, to avoid taking with full seriousness the life of his fiction.

My third and fourth citations magnify this tiny instance into its much larger consequences, and they are the endings of *The Scarlet Letter* and *The Marble Faun*. If one were to ask most readers to describe the ending of *The Scarlet Letter*, the chances are that they would recall the final scaffold scene. Some might offer the fact that after the scene, Pearl, humanized and redeemed, grows up, moves away, lives happily ever after, and that Hester is treated with respect and affection as she lives out her good old age in her cottage. In any case, the ending remembered suggests the typical and central Hawthornian theme of redemptive sin and the necessity of immersing in that destructive element in order to understand sympathetically the human heart and to maintain one's place in the magnetic chain of humanity. The stained dark lady, wrestling honestly with her own sin, develops the possibilities of human oneness, love, and redemption. But, of course, that is not the ending at all. The ending is a peroration calling for the unstained blond lady of light who has never succumbed to human frailty. That is, the ending is a repudiation of the entire book that preceded it, for that book, in turn, was a repudiation of the American sense of millennial possibilities of goodness clearly marked off from sin and darkness from the moment that the beadle says "A blessing on the righteous Colony of the Massachusetts where iniquity is dragged out into the sunshine." The ending is submission to popular beliefs and images—as F. I. Carpenter said long ago, "Puritans preferred blondes"—at the expense of the fiction. And in *The Marble Faun*, when Hawthorne creates that white-clad little lady of light in the character of Hilda, "the daughter of the Puritans," the "simple child of New England," the "American girl," what he actually creates within the context of the dramatic action is not a saint but a moral fungus. Yet not only does he struggle manfully to endorse Hilda throughout his romance, even when she uses St. Peter's cathedral as a spiritual public outhouse, but he even allows the representative "Americans," Hilda and Kenyon, to inherit the stage and the view at the conclusion of the story. The major thematic thrust of the romance is impelled by an imagination obsessed with the idea of the *felix culpa*, certain of a limited human identity rather than a millennial one. Like all of Hawthorne's works, *The Marble Faun* is generated out of a philosophically conservative imagination. Yet at the very moment that Kenyon suggests that there might be validity to the concept of the fortunate fall, Hilda shushes him up with shock and indignation, and Kenyon, with Hawthorne's awkward endorsement, submits: "Oh Hilda, lead me home!" The complexities of *The Marble Faun*, Hawthorne's richest book and his most significantly flawed one, are a reservoir of suggestions about the conflict of allegiances facing American writers of Romantic fiction.

The last and greatest of these four writers, Herman Melville, presents a development of fiction writing that is an exposition of the creative rages loosed by the Romantic-Classicist conflict I have been suggesting. Melville's books seem to begin in agreement with the impulses of Romantic primitivism. *Typee* is all nature, sunniness, and joy; *Omoo* is all fun and frolic; *Mardi* seems to champion the quest for the millennial condition; *Redburn* seems to be rebellion against the economic and political *status quo*; and *White-Jacket* seems to be a democratic rebellion against the military *status quo* in the United States Navy.

But equally present in these books is a repudiation of primitivistic ideologies in *Typee*, a repudiation of Taji's quest in *Mardi*, a recognition that one matures into a fallen state in *Redburn*, and an elitist sense of separation from the commoners who are being championed in *White-Jacket*. In *Moby-Dick*, the most magnificent of our Romantic fictions, the glories of the book are generated by the marvelous tension between allegiances. The wonderful *openness* of the book arises from the tempering of Ahab's millennialistic and all-sweeping wicked nobility by the perspectives of Ishmael, who comically recognizes that we are all slaves in a world where one is a wanderer rather than a commander. In *Pierre* the successful tensions of *Moby-Dick* break into the tortured agonies of repudiation by society and of the artist's repudiation of the Edenic shibboleths of Saddle Meadows. If one considers the image of light, from the sun-drenched brilliance with which *Typee* opens Melville's literary career in 1846 to the complete pitch blackness which is the closing image of *The Confidence Man* in 1857, the end of Melville's publishing of fiction during his lifetime, one finds in *Pierre* a summary of the image. The book begins with the soft brightness of early country morning and the sunny openness of endless, summer expectations in Saddle Meadows, and it ends in the gloomy darkness and the death of both life and expectation in the stony hardness of a city prison. And in the last fiction, the posthumously published *Billy Budd*, Melville tried to relate to actual history the metaphor of his finding that "the angel must hang," and that the moment of redemption, the assumptions of American expectation, never arrive. In no one more profoundly than in Melville does one find Romantic fiction created by recoil from the assumptions inherent in the American self-image. I do not mean to say that our Romantic fiction was only a political artifact. I do mean to say that the complete dimensions of political significance exist within the fiction, and that when one struggles with a full examination of the details of that fiction, the commonplaces I introduce so sparsely here assume fascinating importance both as facts of culture and as facts of the literary imagination. They serve as an illuminating and instructive bridge between the two in our literary history. Of course, one can argue that the conservative strain in Romantic writing derives simply enough from idiosyncratic conservatism within the writers themselves. But the fullest context of a writer's work is the writer's whole life in his whole world, and it is not insignificant that a common link among these otherwise very different writers is that the values with which their classicist-conservatism interacts are, in fact, the popular American shibboleths of a Romantic-radical heritage.

Notes

[1]In this brief space it is not possible to trace out the intricacies of definition involved in the categories "radical" and "conservative." The full development is attempted in a book I am currently writing, which examines the political dimensions of American literature and a fragment of which this essay is a highly condensed version. I warn the reader to be wary of the terminolgy in this essay, for I suggest a connection between Romanticism and radicalism, and there are many lines of radical thought that are quite anti-romantic. Furthermore, there are many lines of thought within Romanticism itself (the later Wordsworth, for instance, the later Germans of the nineteenth century) that are quite antiradical. But because I have room here only for a highly compacted condensation and not for intricacies and modifications, I ask the reader to accept the categories I offer not as full statements of "isms" but merely as labels for certain clusters I bring together. As I suggest much too sketchily in this essay, what I call "social radicalism" and "social

conservatism" both share a philosophically unexamined allegiance to ideological rhetoric; "philosophical radicalism" and "philosophical conservatism" both share a philosophical examination into their antithetical views of the identity of man, God, and nature. "Vocational radicalism" is what I call the work of the artist who dissents from the ideological rhetoric and values of his society. The essence of what I call "social conservatism" is an insistence on conformity to and belief in the values implicit in the ideological rhetoric of the established society. The fun begins with the recognition that social conservatism can insist upon examined assumptions that belong, in the philosophical depths, to versions of radical creeds. Thus, a writer who is a philosophical conservative may become a vocational radical in order to dissent from the social conservatism of culture which adheres to the unexamined, hardened, and distorted surfaces of what was originally a philosophically radical perspective.

²See also Ralph Thompson, *American Literary Annuals and Gift Books: 1825-1865* (New York: H. W. Wilson Co., 1936).

³*America's Heroes: The Models of Success in American Magazines* (New York: Oxford Univ. Press, 1970).

⁴Greene, p. 52.

⁵Hale was not idiosyncratic in her priorities; she reflects the consensus of the day even at the height of cultural nationalism. See *The Ladies' Magazine*, 1 (November, 1828), 526-27.

⁶The complete review, for all its qualifications, is part of the quite copious evidence that suggests that Hawthorne in fact had a considerable and appreciative select audience at the time he thought himself "the obscurest man of letters in America." See the *American Monthly Magazine*, 5 (March, 1838), 281-83.

⁷Hawthorne's letter to his publisher, James T. Fields (February 11, 1860) is quoted by Fields in his autobiographical book, *Yesterdays with Authors* (Boston: James R. Osgood, 1872).

⁸Trollope's essay, well known as it is, remains fresh and instructive in its entirety today. See "The Genius of Nathaniel Hawthorne," *North American Review*, 274 (September, 1879), 203-22.

⁹The reviewer is only partly aware of the profundity of the problem he raises. See the *Christian Examiner*, 55 (September, 1852), 292-95. See also John Caldwell Stubbs, *The Pursuit of Form: A Study of Hawthorne and the Romance* (Urbana: Univ. of Illinois Press, 1970), and Richard H. Brodhead, *Hawthorne, Melville and the Novel* (Chicago: Univ. of Chicago Press, 1976), pp. 1-118.

¹⁰For an intelligent, instructive, and useful discussion of contemporary critical terms, see J. Donald Crowley's introduction to his extremely serviceable edition, *Hawthorne: The Critical Heritage* (New York: Barnes & Noble, 1970).

¹¹Dwight Mayo Amory, "The Works of Nathaniel Hawthorne," *Universalist Quarterly*, 8 (July, 1851), 272-93; Italics mine.

¹²There is no doubt about what Webber would have thought about "The Artist of the Beautiful." He was a constant champion of Whiggism and the remnants of the epistemology that had been taught at Harvard in a previous generation. His essay, "Hawthorne," appeared in the *American Whig Review*, 4 (September, 1846), 296-316.

¹³*Speculations*, ed., Sir Herbert Read (New York: Harcourt, Brace, World, 1924). The essay, though published well after World War I, was written in 1913.

EROTICISM IN
AMERICAN LITERARY REALISM

Joseph Katz
University of South Carolina

The most serious flaw in American realistic literature still seems to be its sexual sterility. During the half century after the end of the Civil War, while the American realists fought for freedom to write about life as they saw it, they apparently made an abrupt retreat from the sexual arena. Sometimes the about-face was reluctant, as indicated in H. H. Boyesen's complaint about "the Iron Madonna who strangles in her fond embrace the American novelist." But more frequently the withdrawal appears to have been voluntary and even amiable, as in William Dean Howells's stricture:

> If the novel were written for men and for married women alone, as in continental Europe, it might be altogether different. But the simple fact is that it is not written for them alone among us, and it is a question of writing, under cover of our universal acceptance, things for young girls to read which you would be put out-of-doors for saying to them, or of frankly giving notice of your intention, and so cutting yourself off from the pleasure—and it is a very high and sweet one—of appealing to these vivid, responsive intelligences, which are none the less brilliant and admirable because they are innocent.[1]

The "Iron Madonna" and her immaculate ward "The Young Girl" became figures of fear or veneration for professional writers whose vision was realistic in both senses of the word.

And with good reason. Those figures represented a principle of female purity that was upheld and guarded by publishers of respectable magazines and novels. Pornography is not the question. There was pornographic literature in America before the Civil War, during it, and in the years after it—as, likely, there always will be. The question is at once more simple and more complex than that of pornography, centering as it does on the admissibility of sex and sexual awareness into literature in any way beyond the mere demarcation of characters as male and female. Looking backwards through the generation of H. L. Mencken to the generations of the realists themselves, it seems that anything more was inadmissible among respectable writers and readers. Affection was commonly rendered, even love, but apparently neither could have physical bases. Gentlemen did not even speak of the subject directly. As late as the first year of the twentieth century, whoever read Theodore Dreiser's *Sister Carrie* on its first submission to a publisher (Harper & Brothers) recommended its rejection mainly on the following grounds:

> His touch is neither firm enough nor sufficiently delicate to depict without offense to the reader the continued illicit relations of the heroine. The long succession of chapters dealing with this important feature of the story begin to weary very quickly. Their very realism weakens and hinders the development of the plot. The final scenes in New York are stronger and better—But I cannot conceive of the book arousing the interest or inviting the attention, after the opening chapters, of the feminine readers who control the destinies of so many novels.[2]

The Iron Madonna and The Young Girl were real enough to bar immediate publication of a great American realistic novel. They were real indeed.

"Puritanism," expostulated H. L. Mencken in an essay written while the storm of World War I was gathering.[3] "Naturally enough," he raged publicly, "this moral obsession has given a strong color to American literature. . . . In none other will you find so wholesale and ecstatic a sacrifice of aesthetic ideas, of all the fine gusto of passion and beauty, to notions of what is meet, proper and nice." Take Howells: "His investigations, one might say, are carried on *in vacuo*; his discoveries are not expressed in terms of passion, but in terms of giggles." The war for absolute sexual frankness was under way in American literature, and the preceding two generations of its native realists were—with their Iron Madonna and Young Girl—chief among the enemies. Whether reluctant or eager in their homage to those icons, writers of that group had been astonishingly reticent in matters of sex. Or so it seemed.

Partly because William Dean Howells was a pivot in the course of American literary realism, and partly because devotees of Howells's works and life usually are sensible, most considerations of questions relative to it tend to begin with him. Two academic critics are especially important in connection with the American realistic writers' treatments of sex, and both are Howellsians. One, Everett Carter, wisely emphasized the need to read Howells in the dual context of his life and time. "From the standpoint of our age, of course," Carter said, "Howells *was* a prude; not a hopeless one, but nevertheless a man of easily offended sensibilities; were he to appear among us we would dismiss him as impossibly neglectful of the physical involvements of love."[4] Moreover, in the eighteen nineties Howells worked in "an age of concealment, an age in which it took very little frankness to be regarded as vulgar and anarchical."[5] And yet anyone flipping through reviews of Howells's works, even as late as the nineties, finds adverse comments of an unexpected kind. Something must have been there. In an essay appropriately entitled "The Howells Nobody Knows," Edwin H. Cady demonstrated that this "something" was sex.[6]

For although Howells talked most sincerely about deferences due to The Young Girl, he in fact was talking about an approach to literature in which both she and The Iron Madonna were consequences rather than bases. The approach begins with the realists' shared conviction that fiction was serious art, not mere entertainment. Howells admitted that his own tastes lay in considering subjects other than " 'guilty love' "; but that and related matters could be considered in serious literature, he indicates. The requirement was for decorum in their treatment. His clear implication, in context, is that a serious literary artist had no need and ought not to provide instruction on the mechanics of sexual activities in his fiction. Gonadal appeals overpower most else in evocative genres, so the writer who appeals to the gonads—to " 'passion' " of the sexual kind—risks losing his reader's attentions from its overall direction. Treat sexual matters if appropriate, he was saying, but be balanced in the treatment.

Treated they were, and in balance. The sterility of American literary realism is only appearance. What is missing usually—but not even always—is the language of the streets and a hint of the *Kama Sutra*. Sex is approached honestly, openly, and directly from the beginnings of realism in American literature. There it is as early as 1867, in John W. DeForest's *Miss Ravenel's Conversion from Secession to Loyalty*. Although the sexual motif is prominently functional throughout the novel, one passage in chapter 27 is sufficient to make the point. The chapter details how Colonel Carter, husband to the former Miss Ravenel, is seduced by his wife's relative Victorine Larue. He tried to be faithful, but she was persistent; and, isolated on shipboard as they were, he was her captive:

> Carter hoped she would get sea-sick. This great, brawny, boisterous, domineering, heroic fighter had just enough moral vitality to know when he was in danger of falling, and to wish for safety. Those were perilous hours at evening, when the ship swept steadily through a lulling whisper of waters, when a trail of foamy phosphorescence, like a transitory Milky Way, followed in pursuit, when a broad bar of rippling light ran straight out to the setting moon, when the decks were deserted except by slumberers, and Mrs. Larue persisted in dallying. The temptation of darkness, the temptation of solitude, the fever which begins to turn sleepless brains at midnight, made this her possible hour of coquettish conquest. She varied from delicately phrased sentimentalities to hoydenish physical impertinences. He

> was not permitted for five minutes all together to forget that she was
> a bodily, as well as a spiritual presence. He was not checked in any
> transitory license of speech or gesture. Meantime she quoted fine
> rhapsodies from Balzac, and repeated telling situations from Dumas
> le Jeune, and commented on both in the interest of the *sainte passion
> de l'amour.*[7]

In short, Mrs. Larue led Carter to bed. The reader can know that or not.
What is important to the development of story and characters is that
Carter betrayed his wife with her—a passionate kiss would have done to
signify the betrayal. And what is explicitly reported a bit later is such a
kiss. But a reader with any degree of sophistication at all recognizes that
the physical intimacy was complete: the chapter concludes with a letter
from Mrs. Larue to Carter that she playfully signs " 'Your best and most
loving friend, St. Marie Madeleine.' " And the reader alert to the
rhythms, imagery, and allusions in the passage above knows what was
happening there. The latter two readers get far more out of the entire
novel because they are aware in detail of the physical desires that also
drew Miss Ravenel and Carter together. Howells was that third kind of
reader. In reviewing the novel, he mildly complained about Mrs. Larue:
"There is a little too much of her,—it is as if the wily enchantress had cast
her glamour upon the author himself,—and there is too much anxiety
that the nature of her intrigue with Carter shall not be misunderstood."[8]

To understand the realists' uses of eroticism requires, first, the
elemental acceptance of the fact that they did indeed use it; and, second,
the development of the ability to read as they wrote. A useful piece in
both connections is a small thing written by Stephen Crane. Just at about
the time that Crane published the first edition of *Maggie: A Girl of the
Streets*, a magazine published his "Why Did the Young Clerk Swear?;
Or, the Unsatisfactory French."[9] It is a simple enough sketch treating the
growing frustration of a young clerk attending a men's furnishing shop.
The frustration grows because periodically, just as he begins to
concentrate on the novel with which he tries to while away an inclement
day, he is interrupted by trivial requests. Look again. He reached for "a
French novel with a picture on the cover" that he had concealed under a
pile of shirts. He "opened the book and began to read. Soon it could have
been noticed that his blond mustache took on a curl of enthusiasm, and
the refractory locks on his brow showed symptoms of soft agitation."
There was a man and a woman: " 'She crossed the street. The young man
received a shock that sent the warm blood to his brain. It had been
raining. There was mud. With one slender hand Eloise lifted her skirts.
Silvere, leaning forward, saw her——' " *Now* the shop door opens. The
clerk disposes of the intruder quickly, resuming his reading at the point

where he had been interrupted: " 'handkerchief fall in a puddle. . . .' "
He hurriedly skips ahead to find a more promising passage: " ' "Eloise!"
Silvere was murmuring, hoarsely. He leaned toward her until his warm
breath moved the curls on her neck. "Eloise!" murmured Jean.' " Two
men and one woman obviously intrigues the clerk; but now again
someone enters the shop, again to be cast out rudely. But when the clerk
takes up his reading this time he finds that the second man is only a
peasant stopping to inquire about a misplaced cow. And so it goes, the
clerk searching for the "good" parts only to be disappointed each time.
That was why he swore.

Crane was playing for real as well as for laughs. The laughs come
because the knowing reader, like the young clerk, is led to expect sexual
action that does not take place; then, at some point—which, depends on
the reader's own level of gullibility—he catches on. Three directions of
the laughter are called for: towards the clerk for having been gulled, and
for taking so long to realize it; towards the reader, for the same reason;
and towards pornography as a genre. That last is the way in which Crane
was playing for real, because he already had written a novel—*Maggie*—
which proved that a serious writer could work comfortably with sexual
materials without being in any way pornographic.

Something else about Crane's sketch is interesting in context of the
larger consideration. It first appeared in *Truth*, a magazine that then had
the reputation for being spicy, so a discrete father might choose to not
bring it into his home. But this sketch, at least, could have been brought
home. Either The Iron Madonna or The Young Lady could have read it
without harm for they would have missed everything in it except the
clerk's understandable and amusing frustration at the constant intrusions
on his reading. Crane's sketch demonstrates the foundation on which the
realists based their ability to treat sexual matters without violating
prevailing moral codes. The sketch qualified its readers: only those who
knew the conventions of pornography would know what really was
going on, and they presumably would have the sophistication to handle
it; others, lacking the knowledge and the sophistication, would find it
readable and mildly amusing. Even the title of the sketch is a qualifying
device. The kind of bluenose so azure as to object even to swearing
would pass it by. Potential readers with more normal attitudes, however,
would not be offended. Among those readers—even women only
slightly more world-wise than The Iron Madonna and The Young Girl—
most would pick up one of Crane's two plays on the words "Unsatisfactory French" in the title. As Howells said, the French novelist had the
"tradition of indecency"—meaning not that the French were por-
nographers (for, again, pornography is not the question), but that the

reins on them were looser than on writers in America.[10] Howells argued, and to a reasonably aware readership Crane's title suggests, that this degree of looseness ultimately is unsatisfactory. But Crane's second play on those words in the title would be revealed only to those sufficiently familiar with pornography and its world to recognize its implied promise of oral-genital sexual activity, however unsatisfactory.

What the first publishers' reader of *Sister Carrie* complained about was not "the continued illicit relations of the heroine"; his complaint was about Dreiser's technique, "neither firm enough nor sufficiently delicate" to treat Carrie's behavior without The Iron Madonna and The Young Girl both knowing what was going on. That was bad business, because it limited the potential audience (which means "market" to a publisher) for the novel. Worse, it also was bad art. "It was not written for children," remarked Howells about *Doctor Breen's Practice* when he found his young son reading it, "but if a child may read it without harm, it seems to me something to be glad of."[11] And young John Howells then was "deep in the love-makingest chapter." Pursuing leads like this and those in Howells's discussion of The Young Girl, Everett Carter's musings are particularly valuable here:

> Perhaps there were literary conventions in operation at the time to which a modern reader is insensitive, since his are a different set of symbols relating to sex—different, but still conventional, for in no area of the representation of life does convention operate more strongly. In dealing with this most basic of human drives, surrounded by all of the tabus a culture erects around it, the writer is playing with emotional explosive; it must be handled with the greatest of care or it breaks out of its walls and blows up over the entire story, blurring other nuances and details. It is obvious, further, that save in textbooks, the sexual act can rarely be described accurately in letters, but must always be conveyed by more or less indirection.[12]

Carter followed Howells's train of thought to the correlations of the writer's intentions, the writer's style, and the reader's perception.

That the three are correlatives Nathaniel Hawthorne knew better than any writer to his time. Two of his experiments in handling the relationships may be worth some consideration in a discussion of eroticism in American realistic literature, in part because his enshrinement as a "classic" American writer took place between the years 1876 and 1879 and—as Cady documents—touched off the realism war.[13] Three years after Hawthorne's first novel appeared, *The Token* for 1831 published a curious sketch of his. The narrator of "Sights from a Steeple" had climbed to the highest point in town, its church steeple. From it he can see scenes unfolding below him, including a series of interrupted episodes that become a little drama. A young man saunters slowly down a north-south street. Two young ladies (one slightly prettier than the other) leave "an aristocratic edifice" and walk up that street. The young man and the young ladies encounter one another, and he turns and walks along with them, by the side of the prettier. A gouty, rich old merchant hustles up the street, meets the group, and thrusts the young man aside to hasten the young girls away. Most interesting in this sketch is its narrator: beginning with full acknowledgement that his vantage point sacrifices details to vista, he soon forgets; from his first wonders about whether the young man is in doubt or debt, in love or what, the narrator concludes "How disconsolate the poor lover stands!" Ambiguity has given way to certainty.

"The most desirable mode of existence might be that of a spiritualized Paul Pry," mused the narrator of "Sights from a Steeple" in 1831, "hovering invisible round man and woman, witnessing their deeds, searching into their hearts, borrowing brightness from their felicity, and shade from their sorrow, and retaining no emotion peculiar to himself." Perhaps it was reviewing the sketch again twenty years later, when he collected it in *Twice-Told Tales*, that helped Hawthorne to shape the novel he began that November of 1851. For the character and actions of Miles Coverdale in *The Blithedale Romance* are rooted in those of the sketch's narrator. Like him, Coverdale spies from a vantage point on those around him: in chapter 12, from a tree allowing him to pry into the affairs of Priscilla, Zenobia, and Westervelt; and in chapters 17 and 18, from a hotel room peeping onto the three in a boarding house opposite. Like the narrator of "Sights from a Steeple," Coverdale leaps to conclusions about love affairs—and like him he is all wet.

These and other experiments in the correlation among intention, style, and perception likely influenced the realists. At least William James thought so. Writing to his brother Henry in response to reading *The House of the Seven Gables*, James exclaimed: "It made a deep impression on me and I thank Heaven that Hawthorne was an American. It also tickled my national feeling not a little to notice the resemblance of Hawthorne's style to yours and Howells's. . . . That you and Howells with all the models in English literature to follow, should needs involuntarily imitated (as it were) this American, seems to point to the existence of some real American mental quality."[14] What Howells, James, and others of the American literary realists found in Hawthorne that they could make theirs and extend remains to be fully explored. His techniques of indirection, of inviting perception from those qualified for it, and of styling language for multi-levelled communication were certainly among Hawthorne's bequests to them. In erotic areas especially, he had more that was usable for them than the French or other Continental writers.

Harold Frederic's *Illumination* (the novel that Americans accidentally know as *The Damnation of Theron Ware*) is one novel that follows Hawthorne's experiments directly to the point to which they integrate an erotic motif into native literary realism.[15] Whatever else this genuine American masterpiece is, it is to a great extent a novel about erotic perception. Ware, the backwoods Methodist minister whose ambition outstrips his calling, is taken up by Celia Madden, Father Forbes, and Dr. Ledsmar—people involved in the New Humanism, the New Religion, and the New Science that developed in the nineteenth century. Captivated by his innocence and apparently naive sincerity, Celia and the priest take Ware up and begin a process of enlightening him. But that process leads Ware to three related perceptions: that Forbes is a hypocrite performing the rituals of a religion in which he does not believe; that Celia is a libertine; and that she and Forbes are carrying on a sexual relationship. He receives and computes his information in the same way Miles Coverdale and his anonymous predecessor did theirs: from the outside, by putting two and two together. And like them he comes up with something other than four.

There are rules to this game. Considering the correlatives of intention, style, and perception, the writer must play fair and give the reader the essentials for knowing what is going on. Since American literary realists often are interested in psychology, so long as they play by those rules the game is straight. These were Hawthorne's rules too. For the realist, one of the subparts to the rules evidently was honesty and consistency in developing character. At the outset, Theron Ware is shown plainly to be an opportunist with no values unrelated to his self-interest. He is developed as a husband who decides, for reasons of self-interest and no other, that his wife is having an affair. His mind operates in similar serpentine fashion throughout the novel. Since it is told mainly from Ware's point-of-view, the unsophisticated reader may not understand what is happening until relatively late—the point of understanding coming at any time in which the novel has educated the reader in reading, but not later than the third chapter from the end, in which Ware's point-of-view is completely blasted. Then even such a reader recognizes that he has been shown a peculiarly warped kind of person. He, like Ware, has received illumination.

Illumination, however, can take place at almost any point after the novel opens. Frederic does indeed play fair with his reader, showing him from the beginning Ware's warped orientation towards the world. Moreover, Frederic, like any good writer whether realist or not, indoctrinates the reader into what he is doing by supplying a variety of clues. For example, *Illumination* mainly is told from Ware's point-of-view—but not always. In one instance, Ware visits Dr. Ledsmar to confirm his perception of the relationship between Father Forbes and Celia Madden. Ware feels that Ledsmar disapproves of Celia, but does not understand that the reason for his disapproval is that Ledsmar is purely and only the New Scientist. In all other ways he is conservative, especially in a way that makes him unable to accept a woman who has departed from traditional models for her sex. During Ware's call Ledsmar singlemindedly pursues the topic of his work, misunderstanding the purpose of the call. Each time Ware alludes to Celia, Ledsmar brushes aside the distraction from *his* main interest. When Ledsmar slightingly remarks that Celia's father "ought to have her whipped," Ware interprets the remark wrongly and sees it as an invitation to pursue gossip. With what he evidently believes to be infinite delicacy, he inserts a blunt probe: Celia, he says, commented that she was happy to have the priest to herself all day. The scientist screeches in anguish. At first it seems a cry of anger, but Ware understands it soon as great pain. It was such pain, such an attack, says Ledsmar, as "rendered it impossible for him to shake hands with his guest in parting" as Ware is rushed to the door. When he leaves, the narrator remains behind to see Ledsmar pick up "a long, slim, yellowish-green lizard, with a coiling, sinuous tail and a pointed, evil head. . . . 'Yes, you are the type,' he murmured to it, with evident enjoyment in the conceit. 'Your name isn't Johnny any more. It's the Rev. Theron Ware.' "[16] A reader missing even clues such as these finds the novel an education in the discipline of reading American realism.

However, eroticism was neither merely a game nor a discipline in the literature of the American realistic writers. It was an area of the human condition that *is*—and, therefore, that could be treated and would be when appropriate. But the treatment of sex itself had to be appropriate. A vision of The Iron Madonna about to spring in defense of The Young Girl may have been at least annoying to a good writer; what apparently was truly fearsome was literature destroying itself by imbalance. Howells's evocation of The Young Girl appeared in that unfortunate hash, *Criticism and Fiction*, which since 1891 has summarized his critical stance—much to the detriment of his critical reputation.[17] "Generally, people now call a spade an agricultural implement; they have not grown decent without having also grown a little squeamish, but they have also grown comparatively decent; there is no doubt about that"—statements like these, out of the context of his work, are grist for the mill of anyone who would grind. But in context

Howells is saying something quite different than would appear at first glance:

> The fact, generally lost sight of by those who censure the Anglo-Saxon novel for its prudishness, is that it is really not such a prude at all; and that if it is sometimes apparently anxious to avoid those expriences of life not spoken of before young people, this may be an appearance only.

Fidelity to human experience was one requirement of good literary art: so far as the erotic was concerned, "unless the scheme of the story necessarily involved it, . . . it would be bad art to lug it in, and as bad taste to introduce such topics in mixed company." Which leads to the second requirement, that for the artist's control of his reader by controlling his material:

> "See how free those French fellows are!" . . . "Shall we always be shut up to our tradition of decency?"
>
> "Do you think it's much worse than being shut up to their tradition of decency?"

Howells evidently felt comfortable in exercising his art within the standards of a middle-class community.

So had Frank Norris, once he became used to them.[18] It astonishes critics to discover that *The Pit*, his last novel, was a bestseller almost immediately: it sold 100,000 copies during its first year of publication in America alone. Their astonishment comes from the reasoned conviction—shared without exception—that the novel splits apart. The consensus is that Norris muddles the novel by intruding Laura, Curtis Jadwin's younger wife, into the story of Jadwin's monomaniacal attempt to corner wheat:

> She is both important and unimportant. Though she seems real enough at times, her character is nevertheless intellectually rather than emotionally apprehended. One feels that Norris thinks of new things to do with her as he proceeds with the story: he makes dialectical discoveries of ways to write pages of reasoning about how she should feel and act at particular times. These reasoned pages do not make her come to life. Her whole role, to be sure, is vitiated by the supreme importance of Jadwin's fight over the wheat. Obviously, she is there merely as a foil to set off the great struggle in the Pit, to show the other side of Jadwin's public failure. Thus the story breaks completely in two when Norris devotes considerable time to her connection with Sheldon Corthell, the understanding artist to whom she goes for comfort when Jadwin is deserting her more and more for the Pit.[19]

In fact, Laura Dearborn Jadwin goes to Corthell for much more than "comfort"—and receives it.

Norris began *The Pit* as the story of Laura, not of Jadwin. "*She occupies the center of the stage all the time,*" he wrote to an acquaintance at the end of the novel's planning stage, "and I shall try to interest the reader more in her character and career than in any other human element in the book. The two main themes, consequently, are the story of Jadwin's corner in May wheat and the story of his wife's 'affair' with Corthell."[20] This is not an occasion appropriate to explicating any one work in detail, even a novel that has been generally misunderstood by modern critics. But *The Pit* offers so good an example of the ways in which a realist not only could treat erotic materials successfully, but also could use them as integral in an extensive work of fiction, that it does deserve consideration as a specimen for analysis.

To be fair, there are good reasons for misreading *The Pit*. One is that it was the second volume in Norris's Trilogy of The Epic of the Wheat, preceded by *The Octopus* and to be succeeded by the never-written *The Wolf*. This setting seems to imply a focus on the wheat. Norris, however, was doing something quite different: he was focussing on people whose lives were affected by attempts to manipulate the wheat for industrial purposes. "These novels," he said in a brief preface to *The Pit*, "while forming a series, will in no way be connected with each other save only in their relation to (1) the production, (2) the distribution, (3) the consumption of American wheat." Read *The Pit* as emphasizing Curtis Jadwin's failed attempt to corner the wheat market—the distribution of wheat—and the novel is indeed a failure for just the reason critics have offered. In that reading, Laura Dearborn Jadwin's story is superfluous.

But *The Pit* is a much more complex and carefully wrought novel than it seems to be for modern critics. Of course it is partly the story of Jadwin's failed corner. Mainly, however, it is an exploration of development in a woman with great beauty who has limited capacities in most other areas of life. Laura is ill-educated, egocentric, and without real understanding of her own sexuality or its effects on others. Drawn into marriage with Jadwin almost by whim, therefore, she is unable to make—or even to understand the need to make—the loving compromises that define marriage. *The Pit* is the story of an illumination, an awakening, and like all of Norris's novels its direction is to support middle class values. Extremes of any kind are intolerable to that value system. So, like novelists in the mainstream from Jane Austen on, Norris takes his characters to the extremes in order to bring them back to the middle way. The title of his novel is important. Like the title of Crane's sketch, it functions on three levels. It refers literally to the floor of the wheat exchange, on which men manipulate the grain for their own advantage. Metaphorically, it is a reference to an arena in which beasts tear one another apart for sport. And allegorically it evokes the place to which sinners are relegated.

Most of this will appear to be critical hocus-pocus to the reader who does not recognize the explicit sexual aspects of the novel. Laura is introduced in the first chapter as a beautiful, strong-willed young woman who waits impatiently with her sister Page and their Aunt Wess' for their hosts to arrive so that she she can see her first opera. When she hears the opera begin and they still have not appeared, she boldly introduces herself to Jadwin (whom she had not met, but who she knew was one of the party) and asks him to help. While Laura intentionally makes him feel awkward in punishment for his initial reserve at being accosted by a strange woman in a public place, the rest arrive. Among them is Sheldon Corthell, the comfortably-fixed artist who had been wooing her. He had sent her flowers for the evening; not seeing one on her cape, he asks if she did not like them. She replies that she selected the most beautiful, parts her cape, and shows him the rose pinned to her gown. By the time the group hustles to their box, the first aria of the second act is just finished. "She'll sing it over again, though, just for you, if I have to lead the applause myself," Corthell says. "I particularly wanted you to hear that."

All commentators have acknowledged that first chapter of *The Pit* as a *tour de force*. Always behind the social intercourse and the music of the opera are rumblings about the failure of a wheat corner, presaging what will happen to Jadwin later. But more—much more—is happening. Again, Norris is qualifying his readers. Everyone recognizes that Corthell is courting Laura. Neither The Iron Madonna nor The Young Girl would be repelled by a good love story; romance, in fact, was what they wanted—so long as it did not involve the bedroom. They could find such good, clean romance in *The Pit*. More sophisticated readers, however, would recognize the bounty of literary, musical, pictorial, and mythological symbols with which Norris develops the erotic context in which everything else is to be interpreted. The affair did indeed involve the bedroom. So textured is the novel with this erotic motif that is its base, that it is impossible here to work through its full development and effect. All that is possible are some slight indications.

The opera that Laura hears is Gounod's *Faust*, by Norris's time a cliché. There is no doubt about the identification: in one of the few surviving pages of the novel's manuscript—the first page—he had originally written the title, then canceled it and substituted the words "one of the most popular pieces of its repertoire" (referring to the opera company). The cancellation presumably resulted in part from the technique of qualification; mostly, however, the knowledgable reader of Norris's day could have been counted upon to recognize the opera from his burlesque of it and from clues such as two different libretti being intermixed on stage. For such a reader, interesting things happen in the first chapter.

Corthell's gift of flowers to Laura, for example, reveals both his intentions and her inability to understand them clearly. He particularly wanted her to hear the first aria in the second act because it is "Faites-lui mes aveux," Seibel's plea that his flowers speak his love for Margarita. Corthell evidently wanted Laura to make the connection, but she does not because she had been tutored only to read French, not to converse in it. Her entire education, in fact, had been deficient. But Corthell's miscalculation is just that. He accurately recognizes Laura's smoldering sexuality. Although she has little idea of what really is going on in the opera, its music and embraces stir her. She herself does not identify her capacity for sexual passion, but Corthell does.

When the marriage between Laura and Jadwin begins to disintegrate, Corthell is there patiently educating her. He teaches her the nature of better painting, literature, and music than she knew before; simultaneously, he cultivates her passions with music like Lizst's *Mephisto Waltz* and conversations about subjects that allude to erotic love, even evoking such figures of feminine sexuality as Phedre and Isolde. In chapter 8, Laura's marriage completely breaks down. Jadwin is so caught up in the pit that he neglects her almost entirely. Despite repeated direct requests that he spend particular evenings with her, he absents himself on business. "Let those who neglected her look to it," she finally declares, considering adultery. That is in her mind one evening when Jadwin is away and Corthell calls. Past visits had been spent in the formal rooms of the house; now she impulsively invites him into her sitting-room, the room off her bedroom that is considered her next most personal and intimate room. There, after a few moments in harmless conversation, she begins to tell Corthell her loneliness, unhappiness, and need for love. His response is to offer her himself. Laura immediately changes the subject, but neither eases him out of the room nor rejects his offer. She is taking time to consider it. With his invariable tact and patience, and his instinctive understanding of her emotions, Corthell participates in the change of subject and waits. Laura invites him to smoke and points him towards matches.

> But Corthell, as he lit his cigarette, produced his own match box.
> It was a curious bit of antique silver, which he had bought in a

Viennese pawnshop, heart-shaped and topped with a small ducal
coronet of worn gold. On one side he had caused his name to be
engraved in small script. Now, as Laura admired it, he held it
towards her.

"An old pouncet-box, I believe," he informed her, or possibly it
held an ointment for her finger nails." He spilled the matches into his
hand. "You see the red stain still on the inside; and—smell," he added,
as she took it from him. "Even the odour of the sulphur matches
cannot smother the quaint old perfume, distilled perhaps three
centuries ago."

An hour later Corthell left her. She did not follow him further
than the threshold of the room, but let him find his way to the front
door alone.[21]

They had had sexual intercourse.

Neither the Iron Madonna nor The Young Girl would understand
what happened during the intervening hour between the time Laura
accepted the box and the time Corthell left, but any reader of the day
capable of accepting the situation unshocked would know it. Norris had
carefully developed the episode not only through readily-available
cultural symbols, but also through symbols internal to the novel which
link its elements together. The shape of the matchbox and the blended
odors of sulphur and perfume function obviously enough. What does
require noting, in this summary, is a passage in the first chapter that ties
the ducal coronet and Corthell's signature. Aunt Wess', more puzzled
than Laura by the opera, does not at all understand what is going on
between Faust and Margarita at the end of the third act, just before
Valentine enters to be slain. She asks about "the gentleman with the
beard"—Faust. " 'Why, that's the duke, don't you see, Aunt Wess'?' "
Laura explains, wrongly. A few days after Laura's episode with Corthell,
Jadwin begins to feel that all is not well. He comes to her, looking odd
enough for her to enquire about his health. " 'Sick?' he queried. 'No
indeed. But—I'll tell you. Since a few days I've had,' he put his fingers to
his forehead between his eyes, 'I've had a queer sensation right
there. . . .' " The allusion is to the cuckhold's horns. But by the end of the
novel both Laura and Jadwin had risen from their respective pits,
obviously battered by their experiences but just as obviously determined to make their marriage work. Laura dismissed Corthell, Jadwin
lost his fortune, and they are waiting for the movers to take them to a
more modest house that would become a home. While they wait, Laura
asks if Jadwin would like to hear a letter that had arrived from her sister
Page and which Laura herself had not had time to completely read.
There are things in the letter that recall painful parts of the past, but
Jadwin asks her to continue. The most painful reference comes in a
postscript—a reference to Corthell. Laura quickly puts the letter

away. Jadwin covers her awkwardness by feigning vagueness about Corthell. "I told you—told you all about it," she responds. Jadwin replies that his only memory is that he himself had been to blame for everything: "I told you once—long ago—that I understood." Certainly, *The Pit* is concerned with Jadwin's failure to corner the wheat. But its real concerns are far larger than only that.

William Dean Howells was right: serious fiction could be written by the American realists in ways to range freely through the passions without disturbing The Young Girl. Carter was right: there were indeed conventions through which the realists could treat erotic love without causing damage to their work. Ironically, H. L. Mencken was wrong. Less than a decade after his blast at the "Puritans," he wrote another essay, "The American Novel." In it he complained that although the battle for freedom to treat anything in literature had been won, for all practical purposes, writers of the day were producing shoddy instead of good literature.[22] The discipline with which the American realists had worked gave their writing strength and depth of a kind that has gone unrecognized.

Notes

[1]*Criticism and Fiction* (New York: Harper & Brothers, 1891), pp. 149-50.

[2]In Robet H. Elias, ed., *Letters of Theodore Dreiser* (Philadelphia: Univ. of Pennsylvania Press, 1959), I, 210. The report is dated 2 May 1900.

[3]"Puritanism as a Literary Force," in Mencken's *A Book of Prefaces* (New York: Alfred A. Knopf, 1917).

[4]*Howells and the Age of Realism* (Philadelphia: J.B. Lippincott, 1954), p. 140.

[5]Carter, p. 147.

[6]In Edwin Cady, *The Light of Common Day* (Bloomington: Indiana Univ. Press, 1971), pp. 138-60.

[7]*Miss Ravenel's Conversion from Secession to Loyalty* (New York: Harper & Brothers, 1867), pp. 376-77.

[8]Reprinted in Clara Marburg Kirk and Rudolf Kirk, eds., *European and American Masters* (New York: Collier Books, 1963), p. 145. The review had originally appeared in the *Atlantic Monthly* for July 1867.

[9]*Truth*, 12 (18 March 1893), 4-5.

[10]*Criticism and Fiction*, p. 150.

[11]Howells to John Hay, 18 March 1882; in Mildred Howells, ed., *Life in Letters of William Dean Howells* (Garden City: Doubleday, Doran & Co., 1928), I, 311.

[12]Carter, pp. 147-48.

[13]" 'The Wizard Hand": Hawthorne, 1864-1900," in *The Light of Common Day*, pp. 120-37.

[14]Quoted in *The Light of Common Day*, pp. 134-35. The letter is dated 19 January 1870.

[15]For the title of Frederic's novel see Stanton Garner, *"The Damnation of Theron Ware* or *Illumination:* The Title of Harold Frederic's Novel," *Proof 5* (Columbia: J. Faust & Co., 1977), 57-66.

[16]*The Damnation of Theron Ware* (New York: Stone & Kimball, 1896), p. 337. But see most of the end of chapter 21.

[17]Howells scholars in recent decades have established that *Criticism and Fiction* was put together quickly as a favor and does not represent accurately Howells's critical stance.

[18]In his first published novel, Norris went a little too far in his treatment of erotic love and modified it for book publication. Again, in *McTeague* and *A Man's Woman*, he offended readers with the strength of his treatment of other areas of life and modified those treatments. See my and John Manning's "Frank Norris' Revision of Two Novels," *PBSA*, 62 (1968), 256-59.

[19]Charles Child Walcutt, *American Literary Naturalism, A Divided Stream* (Minneapolis: Univ. of Minnesota Press, 1956), pp. 153-54. But any modern critic of the novel could have been cited as well. Walcutt is representative of the consensus.

[20]Norris to I. F. Marcosson [November 1901]; in Donald Pizer, "Ten Letters by Frank Norris." Book Club of California *Quarterly News-Letter*, 27 (Summer, 1962), 59-60.

[21]*The Pit* (New York: Doubleday, Page, 1902), p. 267.

[22]In *Prejudices (Fourth Series)* (1924).

AMERICAN LITERARY NATURALISM:
THE EXAMPLE OF DREISER

Donald Pizer
Tulane University

American literary naturalism has almost always been viewed with hostility. During its early years the movement was associated with Continental licentiousness and impiety and was regarded as a literature foreign to American values and interests. "We must stamp out this breed of Norrises," a reviewer of *McTeague* cried in 1899.[1] In our own time, though antagonism to naturalism is expressed more obliquely, it is as deeply rooted. A typical discussion of the movement is frequently along the following lines.[2] The critic will examine the sources of naturalism in late nineteenth-century scientism, in Zola, and in post-Civil War industrial expansion. He will note that to a generation of American writers coming of age in the 1890s the mechanistic and materialistic foundations of contemporary science appeared to be confirmed by American social conditions and to have been successfully applied to the writing of fiction by Zola. But he will also note that Stephen Crane, Frank Norris, and Theodore Dreiser were often muddled in their thinking and inept in their fiction, and he will attribute these failures to their unfortunate absorption of naturalistic attitudes and beliefs. Our typical critic will then discover a second major flowering of naturalism in the fiction of James T. Farrell, John Steinbeck, and John Dos Passos in the 1930s. He will remark that scientism has been replaced by Marxism and that the thinking of this generation of naturalists is not so much confused as doctrinaire, but his account of their work will still be governed by the assumption that naturalism is a regrettable strain in modern American literary history.

Indeed, the underlying metaphor in most accounts of American fiction is that naturalism is a kind of taint or discoloration, without which the writer would be more of an artist and through which the critic must penetrate if he is to discover the essential nature and worth of the writer. So those writers who most clearly appear to be naturalists, such as Dreiser and Farrell, are almost always praised for qualities which are distinct from their naturalism. We are thus told that Dreiser's greatness is not in his naturalism[3] and that he is most of all an artist when not a

philosopher.[4] And so the obvious and powerful thread of naturalism in
such major figures as Hemingway, Faulkner, and (closer to our own
time) Saul Bellow is almost always dismissed as an irrelevant and
distracting characteristic of their work.

This continuing antagonism to naturalism has several root causes.
One of the clearest is that many critics find naturalistic belief morally
repugnant. But whereas earlier critics stated openly their view that
naturalism was invalid because man was as much a creature of divine
spirit as animal substance, the more recent critic is apt to express his
hostility indirectly by claiming that naturalistic novelists frequently
violate the deterministic creed which supposedly informs their work
and are therefore inconsistent or incoherent naturalists. On one hand,
this concern with philosphical consistency derives from the naturalist
writer's interest in ideas and is therefore a justifiable critical interest. On
the other, there seems little doubt that many critics delight in séeking out
the philosophically inadequate in naturalistic fiction because man is
frequently portrayed in this fiction as irredeemably weak and deluded
and yet as not responsible for his condition. It is the rare work of fiction
of any time in which threads of free will and determinism do not
interweave in a complex pattern that can be called incoherent or
inconsistent; on strictly logical grounds man either has free will or he
does not. Yet it is principally the naturalistic novel which is damned for
this quality, which suggests that it is the weighting of this inconsistency
toward an amoral determinism—not its mere presence—that is at stake.[5]

Another source of the hostility of modern critics to the naturalistic
novel lies in recent American political history. American naturalism of
the 1890s was largely apolitical, but in the 1930s the movement was
aligned with the left wing in American politics and often specifically
with the Communist Party. In the revulsion against the Party which
swept the literary community during the 1940s and 1950s, it was
inevitable that naturalistic fiction of the 1930s would be found wanting
because the naturalists of that decade, it was now seen, had so naively
embraced some form of communist belief. The most influential critical
discussions of American naturalism during the 1940s and 1950s—Philip
Rahv's "Notes on the Decline of American Naturalism," Malcolm
Cowley's "A Natural History of American Naturalism," and Lionel
Trilling's "Reality in America"[6]—have as an underlying motive a desire
to purge American literature and its historiography of an infatuation
with an alien and destructive political ideal.

A final reason for the antagonism toward naturalistic fiction is that
several generations of academic critics have been attracted by an

increasingly refined view of the aesthetic complexity of fiction. They have believed that a novel must above all be organic—that is, the product of a romantic imagination—and they have found principally in the work of Hawthorne, Melville, Faulkner, and to a lesser extent James, that enlargement of metaphor into symbol and that interplay of irony and ambivalence which bring fiction close to the complex indirection of a metaphysical lyric. Stephen Crane is the only naturalistic writer whose fiction satisfies these expectations, and his work is generally held to be uncharacteristic of the non-artistry of a movement more adequately represented by Dreiser.[7]

I do not wish to suggest by this brief survey of the critical biases which have led to the inadequate examination of American naturalism that there are not naturalistic novels which are muddled in conception and inept in execution. But just as we have long known that the mind-set of an early nineteenth-century critic would little prepare him to come to grips with the essential nature and form of a romantic poem, so we are coming to realize that a generation of American critics has approached American literary naturalism with beliefs about man and art which have frequently distorted rather than cast light upon the object before them.

Theodore Dreiser is the author whose work and career most fulfill the received notion of American naturalism; indeed, it is often difficult to determine the demarcation between literary history and critical biography in general discussions of American naturalism, so completely is Dreiser as thinker and writer identified with the movement in America. It would be instructive, therefore, to test the example of Dreiser—to note, initially and briefly, those characteristics of his career and work which lead us to describe him as a naturalist; and then, more fully, to examine some of the naturalistic elements in his fiction. But unlike so much of the criticism of naturalism which I have been describing, I do not wish to undertake this test with the assumption that Dreiser's fiction is confused in theme and form because he is not a consistent naturalist or that his work is best when he is least naturalistic. In short, I do not wish to consider his naturalism as an unfortunate excrescence. Rather, I want to see how his naturalistic predispositions work in his fiction and whether or not they work successfully.

Dreiser was born an outsider. His parents were of Catholic, German-speaking immigrant stock and throughout Dreiser's youth the large family was agonizingly poor. As a young man Dreiser sought the success and position which his parents had lacked and also shed the religious and moral beliefs which, he believed, had appeared to shackle them. While a young reporter in Pittsburgh in the early 1890s, he found his deepest responses to life confirmed by his reading of Herbert Spencer and Balzac. There were, he believed, no discernible supernatural agencies in life, and man was not the favored creature of divine guidance but an insignificant unit in a universe of natural forces. Although these forces, whether biological or social, were the source of racial progress, they often crushed the individual within their mechanistic processes. Like many of his generation, Dreiser found that the observed realities of American society supported this theory of existence. The mills and libraries of Pittsburgh were evidence of progress, but the lives of the immigrant foundry workers—to say nothing of the lives of Dreiser's own errant sisters and brothers— appeared dwarfed and ephemeral compared with the grinding and impersonal power of a vast economic system and a great city. Yet the city itself, as Balzac had amply demonstrated, was exciting and alluring, and not all were crushed who sought to gain its wonders. In *Sister Carrie* Dreiser was to write, "Among the forces which sweep and play throughout the universe, untutored man is but a wisp in the wind."[8] But though Hurstwood is swept away by these forces, and though Carrie's career is that of a storm-tossed ship, Carrie survives and indeed grows in understanding by the close of the novel. So accompanying Dreiser's endorsement of an amoral determinism there exists a disconcerting affirmation of the traditionally elevating in life—of Carrie, for example, as a figure of "emotional greatness," that is, of imaginative power. Forty-five years after *Sister Carrie* Dreiser joined the Communist Party while celebrating in his last two novels the intuitive mysticism at the heart of Quaker and Hindu belief. Here, in brief, at the two poles of his career and work is the infamous intellectual muddle of Dreiser and, by extension, of naturalism itself. And this muddle appears to be matched by a corresponding lack of control and firmness in fictional technique. Dreiser documents his social scene with a pseudo-scientific detachment yet overindulges in personal philosophical disquisitions; he attempts to write a "fine" style but produces journalistic cliché and awkwardness.

So in most important ways Dreiser fulfills the conventional definition of the American naturalist. All the major paradoxes are present: his identification with the "outsider," which was to lead to a contemptuous view of the main stream of middle class American life, yet his lifelong worship of "success"; his acceptance of a "scientific" mechanistic theory of natural law as a substitute for traditional views of individual insight and moral responsibility, yet his affirmation of many of these traditional views; and his deep response to a major European novelist, including the form of his fiction, yet his seeming neglect of style and form. I cannot hope to discuss these major characteristics of Dreiser as a naturalist as each appears in his eight novels. But I can pursue the vital naturalistic theme of mechanistic determinism in two of his principal novels, *Jennie Gerhardt* and *An American Tragedy*, and thereby reach toward at least a modest understanding of the example of Dreiser.[9]

Dreiser began *Jennie Gerhardt* in early 1901, soon after the publication of *Sister Carrie*. He wrote most of the novel during the next two years, though he did not complete it until late 1910. Like *Sister Carrie*, *Jennie Gerhardt* is about a girl from a poor family who has several sexual affairs with men of higher station but who emerges from her adventures not only unsullied but also elevated in character and insight. The novel differs from *Sister Carrie* primarily in Dreiser's characterization of Jennie and of Lester Kane, the principal man in Jennie's life. Kane, at least on the surface, is a more powerful, successful, and contemplative figure than Hurstwood, and Jennie differs from Carrie in that she is a warm and generous giver rather than a taker.

In the course of the novel, Jennie is seduced first by Senator Brander, by whom she has a child, Vesta, and then by Lester Kane. She and Kane are attracted to each other by a powerful natural "affinity" and they live together contentedly for several years. But because Lester is gradually forced to accept that a permanent union with Jennie would adversely affect his business career and the comfortable certainties of his social and family life, they do not marry. Eventually they part, Lester marries Letty Gerald, a woman of his own class, and Jennie suffers the death of both her father and Vesta.

One of the major scenes in *Jennie Gerhardt* is Lester's visit to Jennie after the death of Vesta. Deeply depressed by Vesta's death and by his realization that he erred in leaving Jennie, Lester tells her

> it isn't myself that's important in this transaction [that is, life itself] apparently; the individual doesn't count much in the situation. I don't know whether you see what I'm driving at, but all of us are more or less pawns. We're moved about like chessmen by circumstances over which we have no control.[10]

This famous pronouncement, which has supplied several generations of literary historians with a ubiquitous image for the philosophical center of American naturalism, requires careful analysis both in its immediate context and in relation to the novel as a whole if it is to be properly understood.

Whatever the general truth of Lester's words, they represent a personal truth. His pawn image expresses both his sense of ineffectuality in the face of the central dilemma of his life and a covert supernaturalism

which has characterized his thought throughout the novel despite his
overt freethinking. Earlier he had attributed his difficulties merely to bad
luck. But by the time he and Jennie separate, he has elevated and
generalized "fate" into a specific force which is at once social,
supernatural, and (as far as he is concerned) malevolent:

> It was only when the storms set in and the winds of adversity blew
> and he found himself facing the armed forces of convention that he
> realized he might be mistaken as to the value of his personality, that
> his private desires and opinions were as nothing in the face of a
> public conviction; that he was wrong. The race spirit, or social
> avatar, the "Zeitgeist," as the Germans term it, manifested itself as
> something having a system in charge, and the organization of society
> began to show itself to him as something based on possibly a
> spiritual, or, at least, supernatural counterpart (pp. 373-74).

Lester's speculative statement that men are but pawns in the control of
circumstances is thus in part an explanation and a defense of his own
conduct. In particular, it is a disguised apology to Jennie for his failure to
marry her when he could have done so. But it is also a powerful means of
characterizing Lester. Throughout his life he had lived for the moment
and had postponed making decisions about the direction of his life. But
the decisionless flow of time contained an impetus of events which
constituted an implicit and irreversible decision, and when Lester at last
awoke to the fact that his life had been decided for him, he bitterly and
angrily blamed fate.

Because Lester is a perceptive and on the whole an honest figure, his
belief that men are pawns involves more than a rationalization of his own
indecisiveness and ineffectuality. His belief also aptly characterizes
social reality as that reality has been dramatized in the novel. The
pressure of circumstances on Lester in his relationship with Jennie has
indeed been intense, from their initial meeting within the convention of a
seduction—a convention which appeared to preclude marriage—to the
later opposition of Lester's personal, business, and social worlds to the
continuation of the relationship. In a passage cut from Chapter XL of the
final holograph of the novel, Dreiser himself, as narrator, echoed Lester's
attribution of superhuman powers to social force. "The conventions in
their way," he wrote, "appear to be as inexorable in their workings as the
laws of gravitation and expansion. There is a drift to society as a whole
which pushes us on in a certain direction, careless of the individual,
concerned only with the general result."[11]

In his final position as one deeply puzzled by the insignificance of
the individual, Lester therefore reflects a persistent strain in Dreiser's
thought. Before making his pawn speech to Jennie, Lester had "looked

down into Dearborn Street, the world of traffic below holding his attention. The great mass of trucks and vehicles, the counter streams of hurrying pedestrians, seemed like a puzzle. So shadows march in a dream" (p. 400). The scene effectively images both Lester's and Dreiser's belief that life is a helter-skelter of activity without meaning either for its observers or for the "shadows" who give it motion. As a man aware of the direction of modern thought, Lester is able to give this view of life an appropriate philosophical framework. In the years that pass after Vesta's death, his response to life, Dreiser tells us, becomes "decidedly critical":

> He could not make out what it was all about. In distant ages a queer thing had come to pass. There had started on its way in the form of evolution a minute cellular organism which had apparently reproduced itself by division, had early learned to combine itself with others, to organize itself into bodies, strange forms of fish, animals, and birds, and had finally learned to organize itself into man. Man, on his part, composed as he was of self-organizing cells, was pushing himself forward into comfort and different aspects of existence by means of union and organization with other men. Why? Heaven only knew. . . . Why should he complain, why worry, why speculate?—the world was going steadily forward of its own volition, whether he would or no. Truly it was (pp. 404-05).

It must not be assumed, however, that Lester's pessimistic response to the "puzzle" of man's role in a mechanistic world is Dreiser's principal and only philosophical theme in *Jennie Gerhardt*. For Jennie, though not Lester's equal in formal knowledge or in experience, is his equal in the "bigness" of her responsiveness to the underlying reality of life, and she discovers not only puzzlement and frustration in life but also an ineradicable beauty. Dreiser therefore follows his comments on Lester's critical outlook with an account of Jennie's final evaluation of life. This evaluation, because of its source and its strategic location, has significance equal to Lester's beliefs. Jennie, Dreiser writes,

> had never grasped the nature and character of specialized knowledge. History, physics, chemistry, botany, geology, and sociology were not fixed departments in her brain as they were in Lester's and Letty's. Instead there was the feeling that the world moved in some strange, unstable way. Apparently no one knew clearly what it was all about. People were born and died. Some believed that the world had been made six thousand years before; some that it was millions of years old. Was it all blind chance or was there some guiding intelligence—a God? Almost in spite of herself she felt that there must be something—a higher power which produced all the beautiful things—the flowers, the stars, the trees, the grass. Nature was so beautiful! If at times life seemed cruel, yet this beauty still persisted. The thought comforted her; she fed upon it in her hours of secret loneliness (p. 405).

Jennie and Lester's complementary views of life represent Dreiser's own permanent unresolved conception of the paradox of existence. To both figures the world "was going steadily forward of its own volition," apparently guided by some unknowable power. Individuals counted for little in this process, but individuals of different temperaments might respond to the mechanism of life in different ways. One kind of temperament might be bitter and despairing, another might affirm the beauty which was inseparable from the inexplicable mystery of life. It has frequently been noted that Dreiser himself held both views at different stages of his career—that he stressed a cruelly indifferent mechanistic universe in *Hey Rub-a-Dub-Dub* (1920) and a mechanistic world of beauty in *The Bulwark* (1946). It has not been as fully realized that he held the two positions simultaneously as well as consecutively and that he gave each position equal weight and dramatic expression in *Jennie Gerhardt* without resolving their "discrepancy." For to Dreiser there was no true discrepancy; there was only the reality of distinctive temperaments which might find truth in each position or, as in his own case, of a temperament which might find an element of truth in both. Dreiser's infamous philosophical inconsistency is thus frequently a product of his belief that life is a "puzzle" to which one can respond in different ways, depending on one's makeup and experience.

The naturalistic "philosophy" of deterministic mechanism in Dreiser's novels is therefore usually secondary, within the fictional dynamics of each novel, to the role of the concept as a metaphor of life against which various temperaments can define themselves. Or, to put the matter another way, Lester's belief in one kind of mechanistic philosophy and Jennie's in another are less significant fictionally than the depiction of Jennie as a woman of feeling and of Lester as a man of speculative indecision. But it should also be clear that in attributing a secondary fictional role to the mechanistic center of *Jennie Gerhardt* I am not saying that the philosophy muddles the novel or that the novel is successful for reasons other than the philosophy. I am rather saying that the philosophy and the fiction are one and inseparable. As a late nineteenth-century novelist, Dreiser absorbed and used naturalistic ideas. But he did not do so, at his best, in a way which can be distinguished from his absorption of an understanding of character and of experience in general. It is this unity of understanding and of purpose which gives Dreiser's novels their power. At his most successful, Dreiser embodies in his novels the permanent in life not despite the ideas of his own time but because, like most major artists, he uses the ideas of his own time as living vehicles to express the permanent in man's character and in man's vision of his condition and fate.

Most students of American literature are aware that Dreiser derived the central plot and much of the detail of *An American Tragedy* from the Chester Gillette-Grace Brown murder case of 1906. Less commonly known is that although Dreiser's principal source—the reports of Gillette's trial in the New York *World*—presented him with a wealth of detail about Gillette's life in Cortland (the Lycurgus of the novel) leading up to the murder of Grace Brown, it offered only a few hints about Gillette's experiences before his arrival in that city. Thus, Book One of *An American Tragedy*, which deals with Clyde's early life in Kansas City, is in a sense "invented." Such major events of this portion of the novel as Clyde's sister's pregnancy, his job at the Green-Davidson Hotel, his longing for Hortense, and the automobile accident which concludes the book have no source in Gillette's life.

Because Dreiser in Book One is "inventing" a background for Clyde it is possible to view this section of the novel as the application to fiction of a simplistic deterministic ethic in which the author crudely manufactures hereditary and environmental conditions that will irrevocably propel the protagonist toward his fate. So, in Book One, we are offered Clyde's weak and fuzzy-minded father and coldly moralistic mother. We discover that Clyde is a sensitive youth who longs for the material and sensual pleasures of life but lacks the training, strength, and guile necessary to gain them. Ergo: weakness and desire on the one hand and irresistible attraction yet insurmountable barriers on the other will resolve themselves into an American tragedy.

Dreiser in this opening section of the novel is indeed seeking to introduce the deterministic theme that a young man's nature and early experience can solidify into an inflexible quality of mind which will lead to his destruction. Yet once said this observation is as useless to criticism as the equally true statement that *King Lear* is about the failure and triumph of love. For Dreiser in Book One of *An American Tragedy* is not a simple and simple-minded naturalist applying a philosophical theory to documentary material but rather a subtle fictional craftsman creating out of the imagined concrete details of a life an evocative image of the complex texture of that life.

Clyde's desire for "beauty and pleasure"[12] in Book One is in direct conflict with his parents' religious beliefs and activities, and thus Clyde's dominant impulse from early boyhood is to escape. At fifteen he makes his first major break from his parents' inhospitable mission existence and toward the life he desires when he gets a job as assistant clerk at a drugstore soda fountain. This position, with its accompanying "marvels" of girls, lively talk, and "snappy" dressing, offers a deeply satisfying alternative to the drab religiosity of Clyde's boyhood. He recognizes the appeal of this new world "in a revealing flash":

> You bet he would get out of that now. He would work and save his money and be somebody. Decidedly this simple and yet idyllic compound of the commonplace had all the luster and wonder of a spiritual transfiguration, the true mirage of the lost and thirsting and seeking victim of the desert (I, 26).

Dreiser's summary of Clyde's response to the lively worldliness of the soda fountain introduces a theme, and its imagery and tone, which pervades the entire novel. Clyde's need—his thirst—has the power to transform "spiritually" the tawdry and superficial world of the drugstore into the wondrous and exalted. So frequent and compelling is Dreiser's use of "dream" in connection with Clyde's longing that we sometimes fail to realize that his desires also have a basically religious context in which his "dream" is for a "paradise" of wealth and position ruled by a "goddess" of love. Clyde, this moment of insight at the soda fountain, is truly converted. He has rejected the religion of his parents only to find a different kind of heaven to which he pledges his soul with all the fervor and completeness of his parents' belief. Yet like their "cloudy romance" of a heaven above, Clyde's vision of a "paradise" below is a "true mirage." He has thus not really escaped from his parents, and his initiation into life at the soda fountain and later at the Green-Davidson is no true initiation, for he has merely shifted the nebulous and misdirected longings of his family from the unworldly to the worldly. He still has the naiveté, blindness, and absolute faith of his parents' enthusiasm and belief. And because he is, like them, a true believer, he does not learn from experience and he does not change.

Clyde's job as a bellhop at the Green-Davidson is both an extension and an intensification of his conversion experience at the soda fountain. To Clyde, the hotel is "so glorious an institution" (I, 33), a response which at once reflects the religiosity of its sexual attractions and their embodiment in a powerful social form. The Green-Davidson has both an intrinsic and an extrinsic sexuality. So deep and powerful is Clyde's reaction to its beauty and pleasure—to its moral freedom, material splendor, and shower of tips—that he conceives of the hotel as a youth does his first love. The Green-Davidson to Clyde is softness, warmth, and richness; it has a luxuriousness which he associates with sensuality and position—that is, with all that is desirable in life: "The soft brown carpet under his feet; the soft, cream-tinted walls; the snow-white bowl-lights set in the ceiling—all seemed to him parts of a perfection and a social superiority which was almost unbelievable" (I, 42). "And there was music always—from somewhere" (I, 33). Clyde thus views the social superiority which was almost unbelievable" (I, 42). "And there was music always—from somewhere" (I, 33). Clyde thus views the hotel both as "a realization of paradise" and as a miraculous gift from Aladdin's lamp, two images of fulfillment which, in their "spiritualizing" of his desires, appropriately constitute the center of his dream life.

But the hotel has a harsh and cruel sexuality in addition to its soft, warm, and "romantic" sensuality. Older women and homosexuals prey on the bellhops, who themselves frequent whores, and the hotel offers many instances of lascivious parties on the one hand and young girls deserted by their seducers on the other. Clyde, because of his repressed sexuality, cannot help responding to this aspect of sex with "fascination" despite his fears and anxieties. The sexual reality of the hotel is thus profoundly ambivalent. Clyde longs above all for the "romance" of sex and for warmth and a sense of union, but the overt sexuality which he in fact encounters is that of hardness, trickery, and deceit—of use and discarding. Both Clyde's unconscious need and his overt mode of fulfillment join in his response to Hortense. " 'Your eyes are just like soft, black velvet . . . ,' " he tells her. " 'They're wonderful.' He was thinking of an alcove in the Green-Davidson hung with black velvet" (I, 112). Clyde unconsciously desires "softness" and later finds it in Roberta, but he is also powerfully drawn by the "hardness" of wealth and sexual power which he is to find in Sondra and which he first encounters at the Green-Davidson. Thus he endows Hortense with an image of warm softness which reflects his muddled awareness of his needs. For though Hortense is properly associated in his mind with the Green-Davidson because of their similar sexual "hardness," she is incorrectly associated with an image of softness and warmth.

Clyde's belief that the Green-Davidson is a "glorious . . . institution" also represents his acceptance of the hotel as a microcosm of social reality. So he quickly learns that to get ahead in the world—that is, to ingratiate himself with his superiors and to earn large tips—he must adopt various roles. So he accepts the hierarchy of power present in the elaborate system of sharing tips which functions in the hotel. So he realizes that he must deceive his parents about his earnings if he is to have free use of the large sums available to him as an eager novice in this institution. And because the world of the Green-Davidson—both within the hotel and as hotel life extends out into Clyde's relations with the other bellhops and with Hortense—also contains Clyde's introduction into sexual desire and sexual warfare, he assumes that the ethics of social advance and monetary gain are also those of love. Thus, when in Lycurgus he aspires to the grandeur of Sondra and her set, his actions are conditioned by an ethic derived from the Green-Davidson—that hypocrisy, dishonesty, role-playing, and sexual deceit and cruelty are the ways in which one gains what one desires and that these 'can and should be applied to his relationship with Roberta.

The major point to be made about Dreiser's rendering of the Green-Davidson Hotel as an important experience in Clyde's life is that we respond to his account not as an exercise in determinism but as a subtle dramatization of the ways in which a distinctive temperament—eager, sensitive, emotional, yet weak and directionless—interacts with a distinctive social setting which supplies that temperament with both its specific goals and its operative ethic. Again, as in *Jennie Gerhardt*, there is a naturalistic center to this fictional excellence. It is correct to say that Clyde's life is determined by his heredity and environment. But, once more, as in *Jennie Gerhardt*, the naturalism and the fictional strength are inseparable. The naturalism is not an obstacle to the excellence but the motive thrust and center of the bed-rock fictional portrayal of how people interact with their worlds and why they are what they are.

To sum up. One of the major conventions in the study of American naturalism is that naturalistic belief is both objectionable in its own right and incompatible with fictional quality. But the example of Dreiser reveals that the strength often found in a naturalistic novel rests in the writer's commitment to the distinctive form of his naturalistic beliefs and in his ability to transform these beliefs into acceptable character and event. We are moved by the story of Jennie and Lester and by the account of Clyde's career not because they are independent of Dreiser's deepest beliefs but rather because they are successful narratives of man's impotence in the face of circumstances by a writer whose creative imagination was all of a piece. Until we are willing to accept that the power of a naturalistic writer resides in his naturalism, we will not profit from the example of Dreiser.

Notes

[1]Quoted by Franklin Walker, *Frank Norris: A Biography* (Garden City, N. Y.: Doubleday, Doran and Co., 1932), pp. 222-23.

[2]The most characteristic discussions of American naturalism occur in histories of American fiction. See, for example, Harry Hartwick, *The Foreground of American Fiction* (New York: American Book Co., 1934), pp. 3-20; George Snell, *The Shapers of American Fiction, 1798-1947* (New York: E. P. Dutton and Co., 1947), pp. 223-48; Frederick J. Hoffman, *The Modern Novel in America* (Chicago: H. Regnery, 1951), pp. 28-51; and Edward Wagenknecht, *Cavalcade of the American Novel* (New York: Holt, 1952),

pp. 204-29. But see also Oscar Cargill, *Intellectual America* (New York: Macmillan Co., 1941), pp. 82-175, and Lars Ahnebrink, *The Beginnings of Naturalism in American Fiction* (Cambridge: Harvard Univ. Press, 1950).

[3]Charles C. Walcutt, *American Literary Naturalism: A Divided Stream* (Minneapolis: Univ. of Minnesota Press, 1956), p. 220.

[4]Eliseo Vivas, "Dreiser, An Inconsistent Mechanist," *Ethics* (July, 1938); revised version, *The Stature of Theodore Dreiser*, ed. Alfred Kazin and Charles Shapiro (Bloomington: Indiana Univ. Press, 1955), p. 237.

[5]Two extreme examples of this position are Randall Stewart, *American Literature and Christian Doctrine* (Baton Rouge: Louisiana State Univ. Press, 1958), pp. 114-20, and Floyd Stovall, *American Idealism* (Norman: Univ. of Oklahoma Press, 1943), pp. 134-36.

[6]The essays were published originally in 1942, 1947, and 1950 respectively.

[7]See, for example, Charles Thomas Samuels, "Mr. Trilling, Mr. Warren, and *An American Tragedy*," *YR*, 53 (1964), 629-40. Samuels finds *An American Tragedy* inept beyond belief.

[8]*Sister Carrie* (New York: Doubleday, Page and Co., 1900), p. 83.

[9]Portions of the discussion of *Jennie Gerhardt* and *An American Tragedy* which follow appear in different form in my *The Novels of Theodore Dreiser: A Critical Study* (Minneapolis: Univ. of Minnesota Press, 1976). I do not wish by my emphasis on the deterministic thread in naturalism to appear to be supporting a return to a simplistic definition of naturalism as "pessimistic determinism" or some such formula. I have devoted much effort over two decades in various critical studies of individual naturalists as well as in more general essays on the movement as a whole to the position that naturalism is a complex literary movement in which distinctive writers combine in their works distinctive strains of traditional humanistic values and contemporary deterministic belief. Rather, I seek in this essay to suggest that just as we were long guilty of not recognizing the element of covertly expressed traditional value in most naturalists, so we have also been guilty of an uncritical disparagement of the more readily identifiable deterministic strain in their work.

[10]*Jennie Gerhardt* (New York: Harper and Brothers, 1911), p. 401. Citations from this edition appear hereafter in the text.

[11]In the Theodore Dreiser Collection, University of Pennsylvania Library; quoted by permission of the University of Pennsylvania Library.

[12]*An American Tragedy* (New York: Boni and Liveright, 1925), I, 5. Citations from this edition appear hereafter in the text.

TENSION AND TECHNIQUE:
THE YEARS OF GREATNESS

Linda W. Wagner
Michigan State University

Were I a Gail Hightower, my moments of nostalgia would center about those years of literary greatness, the period from 1912 or 1915 to 1940. Exuberance, innovation, temerity, the compulsion to create a new consciousness, in modes and patterns that were equally new: as John Dos Passos recalled, "there was, among many of the young people of my generation, a readiness to attempt great things. . . . It was up to us to try to describe in colors that would not fade, our America that we loved and hated."[1] And were I a Malcolm Cowley or Cleanth Brooks, I could present an "I-was-there" kind of survey, the remarkable listing of Cowley's in *Exile's Return* and *A Second Flowering*. But as it is, I would like—as concisely as possible—to provide a more nearly retrospective view, from the end of glory backward, assessing some of the major writers of the time through the eyes of readers since World War II. No matter which writers from the period we discuss, there are at least four assumptions that unite even the most dissimilar.

(1) Writers after 1900 were struggling toward a new nationalism, and much of the interest in style and language stemmed from the general impatience with the influence (outright dominance) of England. We too often forget that the prevalent view of American literature (evident in its paucity in curricula and anthologies) was that of John Macy, writing in 1913:

> American literature is a branch of English literature, as truly as are
> English books written in Scotland or South Africa. . . . In literature
> nationality is determined by language rather than by blood or
> geography.[2]

Yet, set against that view are Hemingway's excitement over each victory of natural American language; Dos Passos' and William Carlos Williams' fascination with America as both subject and image; the characterizations of Sinclair Lewis, Willa Cather, Sherwood Anderson, and, more obliquely, Gertrude Stein as a means of defining a national persona. Which of America's modernists has not given us some picture of character, whether it be in the perverted tragedies of displaced Americans like Joe Christmas or Jay Gatsby, both men victimized by insidious social patterns; or the romantic epics of Eugene Gant, Robert Jordan, and the Joads, simple Americans who manage to best those social patterns? And yet, criticism, even today's criticism, sometimes balks at such evident chauvinism and appears to penalize the most obviously American of its authors. At times one must wonder whether we share Yvor Winter's 1943 attitude, when he called interest in America a "romantic error," condemning out of hand "the fallacy" that a writer "achieves salvation by being, in some way, intensely of and expressive of his country."[3]

(2) The intense interest in America was only one means of breaking convention, upsetting the expectations of the parental or educational authority figures. The tensions of the time were created largely from the supposed betrayal of beliefs—Wilson's in political and social matters, middle-class conventions in religious and economic ones—and because betrayals were graphically illustrated in carnage and death on the battlefield of World War I, those of this generation who lived came to rebel actively against the rhetoric of amelioration. "Peace in our time" became one ironic war cry, and Ezra Pound's "make it new" became another.

(3) The obsession with innovation and technique was, consequently, much more important philosophically than it might first appear. The reason an entire generation of writers turned to a religion of art, believed so compulsively in their work as both promise and reward, was that nothing else that was left to them seemed valuable. Sherwood Anderson describes modernism as "an attempt on the part of the workman to get back into his own hands some control over the tools and materials of his craft."[4] The impetus behind what John Ciardi was to call "The Age of the Manifesto"[5] was the same kind of search that the Victorians had pursued; but by 1915 or 1920, art had replaced philosophy and was coming close to replacing religion. Robert Penn Warren, too, defines the modern period as marked by "the self-conscious passion for style, and in all forms this will to style—in all its rich manifestations from Pound to Hemingway, Eliot to Faulkner, Yeats to Joyce."[6]

The interest in craft was hardly new, of course, just as the thematic emphasis on quest and search was foreshadowed by many novels before 1900. Henry James had certainly established all the important concepts of novelistic freedom and growth, as had Emerson in poetics; but the discovery of James' theories and the work of Stephen Crane, the real import of Mark Twain and Herman Melville, all came well after 1900.

One important current feeding into the absorption with technique was the quasi-philosophical and poetic interest in Imagism (and, in quick succession, Vorticism and Objectivism). Developing from Henri Bergson's interest in the concrete representation of ideas, T. E. Hulme's notion of Imagistic writing was also related to William James' concepts of pragmatism. As propagandized by Pound, and called "Impressionism" by Ford Madox Ford, it brought to modern prose as well as poetry the use of concrete scenes and images; concision; clear and generally simple language; and a form germane to what was being written.[7]

(4) To speak of technique without mentioning naturalism or realism may seem perverse, but it is possible that the stronger literary impulse was Flaubert's *le mot juste*, not Howells' painterly detail—the precise word, well-seasoned with Emerson's and Cooper's romantic attitudes. For the fourth quality that unites the strongest of modern novels is a trait antithetical to naturalism, the quality Irving Howe calls "wonder,"[8] that aura of belief in a person's capacity to develop, to learn, and even in a culture's ability to progress. The green light at the end of Gatsby's vision becomes a symbol for the promise that, unexpectedly perhaps, nearly all these novelists seem to have shared belief in. Give people love and human contact, wrote Anderson, and social problems disappear; trust the labor organizers, thought Steinbeck and Dos Passos, and economic ills ameliorate. Repeatedly in modern fiction, characters become heroic not so much for what they achieve but for what they dare. The risk for greatness, whether in Carrie Meeber or Thomas Sutpen, is usually presented with sympathy, not condemnation. We hope with Gatsby and Gant that, indeed, they can re-live a happier past; and when Fitzgerald writes in *The Crack-Up* that "the natural state of the sentient adult is a qualified unhappiness,"[9] we don't believe him. Writers such as Barth, Updike, and Bellow, however, would.

In these four ways, then, modern American fiction seems reasonably unified: its absorption with American subject matter, character, and language; its fascination with rebellion against traditions of whatever kind; its obsession with craft (and the corollary to that obsession, innovation); and its affirmation through a sense of promise, wonder, even romanticism.

Promise? Wonder? When these novels could be said to be "monotonous—all those endless drinks with little else happening to the heroes"?[10] So said Boris Pasternak's wife about Hemingway's novels. So said a great many people—not, fortunately, most of the earliest reviewers. But the anomaly—that Hemingway was thought a shockingly permissive and progressive writer, his short fiction called "sketches" instead of "stories"—remains puzzling today. For what was

Hemingway, in fact, if not another prescriptive, quasi-Victorian moralist? What real difference is there between James's duty-bound Lambert Strether, renouncing his Maria Gostrey out of a self-imposed sense of propriety, and the equally circumspect Jake Barnes? For that matter, the flamboyant Brett Ashley is no freer, for all her seeming license, than was Edith Wharton's Lily Bart in the 1905 *House of Mirth.* As Jeremiah Sullivan describes the premise, "conscience over impulse" equals morality;[11] and Winifred Bryher, reminiscing, calls Hemingway "the last of the great Victorians who still believed in loyalty and honor."[12] Not to fault Hemingway for those personal qualities, but when the reader of today faces these characters designated "heroes" (and, admittedly, fewer "heroines") he is all too likely to question the purpose in Robert Jordan's sacrifice for a bridge, and a battle, that he knows is inconsequential. For John Killinger, the dilemma of reading and teaching Hemingway's fiction today is that he is not *of* today; he instead occupies "an era of transition between one tacitly acknowledged world-view and another," the latter the absurd, darkly comic stance of Joseph Heller, Kurt Vonnegut, Jr., and John Hawkes.[13]

I have written elsewhere about Hemingway's importance as stylist and craftsman.[14] His influence on the modern skill of writing is indisputable, yet if the *impact* of that sharp-edged fiction is, for today's reader, blurred, the stylistic force itself lessens. It is, partly, his judgmental positioning of characters that alienates the modern reader, and in his reliance on the foil tactic, Hemingway limits the kind of response these characters *per se* are capable of evoking. Jake Barnes, Brett Ashley, Pilar, Robert Jordan—any one *might* have been a compelling study of twentieth-century bereavement. The women have the possibility of a Molly Bloom; the men, were they not so obviously inflated beside the Robert Cohns, Mike Campbells, and Pablos—capable of equal psychological depth. Suppose Faulkner had chosen Brett Ashley for a Joe Christmas kind of study? For some contemporary readers, Hemingway's lucid and restricted style—magnificent in its purity though it is—is *so* restrictive that his characterization sometimes suffers because the reader does not know enough, does not have enough ways in. The tight-lipped narrative voice creates silhouettes instead of the more involving, full-color canvas which, it now seems, the age demanded.

The seminal question of such a retrospective approach as this is, of course, what *has* the age demanded? What books are we reading in 1976? What books and authors have lasted these 50 years over? In 1930, Sinclair Lewis won the Nobel Prize for Literature and became the first American novelist to be so honored (one supposes the honor to be ambivalent, since Lewis' satiric pictures of Gopher Prairie reinforced the world's concept of a dully primitive America). Yet, even though "Main Street" and "Babbitt" are clichés in the American vocabulary, few people know more about the terms than that they are vaguely demeaning. The fate of our second Nobel Prize winner, Pearl Buck, is even worse; less specifically "American," Buck's novels have no entry into a standard curriculum, and even feminist critics have had difficulty re-introducing Buck's work. Over-simplification of characters and plot-dominated and extended narrative jar on the sensibilities of younger readers who have been conditioned by this century's energy explosions, whether they be located in Vorticism in all its visual and audial interest or in "Sesame Street," "Laugh-In," and other of television's rapid-fire sequences.

For somewhat different reasons, neither are "Dos Passos" or "Stein" household words in 1976. Dos Passos' pervasive concern with picturing American contexts, not judging or propagandizing them, led him to the same fate as the newsreels he immortalized—oblivion with readers and viewers who demanded news analysis instead of objective reportage. Dos Passos was another of this century's gifted craftsmen, one who believed completely in the efficacy of the direct scene or image; and as expert modern craftsman, he deserves to be studied. But in his fiction, Dos Passos was rarely the social critic he was labeled during the 1930s, although the objectivity inherent in his techniques allowed readers to see his characters—those of *USA* particularly—in various slanted perspectives. The slant, however, was usually affixed from without instead of implied from within.

For Gertrude Stein's work, also, a basic physical difficulty prevents the quick assimilation that many modern readers demand. Since the same difficulty applies to Faulkner, Stein's relative obscurity (even though there are more contemporary writers influenced by her work now than at any other time in the century) derives more from lack of introduction than from sheer difficulty. We seldom teach her work, although it is now often available. Indoctrinated as we are to the two main currents in modern literature—realism and naturalism in much of the fiction and in the poems of Sandburg and Lindsay; imagism and symbolism in the poetics—we fail to consider that Stein's prose is an almost direct concretization of some important philosophical attitudes. Teaching Stein would provide a channel back to both William James and Henri Bergson; her writing has affinities with that of Henry James, Dorothy Richardson, the best of Ford Madox Ford, and extends forward into both the prose of Sherwood Anderson, James Joyce, Faulkner, Hemingway, and Kenneth Patchen; and the poetry of Laura

Riding, Kenneth Fearing, Jerome Rothenberg, Diane Wakoski, and others. As Williams said,

> Stein has gone systematically to work smashing every connotation
> that words have ever had, in order to get them back clean. . . .
> Everything we know and do is tied up with words, with the phrases
> words make. . . . We need too often a burst of air in at the window of
> our prose.[15]

Next to Stein, the greatest window opener stylistically was Hemingway, and for that achievement one must echo Faulkner's 1947 "list" and give him a fourth place in this imaginary prolegomena of modern American novelists. Faulkner's infamous list ran Thomas Wolfe, Faulkner himself, Dos Passos, Hemingway, and Steinbeck.[16] My hypothetical list, correspondingly, runs Faulkner, Fitzgerald, West, Hemingway (and the latter half of this essay discusses these three writers). But before turning to them, some brief comments on those writers a bit below Hemingway on this continuum—writers whose names are still household words, or at least appear on American literature course syllabi: John Steinbeck, Sherwood Anderson, Thomas Wolfe, Theodore Dreiser, and Willa Cather.

Each of these five novelists was a story teller, and in that role lay much of their greatness (*story teller* as one who is intrigued by character and plot, building fiction to best display that focus; rather than being a *philosophical writer*, more interested in conveying ideas through fiction [Mann, Proust, and the clumsiest of Dreiser] or a *lyric novelist*, for whom characters and plot exist to express emotional truths [Kafka, Virginia Woolf, Hemingway]). Steinbeck, Anderson, Wolfe, Dreiser, and Cather were aware of modernist techniques, and emphasized craft to some degree, although the degree varied widely. Steinbeck seems to have taken the place that Dreiser held earlier, his writing less remarkable for its style than for its generosity. Steinbeck cared about his characters, and in his usually affirmative resolutions, today's readers can feel promise, a spiritualism that appeals to students reared as these have been on the cry of "Apocalypse." Steinbeck's emphasis on ecological balances makes his treatment of displaced human beings seem more than sentimental.

Steinbeck seems to draw a somewhat more sophisticated reader than do Anderson, Wolfe, Cather, and Dreiser—perhaps because they were all four American, rural American, in their characters and locales; and that in itself may have shaped the prevalent notion that they are nostalgic writers, holding little interest for anyone who does not live in a North Carolina boarding house, a sun-baked Ohio cornfield, or a Nebraska prairie. Beyond locale, each writer begins with an attention to home, the concepts of origin and belonging, and uses as plot structure the journey away from (and often back to) that source of dual stability and frustration. Whether George Willard or Alexandra, the protagonist of these novels often searches for more satisfaction than home can provide; and yet the failures encountered away from the heartland reinforce the notion that middle-American virtues may be valuable. Treated explicitly in Anderson or implicitly in Wolfe, the home-vs.-adventure theme, just like the pastoral-vs.-technological, appears repeatedly, and judgmentally.

Like Hemingway, these novelists claim to see answers to, or—perhaps—panaceas for, a bewildering array of modern problems; and today's reader, caught in a proliferation of these problems of the earlier years, resents what seem to be over-simplifications of the issues. Much of this fiction gave rise, in one way or another, to the "revolt from the village" concept, but now that the revolt is an expected move, the whole *sturm and drang* of the process fails to hold our attention. Masterful characterizations—the strength of these novelists, the creation of the common, uninspiring American characters made compelling, and human; antidotes to the "elevated" subjects and characters of much fiction in English—are in themselves not enough to make today's readers pack *O, Pioneers* in their crowded backpacks. The weight of any object there must be justified in several ways.

I have thus far avoided using the word "relevance," but that is, finally, where a consideration of modern fiction must head. With the death of authority in the classroom, it is seldom enough to assign a book list with the rationale that this is great literature—effective, lasting, germane to our concerns as humanists. So much good fiction was written during the modern years that our problem as teachers of the period is to select the most appealing work for today's students without resorting to the crutch of authority. Perhaps we should ask ourselves what books we do find in students' knapsacks. If *Zen and the Art of Motorcycle Maintenance* is there, it is not because it is a guide to motorcycle repair. If *Gravity's Rainbow* is there, it is not because it has appeal for science majors. And if Doris Lessing's *Four-Gated City* is there, it is not because the reader is learning about life in London. No, it is something Wright Morris was getting at when he spoke about the modern writer's responsibility: "The imagination made us human, but *being* human, becoming more human, is a greater burden than we imagined."[17]

Each of these recent novels centers on the process of becoming human, of living a life, complete with false starts and falls from grace (did any Hemingway hero ever fall from grace?), and unheroic characters—the process (rambling, meandering, sometimes dull, but involving in its psychological accuracy, the protagonist's traditional Achilles heel now becoming a St. Andreas Fault)—leading to the reader's own identification. Very little modern fiction opened the *process* to the reader. It was instead intent on describing the character that resulted from that process. That literature that did speak of process may still find its way into backpacks—that of Nathanael West, Fitzgerald, Faulkner, alongside the work of Dostoevski, Hesse, Shakespeare, Kafka—writers ostensibly very different from each other, but maintaining a relatively strong foothold among today's literate readers.

The reason for the fascination with Nathanael West is easy to see— the judgmental attitude that dominated American fiction is here translated to the mockery of West's comic ribaldry; grotesques made horrible, not sentimentalized; all caught in the speed of glancing satire. Contemporary readers had already come to be familiar with these techniques in the work of West's many followers—Kurt Vonnegut, Jr., John Hawkes, Joseph Heller, James Purdy, Bruce J. Friedman, Donald Bartheleme, Terry Southern, Thomas Pynchon, E. M. Broner, Ronald Sukenick; they worked back, many of them, to West's *Day of the Locust* or *Miss Lonelyhearts*, and understood readily techniques that West's readers in the 1930s had found obscure.

West's comparatively small quantity of fiction has had dispropor- tionate influence partly because post-modern writers were ready for his wry vision, the high seriousness of disappointment turning already to humor, even if despairing humor; partly because the fast-paced, stylized, and heavily imaged prose was a good compromise between the demands of the full catalogues of realism and the objective reticence of the modern concretist. West's was also some of the first fiction to poke fun at American traditions and fetishes. The stranglehold of the great verities—religion, family, patriotism—had been mourned by the modernists, but they had never before been thoroughly, and comically, derided. The fun-making that is fundamental to fiction since 1955 or 1960 is in no way part of Hemingway's vision. And the anti-art stance of *Up*, the tendency of the novelist to either coast on erudition, as Barth does, or to deny it—and all semblance of craft as well—is also a radical shift from the craft-conscious writers of the modern period. The difference has occurred, at least partly, because of the uniform excellence of modern fiction and the more recent writers' refusal to simply imitate that excellence.

Fitzgerald and Faulkner share very few of these qualities, yet students read them widely. There is no challenger, in fact, to the supremacy of the hold they have on the laurels of American fiction; the only problem is finding a way to divide the crown. Fitzgerald, in *Gatsby*, gave readers a clearly-articulated novel about the tragedy of naive (American) optimism and belief; and yet, even though we know the novel is tragic, it also—like Gatsby—has its glories. Gatsby dares to dream and, inheritor of James' peculiarly American philosophy, also dares to force those dreams into reality. Jake Barnes may have shared some qualities with Lambert Strether; Jay Gatsby takes a step beyond the American need for self-preservation, prudence, and propriety, and shows a heritage from Emerson and Melville in his defiance of the system: " 'Can't repeat the past?' he cried incredulously. 'Why of course you can! ' "[18] "*Flat-out, Gatsby*," today's students say.

The complexity of the American life, and the American identity, is perfectly caught in Fitzgerald's impressionistic novel of Nick and Jay, pointed to in the explicit frame chapters, and reinforced throughout with the motifs and images that the novelist employs like the best post-imagist poet. No wonder T. S. Eliot admired *Gatsby*; no wonder he later suggested that the best fiction "demands something of the reader that the ordinary novel-reader is not prepared to give. . . . Only sensibilities trained on poetry can wholly appreciate [modern fiction]."[19]

And yet, for all its imagery and counterpoint—some of it as simple as Steinbeck's, some equal to Hemingway's best—*The Great Gatsby* is an easy novel to read. Chapter divisions set up, and off, each interrelated scene; every line of dialogue feeds into the total characterization, as well as plot (as when Daisy says, "radiantly," " 'Do you always watch for the longest day of the year and then miss it? I always watch for the longest day in the year and then miss it?' "). Tempo is an expert balance of focus and cohesive yet rapid movement, through carefully selected details. In 1923 William Carlos Williams wrote what he called *The Great American Novel*, but the book that deserves the title appeared in 1925, the first carefully structured portrayal of the modern American dream. The stroke of genius on Fitzgerald's part was that the dream belonged *not* to the respectable, well-descended, educated, and sensitive Nick Carraway—as it easily might have, and in the hands of a British novelist, would have—but rather to a fugitive from the system, a man who had no pedigree but sheer will, a man who shot the naturalists' theories into a cocked hat, even while using some of their methods, and thus became the prototype of the outrageous low-born, even criminal American "hero." That Gatsby is descended from that earlier low-born, Huck Finn, can be excused since Fitzgerald worked to give the novel an ending that forced social codes into confrontation with the ageless codes of human feeling; in the last third of the book, Fitzgerald suceeeds in creating his own American hero.

There is no single Faulkner novel that rivals *Gatsby*. Faulkner's genius is collective, and the Faulkner readers have usually absorbed much of his fiction. Drawn in by his empathetic portrayal of even the strangest characters, readers quickly come to see that—if Fitzgerald's concern is with the American character, the American dilemma—Faulkner's is with the human dilemma. His little postage stamp of soil lies in northern Mississippi, but it franks a letter that travels the world. Love, hope, anger, hatred, grief, joy—Faulkner gives us the range of human emotion, and his psychological dexterity is second only to his technical prowess. Yet he seldom resorts to the simple device of using a narrator, unless it be in such a complex guise that the act of narration becomes the focus of the fiction; Faulkner purposely cuts off readers by refusing to use the obvious narrative devices.

As teachers, then, our work with Faulkner is to give students the background in craft so that they can read juxtaposition, incrementation on themes or images, stream-of-conscious writing, objectively presented fiction, in order to explore for themselves some of the greatest scenes in modern literature: Caddy chasing the buggy to glimpse her daughter; Bayard climbing the stairs; Quentin's "*I don't hate it! I don't hate it!*"; Addie Bundren's stoic death; Joe Christmas with his eager mouth filled with toothpaste. In giving us the human experience, Faulkner more often than not creates the experience of the child or of the deranged. The grotesques that so fascinated Sherwood Anderson and were so touchingly caught in the best of his stories, are in Faulkner given full-scale treatment, with the effect of lamenting the love and dignity so often missing from these crippled lives. Concern for his characters, both female and male, was Faulkner's forte, and that he had the power of his technique to implement his compassion makes him the century's genius. Just as he was not afraid of involvement with his characters, so Faulkner was not afraid of passion—both in his stories, and in his style. And, contrary to the fears of the sociologists, neither have we become children of the computer; we are, humanely, attracted by that passion, by that daring to create a structure—both rhythmically and imagistically—to encompass these stories that had to be told:

> I turned out the light and went into my bedroom, out of gasoline but I could still smell it. I stood at the window the curtains moved slow out of the darkness touching my face like someone breathing asleep, breathing slow into the darkness again, leaving the touch. *After they had gone up stairs Mother lay back in her chair, the camphor handkerchief to her mouth. Father hadn't moved he still sat beside her holding her hand the bellowing hammering away like no*

place for it in silence When I was little there was a picture in one of
our books, a dark place into which a single weak ray of light came
slanting upon two faces lifted out of the shadow. *You know what I'd
do if I were King?* she never was a queen or a fairy she was always a
king or a giant or a general *I'd break that place open and drag them
out and I'd whip them good* It was torn out, jagged out. I was glad.
I'd have to turn back to it until the dungeon was Mother herself she
and Father upward into weak light holding hands and us lost
somewhere below even them without even a ray of light. Then the
honeysuckle got into it. As soon as I turned off the light and tried to go
to sleep it would begin to come into the room in waves building and
building up until I would have to pant to get any air at all out of it until
I would have to get up and feel my way like when I was a little boy
*hands can see touching in the mind shaping unseen door Door now
nothing hands can see* My nose could see gasoline, the vest on the
table, the door. The corridor was still empty of all the feet in sad
generations seeking water. . . .[20]

Quentin's view of life was a rich, if uncomfortable, composite of
past and present, and a future that was largely fear. There were no
verities; everything in his mind was as fluid and chaotic as the prose that
represents his distorted, yet strangely understandable, thinking. Love
for his parents and Caddy runs with jealousy, fear, active dislike; and
serves as a kind of miniature for the attitudes of the American modernist
writers, trying their best to present, "in colors that would not fade," the
America that they both "loved and hated." For all these writers, life in
the twentieth century provided a tension, an ambivalence toward the
truths that culture loves to pimp, that made their views of that life fresh
and interesting. And for most of them, experimental techniques became
the means to craft their vision, well, superbly well, perhaps with an
expert care that we will not see again. I would have to disagree with
Hugh Kenner when he claims in *A Homemade World* that "The
American tradition—look at *Moby Dick*—is to offer discoveries, not
virtuoso performances."[21] It seems instead that modern American fiction
is filled with just these virtuoso performances, so many that we,
critically, are still creating the terminology to discuss them.

When some full evaluation of this modernist fiction is made, critics
will have to come to grips with the fact that much of the best writing
came from middle America (both geographically and financially), and
that very little of it was written by women. But for now, I am content to
praise the amazing wealth of talent, the promise that *was* often fulfilled,
and the reciprocity between technical innovation and the effectiveness
of the modern vision. America's modern novelists, for all their
innovation, or perhaps because of it, seem to fit Irving Howe's
description of American literature as dominated by a voice of promise, a
voice of wonder:

Linda W. Wagner

> With America, a new idea comes into the world; with American
> literature a new voice. . . . Thought and language, idea and image
> fold into a new being, and we have the flowering of our literature.[22]

To no period are Howe's remarks more applicable than to the modern,
when American writers dared to write as if what they were creating was
truly valuable. It *was*, of course; and it *is*; and it, hopefully, will remain
so, regardless of whether it lives in university literature classes or in
remote canvas backpacks.

Notes

[1]John Dos Passos, "What Makes a Novelist," *National Review*, (1968), 30.

[2]John Macy, *The Spirit of American Literature* (Garden City, N. Y.: Doubleday, Page, & Co., 1913), p. 3.

[3]Yvor Winters, *Anatomy of Nonsense* (Norfolk, Conn.: New Directions, 1943), p. 99.

[4]Sherwood Anderson, *The Modern Writer* (San Francisco: The Lantern Press, 1925), p. 32.

[5]John Ciardi, "Edna St. Vincent Millay," *Saturday Review*, 33 (Nov. 11, 1950), p. 8.

[6]Robert Penn Warren, *A Plea in Mitigation: Modern Poetry and the End of an Era* (Macon, Ga.: Wesleyan College, 1966), p. 5.

[7]Tony Tanner notes this correspondence as well in *The Reign of Wonder, Naivety and Reality in American Literature* (Cambridge: Cambridge Univ. Press, 1965), p. 213, and it is the subject of the first chapters of my own *Hemingway and Faulkner: inventors/masters* (Metuchen, N. J.: The Scarecrow Press, 1975) and "The Poetry in American Fiction," *Prospects*, 2, ed. Jack Salzman (New York: Burt Franklin Co., 1976).

[8]Irving Howe, "The American Voice—It Begins on a Note of Wonder," *New York Times Book Review* (July 4, 1976), pp. 1-3.

[9]F. Scott Fitzgerald, *The Crack-Up*, ed. Edmund Wilson (Norfolk, Conn.: New Directions, 1945), p. 84.

[10]"Boris Pasternak," [*Paris Review* interview], *Writers at Work*, (New York: Viking Press, 1963), II, 134. Pasternak himself did not share that opinion.

[11]Jeremiah Sullivan, "Conflict in the Modern American Novel," *BSUF*, 15 (1975), 28-35.

[12]Winifred Bryher, *The Heart to Artemis* (New York: Harcourt, Brace and World, 1962), pp. 213-14.

[13]John Killinger, *The Fragile Presence, Transcendence in Modern Literature* (Philadelphia: The Fortress Press, 1973), p. 25.

[14] See note 7, and Introduction to my *Ernest Hemingway: A Reference Guide* (Boston: G. K. Hall, 1977).

[15]William Carlos Williams, "A 1 Pound Stein," *Selected Essays of William Carlos Williams* (New York: Random House, 1954), p. 163.

[16]William Faulkner, "1947 Classroom Statements at the University of Mississippi," *Lion in the Garden*, eds. James B. Meriwether and Michael Millgate (New York: Random House, 1968), p. 58.

[17]Wright Morris, *About Fiction* (New York: Harper & Row, 1975), p. 182.

[18]F. Scott Fitzgerald, *The Great Gatsby* (New York: Charles Scribner's Sons, 1925), p. 111.

[19]T. S. Eliot, "Introduction to *Nightwood*," *The Selected Works of Djuna Barnes* (New York: Farrar, Straus, Cudahy, 1962), p. 228.

[20]William Faulkner, *The Sound and the Fury* (New York: Random House, 1929), pp. 214-15.

[21]Hugh Kenner, *A Homemade World: The American Modernist Writers* (New York: Alfred A. Knopf, 1975), p. 217.

[22]Howe, p. 1.

DISLOCATIONS OF SETTING AND WORD: NOTES ON AMERICAN FICTION SINCE 1950

Melvin J. Friedman
University of Wisconsin—Milwaukee

There has been some disagreement of late about what should constitute a novel. John Hawkes admitted forthrightly in an interview in the Summer, 1965, *Wisconsin Studies in Contemporary Literature*: "I began to write fiction on the assumption that the true enemies of the novel were plot, character, setting, and theme. . . ." William Styron's pleading in the August, 1972, *Esquire* was for a fiction with a "narrative flow. It's when there is no narrative flow that I think fiction is copping out. I don't mean to say it has to be a 'cracking good yarn,' but there has to be a story." These opposed positions, as stated by two of America's most articulate and accomplished novelists, register persisting and disturbing uncertainties about the form.

Hawkes and Styron (both born in 1925) are as central to the American fictional scene—and as representative of its possibilities and concerns—as any two writers in the last quarter century. Hawkes' first novel, *The Cannibal*, appeared in 1949, and Styron's *Lie Down in Darkness* followed two years later. Just as *Lie Down in Darkness* looks over its shoulder, sometimes uncomfortably, at *The Sound and the Fury* (especially) and *Ulysses*, so does *The Cannibal* look ahead to a postmodern ambience which can accommodate Hawkes himself as well as John Barth, Jerome Charyn, Kurt Vonnegut, Jr., Ronald Sukenick, William H. Gass, and Donald Barthelme. Hawkes' and Styron's first novels have in common a fascination with words and with violence. The difference is that the Styron of *Lie Down in Darkness* is something of an old-fashioned rhetorician, with his Faulknerian indulgences, and he secures his violence in comfortably mythical terms, while the Hawkes of *The Cannibal* seems to have broken down all the classical distinctions between poetry and prose and forced his violence to retreat into the surreal and hallucinatory.

Their careers seem to diverge increasingly as Hawkes continues to grope for new forms and narrative possibilities while Styron respectably holds on to tradition and its undaring storytelling conventions. In certain ways, however, they have gone in similar directions. Both have worked toward first-person narrative. We see Hawkes moving from the "I,

Zizendorf" of parts one and three of *The Cannibal* through the first-person prologues of *The Beetle Leg* (1951) and *The Lime Twig* (1961) to the unrelaxed, continuous first-person of *Second Skin* (1964), *The Blood Oranges* (1971), and *Death, Sleep & the Traveler* (1974). Styron used a fifty-page interior monologue in the midst of third-person discourse in *Lie Down in Darkness*, set up a controlled, almost background, first-person voice which gradually gave way to the more staccato, irregular language of diary notations and notebook jottings in *Set This House on Fire* (1960), and finally turned to the unrelieved, unbroken first-person of *The Confessions of Nat Turner* (1967). Styron grimly holds on to the first-person (the confessional "I" of the novelist-turned-diarist) in the excerpts from two novels-in-progress[1] which have appeared in periodicals since the publication of *Nat Turner*, while Hawkes detours somewhat to the familiar second-person of dramatic monologue, never quite abandoning the "I", in his latest novel, *Travesty* (1976).

Hawkes and Styron, in the way of further similarity, both tried their hands at playwrighting after their reputations as novelists were assured. The four plays of Hawkes, contained in a volume called *The Innocent Party: Four Short Plays* (1966), and Styron's *In the Clap Shack* (1973), seem more limbering-up exercises than firm commitments to the dramatic form. Hawkes' plays are at best rather minor extensions of his novels, and Styron's single play is little more than an exploded anecdote casually lifted from his frustrated military past.

Hawkes and Styron also share—along with other American contemporaries—a French "birthmark." It has been suggested several times that Hawkes' principal forebears are the Symbolist poets, with their poetics of the blank page and their addiction to the hallucinatory and alchemical property of words. Hawkes, in his *Wisconsin Studies in Contemporary Literature* interview, speaks of a lineage in prose fiction which starts with Quevedo and Thomas Nashe and comes down to himself and which includes along the way Lautréamont and Céline. Céline's *Voyage au bout de la nuit* (translated as *Journey to the End of the Night*) must indeed be thought of as one of the half-dozen texts which help most to illuminate Hawkes' work; he even took from the English translation the title of his *Second Skin*: ". . . the Admiral Bragueton had a sort of second skin like an onion."[2]

Styron's kinship seems strongest with the French New Novelists and the Existentialists.[3] His *Set This House on Fire* is a mock-detective novel with mythical parallels, which has a good deal in common with works like Robbe-Grillet's *Les Gommes* (*The Erasers*) and Butor's *L'Emploi du temps* (*Passing Time*). (Butor, in fact, wrote the preface for the French translation of Styron's novel and revealingly called it "Oedipus Americanus.") Styron admitted in an interview in the *New York Times Book Review* (October 8, 1967) that the first-person discourse of *Nat Turner* was suggested to him by Camus' *L'Etranger* (*The Stranger*).

Hawkes and Styron—who appeared on the literary scene about the same time, freshly out of creative writing programs—seem to go in quite different directions yet converge interestingly along the way. Saul Bellow and Norman Mailer, as another pairing of alternatives, often appear more dominant than Hawkes and Styron if not more representative. Ihab Hassan allows them to share in solitary splendor a section called "Major Novelists," in his recent book, *Contemporary American Literature 1945-1972*. Nathan Scott places them together with Lionel Trilling "at the absolute center of what is most deeply animating in American literature of the present and the recent past," in his *Three American Moralists: Mailer, Bellow, Trilling* (University of Notre Dame Press, 1973, p. 11). Bellow continues to honor tradition, especially as conceived of by the modernist writers of the 1920s and early 1930s, while Mailer changes his stances to accommodate disruptions and fragmentations of our collective psyche, as he moves with ease from anti-war novelist, to spokesman for American existentialism, to nonfiction novelist, to popular culturist, to the most exacting literary barometer we have had since Walt Whitman. (Nathan Scott revealingly calls him "our Whitman.")

Bellow has created an. *oeuvre* which places him squarely in the center of everything literary in this country, makes him heir apparent to the Nobel Prize, and allows him to continue as the darling of the Establishment. All of his fiction is enviably finished, even the excessively lean *Dangling Man* (1944) and the rather too bloated *Humboldt's Gift* (1975). His admirably svelte *Seize the Day* (1956), perhaps his most successful effort, belongs with the handful of best American novellas: *Billy Budd*, *The Great Gatsby*, and *The Bear*. While most of his work comfortably enjoys a modernist cast, there are occasional rumblings of postmodernism. It is not impossible that when his Israel diaries appear in book form later this year, reviewers will regard it as a contribution to the "fact-fiction" mode which Mailer, E. L. Doctorow, and others have recently made fashionable.

Mailer's career has been as jagged and irregular as Bellow's has been rectilinear. Mailer, like the phoenix, keeps rising rejuvenated from his own ashes, assuming an unending variety of masks. He even posits Norman Mailer as the pivotal figure of *Armies of the Night* (1968), a very "surfictionist"[4] thing to do: witness, for example, Ronald Sukenick's central presence in Sukenick's first novel, *Up*, which appeared the same year as Mailer's book. Hassan is quite right in saying that Mailer's position "rests, indeed, on his power to shape the moment rather than on any specific masterpiece of fiction."[5]

Bellow and Mailer have less in common than Hawkes and Styron. They have indeed few genuine points of convergence. One is certainly the fact that they are both Jews, although Mailer's Jewishness seems an accident of birth while Bellow's is a staple of his art: the movement of Bellow's prose appears often to be tuned by Yiddish cadences and inflections. Another might be their early flirtations with French existentialism which informed Bellow's *Dangling Man* and *The Victim* (1947) and much of Mailer's work through *Advertisements for Myself* (1959).

But in the end their careers are irreconcilable. Here is Mailer—at his crankiest and ill-tempered best—on Bellow: "To tell the truth I cannot take him seriously as a major novelist. I do not think he knows anything about people, nor about himself. He has a whacky, almost psychotic lack of responsibility to the situations he creates, and his narrative disproportions are elephantiastical in their anomaly."[6] Hawkes, Styron, Bellow, and Mailer are strikingly representative of the period in American fiction when the techniques and concerns of modernism gradually, if reluctantly, gave way to postmodernism and surfiction. They had all done important work by the early 1950s and they continue, if occasionally in an avuncular way, to oversee and contribute to the resuscitation of the novel form which had been pronounced dead more times than one can count since T. S. Eliot declared its demise with James and Flaubert.

Eugene Wildman commented tellingly on the final page of a recent gathering of short fiction, *Statements: New Fiction from the Fiction Collective* (Braziller, 1975): "We are just about at the absolute edge of the silent '50s." He said this from the vantage point of a practicing fiction writer who has watched the exhaustion of a type of literary mentality and its replacement by a "self-conscious" (in Robert Alter's sense)[7] set of fictional alternatives in which subject matter and verbal constructs conspire in a uniquely autotelic way.[8] The "silent '50s" have clearly given way to what Jerome Klinkowitz has called the "literary disruptions" of the late 1960s and the 1970s.

There seemed, predominantly, to be three kinds of novels written in the 1950s, fiction distinguished as much (if not more) by its subject matter as by its techniques: the college or academic novel, the Jewish American novel, and the Southern novel. (One might think of the "Beat" novel, with its many variations—given a certain critical respectability by

Kerouac's *On the Road* (1957) and Ferlinghetti's *Her* (1960)—as a fourth
type but this seems in the end more ephemeral than the other three.)

Typical of the academic novel is Robie Macauley's *Disguises of
Love* (1952). It is the enviable product of years spent in close and
sympathetic relationship with the best novels of the modernist period.
The setting is an American university in the 1940s, in the heart of the New
Critical era (with much the same ambience as Lionel Trilling's 1944
story, "Of this Time, of that Place") and the situation involves the
clandestine relationship between a straight-laced college professor and a
coed. The novel is shaped by the twists and turns of their love affair.
Macauley sets up three "successive centres" (Henry James' expression in
his preface to *The Wings of the Dove*) who alternate in the telling of the
story; they are: the professor (Howard Graeme), his wife Helen, and
their son, Gordon. The eleventh chapter, in contrast to the rest of the
novel, offers a babel of voices which open on "the successive windows of
other people's interest" (another quotation from the preface to *The
Wings of the Dove*). This eleventh chapter, in fact, seems to have
something in common with the "Wandering Rocks" section of Joyce's
Ulysses. The tellings of the story have in common an ambiguity and
unreliability. The unraveling of the various threads of misunderstanding
is managed by outsiders, especially by the succession of gossips in the
eleventh chapter (who perform a role not unlike that of the townspeople
in Faulkner's *As I Lay Dying*).

When we read the novel we are reminded of the techniques of
Henry James, Joyce, and Faulkner. Several reviewers invoked the name
of Proust, the other great modernist, when they thought they found in
Disguises of Love a "reversal of masculine and feminine roles" (Anthony
West in *The New Yorker*) and "accounts of homosexual relations . . .
disguised as accounts of heterosexual relations" (Stanley Edgar Hyman
in *The Hudson Review*). Macauley continues certain of these preoccupations in the stories collected in *The End of Pity and Other Stories*
(1957), especially in those three which are concerned with academics,
"The Academic Style," "The Chevigny Man," and "A Guide to the
Muniment Room." Stuffiness, phoniness, the narrow devotion to one's
"special subject" are exposed in all three.

These concerns are also evident in other academic fiction of the
period, like Mary McCarthy's *The Groves of Academe* (1952), Randall
Jarrell's *Pictures from an Institution* (1954), and, in a far more serious
vein, May Sarton's *Faithful are the Wounds* (1955). The genre continues
uninterruptedly into the late 1950s and 1960s, perhaps with a nod to the
Angry Young Man motif imported from England, in such novels as John

Barth's *The End of the Road* (1958), Mark Harris' *Wake Up, Stupid* (1959), and Bernard Malamud's *A New Life* (1961).

The End of the Road is the most intriguing and curious of these. It is a novel which seems to acknowledge modernist practices and concerns yet remains steadfastly uneasy with them. Each of the chapters is dutifully summarized before the chapter proper begins but in the same mocking, irreverent way that Pynchon later does this in *V.* and Vonnegut in *Cat's Cradle* (both of which appeared in 1963). The summary is repeated verbatim in the opening sentence of the chapter, retaining the italics of the heading. The opening chapter, for example, has this surprising heading: *"In a Sense, I Am Jacob Horner."* The sentence sets the ambiguous tone of the first-person narration by the recently turned college teacher who has an affair with a colleague's wife. Horner is another of these thirty-year-old outsiders who haunt the twentieth-century novel from Kafka's K. and Fitzgerald's Nick Carraway through Camus' Meursault, Sartre's Roquentin, and Grass' Oskar Matzerath. Like so many characters in modernist works he is associated with a myth: in his case, Laocoon. Like Beckett's Murphy he enjoys long sieges in his rocking chair. The furnishings of this college novel, then, are familiar but the twists and turns they are subjected to are not. Jacob Horner, for example, is under rather unorthodox psychiatric care at the so-called Remobilization Farm and teaches at Wicomico State Teachers College merely to satisfy certain conditions of his therapy. One of the basic texts connected with the therapy—it is referred to as his "breviary"—is the 1951 *World Almanac*. He finally graduates into "Mythotherapy" which seems almost to be the cure Barth later took for himself to rid himself of traditional fictional modes and pass into his myth-refashioning later work from *The Sot-Weed Factor* (1960) through *Chimera* (1972).

The End of the Road is clearly not an orthodox academic novel just as Nabokov's *Pnin*, published a year earlier, is not.[9] Like Barth's first novel, *The Floating Opera* (1956), *The End of the Road* is self-consciously ill-at-ease with its own form as the author, as one critic remarked, "is caught in conflict between his affinity for traditional fiction and his acute sense of its exhaustion."[10] Both *The End of the Road* and *The Floating Opera* use first-person storytellers who question their narrative functions and even their competence to tell the stories they are telling. Here is Todd Andrews, the narrator of *The Floating Opera*: "No doubt when I get the hang of storytelling, after a chapter or two, I'll go faster and digress less often."[11] At another point he tells us that he must begin a chapter "in two voices, because it requires two separate introductions delivered simultaneously" (p. 168). The result is two pages of parallel columns before the usual format is resumed. These first-person presences are disruptive and self-mocking and clearly look ahead to those surfictionist voices which tell us, like the narrator of Raymond Federman's *Take It or Leave It*: "I want to tell a story that cancels itself as it goes I replied."[12]

A novel published four years after *The End of the Road*, Philip Roth's *Letting Go*, has curiously much in common with it. Roth's Gabe Wallach, another self-conscious narrator, is a more aggressive Jacob Horner who settles uncomfortably into the academic life and gets involved with a married couple. The major difference is perhaps that *Letting Go* has a strong Jewish component so that it includes not only the idiosyncrasies of university faculties, ill-suited love relationships, and unsavory abortionists, but also of the urban Jewish way of life. Roth is perhaps more sensitive to the verbal rhythms and pulse beat of the second and third-generation American Jew than any of his contemporaries. The importance of *Letting Go* may be more in this area than in the Barthian way of *The End of the Road*.

Roth published his first book, *Goodbye, Columbus*, in 1959. It was immediately apparent that he was dealing with a quite different Jewish milieu from the one which engaged the attention of Henry Roth and Daniel Fuchs in the 1930s or Bellow and Malamud in the 1950s. The New York immigrant societies of Henry Roth's *Call It Sleep* (1934), Fuchs' *Williamsburg Trilogy* (1934-37), or Malamud's *The Assistant* (1957), which struggle to keep their ethnic and religious identities and distinctions alive, are very different from Philip Roth's suburbanites with their assimilative urgencies. The conflict between the lower middle-class urban Jew and the affluent suburban Jew is the central concern of many of the stories in *Goodbye, Columbus*. The Yiddish-speaking immigrant, who intones a kind of poetry in *Call It Sleep*, or in Alfred Kazin's autobiographical *A Walker in the City* (1951), has no place in this fiercely unpoetical world. In the title story, "Goodbye, Columbus," for example, the somewhat deprived Neil Klugman confronts the affluent Jewish society of Short Hills, as represented by Brenda Patimkin and her family, where "fruit grew in their refrigerator and sporting goods dropped from their trees!" Neil's wrong-side-of-the-track Judaism fails to make the proper concessions and adjustments. In "Eli, the Fanatic," the assimilated Jews of another suburban community, Woodenton, employ the lawyer Eli Peck to force a Yeshivah to move elsewhere or at least to modernize. Eli ends by donning the Hasidic garb of one of the Yeshivah instructors, which conveniently suggests to his fellow Jews of Woodenton the return of an earlier nervous breakdown. In "Defender of the Faith" the conflict shifts ground a bit as a Jewish sergeant of unquestioned integrity feels seriously threatened by three Jewish

recruits in his training company. The outrageous scheming of one of
them finally forces the sergeant to retaliate despite his misgivings about
taking punitive action against a coreligionist. Jew is also pitted against
Jew in "The Conversion of the Jews." This time a questioning Jewish
schoolboy, Ozzie Freedman, forces embarrassing ideological concessions from Rabbi Binder (the first of Roth's pompous, bloated rabbis)
and the Jewish Establishment when he threatens to jump from the roof
of the synagogue.

Letting Go, Roth's first novel, is still concerned with the Jew of
privileged circumstances, at least a generation removed from the ghetto.
Gabe Wallach's voluntary "exile" to the midwest, not unlike S. Levin's
removal to the Pacific Northwest in Malamud's *A New Life*, never quite
dissipates the burden of his Jewishness. The first words of the novel are
the deathbed letter of Wallach's mother tucked, inadvertently, between
the pages of Gabe's copy of James' *The Portrait of a Lady*. (This
bringing together of two inheritances, the Jewish past and the modernist
past, is not uncommon with Jewish American writers.) Wallach's
midwestern pilgrimage, which brings him from the University of Iowa
to the University of Chicago, still allows him to remain in touch with his
New York origins.

Roth continues his flirtation with the midwest in *When She Was
Good* (1967), but this time a midwest without Jews. *Portnoy's Complaint*
(1969) marks a return, with a vengeance, to Roth's earlier manner. This
novel seems to come out of the best pages of *Goodbye, Columbus* and
Letting Go. Roth settles here on all the things he knows how to do best,
especially in his creation of the urban Jewish family with the mother at
its moral center. Sophie Portnoy, the most imposing of the new breed of
Jewish mother, dominates not only the family but also the "confessions"
of her son. Everything in this novel, it would seem, "can be traced to the
bonds obtaining in the mother-child relationship" (as Alexander
Portnoy's psychiatrist is quick to point out).

Roth's novels of the 1970s seem to veer away somewhat from the
concerns of his earlier fiction. He ably manages the rhetoric of political
corruption in his Nixon novel, *Our Gang (Starring Tricky and His
Friends)* (1971). He submits to the temptation experienced by other
American Jewish writers like Malamud and Mark Harris and writes a
baseball novel in *The Great American Novel* (1973). Only in *The Breast*
(1972) and *My Life As a Man* (1974) does he deal, if obliquely, with
Jewish settings and concerns. One can perhaps think of *The Breast* as
marking a return to *Portnoy's Complaint* if one views this novella—with
its Jewish college professor narrator, David Alan Kepesh, who turns into

a female breast—as a working out of certain fantasies suggested by *Portnoy* with a helping hand from Kafka, Gogol, and Swift. *My Life As a Man* is more than passingly indebted to *Letting Go*; the Jewish ingredients are far less pronounced than in the earlier novel but the ambience seems unmistakably the same.

Roth's work is central to any consideration of the Jewish American novel after it has abandoned its immigrant, ghetto-life phase. The experience of being a Jew, with its urban and suburban variations, has become an increasingly tempting subject since Roth published *Goodbye, Columbus.* Even older Jewish writers, like Bellow and Malamud, have somewhat shifted ground to accommodate this new *Weltanschauung.* The implied Jewishness of much of Bellow's earlier fiction turns into the more emphatic urban Jewish rhythms of *Herzog* (1964). The old world Jewish values of *The Assistant* and the stories in *The Magic Barrel* (1958) give way to the preoccupations of dislocated-modern urban Jews in *A New Life* and *Pictures of Fidelman* (1969).

The new breed of American Jewish writer, like Bruce Jay Friedman, Wallace Markfield, and Burt Blechman, has continued the fascination with the second generation Jew who has made his way out of the ghetto. Both Friedman and Blechman have been classified as "black humorists"[13] and join, in this category, such non-Jewish novelists as Hawkes and Vonnegut. Friedman and Markfield have been linked with the stand-up comic tradition of Lenny Bruce and Woody Allen, and, indeed, Markfield's latest novel, *You Could Live If They Let You* (1974), offers a thinly-disguised portrait of Bruce under the name Jules Farber.

Friedman, like Philip Roth, is concerned with the American Jew who has left the city for the suburbs, who has exchanged the suffering which goes with being a part of the Diaspora for a more personal *Angst.* Friedman's heroes are invariably misfits, a condition they associate very often with their Jewishness. Friedman has published four novels to date and three of them, *Stern* (1962), *The Dick* (1970), and *About Harry Towns* (1974), have main characters who are intense worriers, who have an uncomfortable inheritance of guilt: their laughs come always at the expense of overbearing psychic pain. The art of these novels depends heavily on incongruity; the use of the unlikely juxtaposition becomes almost a compositional principle with Friedman.

Markfield is the most Joycean of this latest group of Jewish novelists. His first novel, *To an Early Grave* (1964), was accurately described by Stanley Edgar Hyman as "Mr. Bloom's Day in Brooklyn." One can go beyond this and say that the novel has a great deal to do with the sixth episode of *Ulysses,* "Hades." Joyce's "creaking carriage" has been replaced by a Volkswagen; Paddy Dignam has turned into a young writer named Leslie Braverman; and the four mourners who attend the Dignam funeral, Martin Cunningham, Leopold Bloom, John Power, and Simon Dedalus, give way to the more literary foursome of Morroe Rieff, Holly Levine, Felix Ottensteen, and Barnet Weiner. The Jew, Leopold Bloom, feels uncomfortable and unwanted among his Christian companions during the ride to the cemetery. Braverman and his mourners are Jews, as are the other characters who figure prominently in *To an Early Grave*. The Jew in exile in Dublin gives way to the Jew at home in Brooklyn.

Brooklyn, Joyce, and the urban Jewish experience remain central also to Markfield's second novel, *Teitlebaum's Window* (1970). This is a kind of Brighton Beach-Coney Island version of the *Bildungsroman*, with the Jewish boy, Simon Sloan, coming of age between the Depression years and the beginnings of World War II. The mother-son confrontation in this novel reminds one a bit of the similar encounters in *Portnoy's Complaint* and in Friedman's *A Mother's Kisses* (1964).

While Isaac Bashevis Singer is older than any of the other writers considered here (he was born in 1904) and has devoted the larger part of his writing years to Polish ghetto and *shtetl* subjects, he has of late begun to cast a knowing glance at the American scene. His latest novel, *Enemies, A Love Story* (1972), has a New York setting, with much of the action taking place in the Brighton Beach-Coney Island area of Brooklyn, the area dear to the hearts of Markfield's characters. The people in the novel, especially the protagonist Herman Broder, are haunted by memories of the Holocaust. The Holocaust affords a European backdrop for this only novel of Singer which is set in America; all this would seem to indicate that he is only willing to ease himself gradually, at least in his life as a fiction writer, into a country he has known with great intimacy for forty years. The levity of *Enemies, A Love Story*, gained despite the terrifying background of the gas chambers and concentration camps, is in marked contrast with another novel with some of the same concerns, Edward Lewis Wallant's *The Pawnbroker* (1961).

Jewish subjects continue to prove intriguing even to non-Jewish writers. Thus John Updike has entered the arena with *Bech: A Book* (1970). These lines from Henry Bech's foreword set the American Jewish legacy of Updike's literary pilgrim:

> I sound like some gentlemanly Norman Mailer; then that London glimpse of *silver* hair glints more of gallant, glamorous Bellow, the King of the Leprechauns, than of stolid old homely yours truly. My childhood seems out of Alex Portnoy and my ancestral past out of

I.B. Singer. I get a whiff of Malamud in your city breezes, and am I
paranoid to feel my "block" an ignoble version of the more or less
noble renunciations of H. Roth, D. Fuchs, and J. Salinger?

William Styron's current work-in-progress is to be called *Sophie's
Choice* and, according to "Backstage with Esquire" (*Esquire*;
September, 1976), concerns a young Southerner who comes to New
York, becomes involved with Jewish intellectuals, and falls in love with a
former captive at Auschwitz. The excerpt in this same *Esquire*, "The
Seduction of Leslie," is a first-person telling by a twenty-two-year-old
would-be novelist, transplanted to Flatbush in the summer of 1947, who
tries to have an affair with a 1940s Jewish princess. His failure is
predictable: "The disparity between what Leslie had promised and
what she delivered was so wounding to my spirit that I became
physically ill" (p. 138). This sentence could almost have been written by
the Philip Roth of "Goodbye, Columbus." Styron has clearly caught the
bug. Urban Jewish subjects now seem as irresistible as the dilemma of
the innocent American in Europe once did.

One last observation about the American Jewish writer who has
been nurtured on the modes of traditional storytelling. He seems
invariably uncomfortable when he tries to go experimental. Thus
Malamud's verbal and visual oddities in chapter 5 of *Pictures of
Fidelman* (which includes, among other things, running the Yiddish
veyizmir across an entire line of text) and his similar gestures at the end
of *The Tenants* (1971) do not quite work. Roth's attempt in *My Life As a
Man* to offer a clever variation on the novel-within-the-novel device, by
prefacing the main part of his novel, "My True Story," with two of his
protagonist's stories—giving the sense that truth and fiction are
ultimately interchangeable—is not always convincing.

The Southern writers have largely avoided these experimental
temptations. Even Faulkner, in his novels after *Absalom, Absalom!*
(1936), turned to relatively traditional means of narrative. Faulkner's
inheritors are almost all rather sober storytellers who consider plot,
character, setting, and theme (those four declared enemies of the novel,
according to John Hawkes) before anything else. There is very little, in
the telling, to distinguish a story by Flannery O'Connor from a Carson
McCullers story, or a Truman Capote story, or, for that matter, a
Chekhov or a Maupassant story. Nor has the most recent generation of
Southern writers markedly changed the face of fiction. In fact, one of
them, Reynolds Price, when interviewed in a French journal earlier this
year and asked what he thought of the postmodernists and the
practitioners of the experimental novel, gave this answer:

> I don't enjoy them or feel that I learn from them; therefore I can't
> read them. What they are most famous for—their alleged newness,
> their alleged groundbreaking experimentation—seems to me rough-
> ly as new as the *Satyricon* of Petronius, *Don Quixote*, *Tristram
> Shandy*; and worst of all, their methods doom them to un-
> truthfulness, a woeful incompleteness of sight and speech. . . . My
> own work and the contemporary work I admire and love is free to do
> a number of things not free for, say, the great novelists of the
> nineteenth century; but our *method* is very nearly identical—long
> watching; slow and incremental description.[14]

Indeed Price and contemporaries like Madison Jones, Shirley Ann Grau,
Elizabeth Spencer, Joan Williams, and Thomas Hal Phillips use
nineteenth-century narrative techniques and seem to feel that our
patience for elaborately turned plots and other contrivances is endless.

Much has been written about the Southern writer's sense of place.[15]
From Faulkner through the latest novels of Reynolds Price and Madison
Jones there is a very precise feeling for landscape and terrain. And
almost all of this fiction has a rural setting. The Fugitives who gathered at
Vanderbilt in the 1920s and produced that *vade mecum* of Agrarian
sensibility, *I'll Take My Stand* (1930), still offer an appeal to Southern
writers and supply them with their ideological building blocks and
foundation stones.

The Georgian Carson McCullers and the Mississippian Eudora
Welty appeared almost simultaneously on the literary scene: McCullers
published *The Heart Is a Lonely Hunter* in 1940 and Welty followed with
A Curtain of Green the following year. It became clear that the female
sensibility was to be a dominant force in Southern letters when another
Georgian, Flannery O'Connor, published *Wise Blood* in 1952. This last
was a sterner, less forgiving work than anything McCullers or Welty had
published. O'Connor was to produce another novel, *The Violent Bear It
Away* (1960), and two collections of stories, *A Good Man Is Hard to Find*
(1955) and *Everything That Rises Must Converge* (which appeared
posthumously in 1965).

Despite her lack of experimentation and the numbing sameness of
her themes and preoccupations, Flannery O'Connor is probably the best
of the Southern writers after Faulkner—at least the best of those who
remained in the South and devotedly tilled its literary soil. She is
probably a better short story writer than novelist although her narrative
techniques remain unchanging from the shorter to the longer form. Like
so many other Southern writers she seems to spring from an oral
tradition. She has impeccable pitch and knows the precise cadences of
rural Southern speech and gesture.

Her two novels are neatly patterned, with the same sure sense of design that Flaubert (whom she admired a great deal) and E. M. Forster possessed. *Wise Blood* and *The Violent Bear It Away* both fall into three parts which approximate a transplantation-prophecy-return rhythm. Hazel Motes and Francis Marion Tarwater, the heroes of these novels, leave familiar settings for alien and hostile surroundings. Hazel becomes the preacher for a Church Without Christ; Tarwater's prophetic urges take on a quite different form and end up with the drowning-baptism of the idiot Bishop. Hazel's "return" is more symbolic than real as it ends in a violent, Kafka-inspired death; Tarwater simply returns to his native surroundings and has a vision in which he is ordered: "GO WARN THE CHILDREN OF GOD OF THE TERRIBLE SPEED OF MERCY." This triadic pattern is not unique to Flannery O'Connor. Something like it is noticeable in novels as different as Isaac Singer's *The Slave* (1962) and Beckett's *Watt* (1953).

Flannery O'Connor's Catholicism separates her from most of her Southern contemporaries. Although her characters are mainly Bible Belt fundamentalist types they seem informed by a sense of Catholic sin and redemption. They are also drawn irresistibly to certain objects which seem to have almost religious properties; they appear to experience, in Mircea Eliade's words, a "manifestation of the sacred in some ordinary object, a stone or a tree."[16] Hazel's near-fanatical concern with his hat, his suit "of glaring blue," his silver-rimmed spectacles, and his black Bible; Tarwater's similar involvement with his hat and with a corkscrew-bottleopener (which he considers as his "talisman") are examples of their devotion to "things." It is tempting to connect this phenomenon with the objectal habits of the French *chosistes*, like Robbe-Grillet, Butor, Nathalie Sarraute, and Claude Simon, but Flannery O'Connor's hats, Bibles, and oddly shaped cars are in the end rather different from Robbe-Grillet's figure eights, erasers, and centipedes, or Butor's Graeco-Roman artifacts. It is unlikely, furthermore, that Flannery O'Connor read any of these French contemporaries. She seemed to share with Reynolds Price a distrust of the "groundbreaking experimentation" of those who resolutely turned their backs on the methods of "the great novelists of the nineteenth century."

It is interesting to note, in passing, that the French have been much drawn to Flannery O'Connor as they have been to a succession of other twentieth-century Southern novelists like Faulkner and Styron. All of her work is now available in French translation and her *A Good Man Is Hard to Find* was on the prestigious *agrégation* list for the academic year 1975-76. A new journal devoted to Southern literature and published at the University of Montpellier, *Delta*, turned over its second issue, published in March 1976, to her.

Capote has not as yet reached the enviable position of Faulkner, Styron, and O'Connor in France. Still, much of his work is available in French translation and he has indicated on various occasions his fondness for things French, especially the literature. His early novels, like *Other Voices, Other Rooms* (1948) and *The Grass Harp* (1951), have been compared to Faulkner, McCullers, and Welty. Their uniquely rural sense of place established Capote's credentials as a "Southern writer." His later work, with its distinguishing urban chic, seems to remove him from the Southern tradition, but the divorce is never quite complete. Thus *In Cold Blood* (1966) is set in western Kansas but Capote keeps reminding us that "one is still within the Bible Belt borders." The rural setting, the equation between morality and church affiliation, the gothic sequences are all staples of Southern fiction. Even the Clutter murders remind us of similar moments of violence in Faulkner, O'Connor, and Styron.[17]

But in a more important way, *In Cold Blood* is related to the *nouveau roman*.[18] It is vintage mock-detective, the very thing Sartre defined in his preface to Nathalie Sarraute's *Portrait d'un inconnu (Portrait of a Man Unknown)* as "an anti-novel that reads like a detective story." The formula is there: the robbery is to no end as the Clutter safe does not exist; the detective is the last one to solve the crime and needs the help of a criminal in doing so; the murderer has a poet's sensibility, dreams of birds, strums a guitar, and carries a "personal dictionary" of multisyllabic words.

Several reviewers of *In Cold Blood* were impressed by its cinematic aspects. Capote admitted as early as his *Paris Review* interview that he "learned and borrowed from the visual, structural side of movie technique." He was already by this time into filmmaking, serving as scriptwriter for *Beat the Devil* and later assisting William Archibald with the script for *The Innocents*. Robbe-Grillet has, of course, been actively involved in filmmaking since *Last Year at Marienbad*. Marguerite Duras, another *nouveau romancier*, did the scenario for *Hiroshima, mon amour*. Both have written novels which have cinematic shapes and are informed by cinematic devices, as have so many other authors of *nouveau roman* fiction, like Claude Mauriac, Nathalie Sarraute, and Michel Butor.

Finally, one should get to Capote's claim that he invented the nonfiction novel with *In Cold Blood*. Indeed he had been mixing reportage with fiction since *The Muses are Heard* (1956) or perhaps even earlier with those brief sketches of places in *Local Color* (1950). Jack Kroll, writing in the January 24, 1966, *Newsweek*, saw something timely in Capote's method: "In its refusal to analyze, to make judgments, *In*

Cold Blood is supercontemporary. This is the attitude of the new international avant-garde—of the French 'anti-novelists' who with bland obsessiveness describe only the surface of reality" (p. 60). Not only is *In Cold Blood* seemingly attuned to certain practices of European contemporaries but it also looks ahead to varieties of experimentation in American fiction during the next decade when fact and fiction began to mingle in unlikely ways.

Jerome Klinkowitz, in his *Literary Disruptions: The Making of a Post-Contemporary American Fiction*, discovers in the publishing season 1967-68 the birth of a new "style" or "school" of American fiction-writing. He describes writers "given to formal experimentation, a thematic interest in the imaginative transformation of reality, and a sometimes painful but often hilarious self-conscious artistry. . . ."[19] He includes in the new group of "literary disruptionists," who have apparently saved the novel from a Barthian exhaustion and death, Jerzy Kosinski, Kurt Vonnegut, Jr., William H. Gass, Ronald Sukenick, and Raymond Federman, among others. These novelists have in common a despair about traditional fiction. Their solutions to the dilemma, however, differ markedly.

Kosinski, at one extreme, seems to be writing fairly conventional fiction, at least on the surface. His syntax is regular. His pages are visually orthodox enough to offer the printer no particular problems. Kosinski seems to be on fairly cordial terms with those "enemies of the novel" which Hawkes identifies as plot, character, setting, and theme. Raymond Federman, at the other extreme, has completely altered the face and possibilities of fiction. His two novels written in English, *Double or Nothing* (1971) and *Take It or Leave It* (1976), are clearly typesetters' nightmares: each page is a discrete visual entity and calls on the unfailing attention and dedication of the printer. *Take It or Leave It* is not even paginated. Federman justifies this lapse: "all sections in this tale are interchangeable therefore page numbers being useless have been removed at the discretion of the author." Marc Saporta, in his *Composition No. 1*, wrote an unpaginated novel in the form of boxed cards which were supposed to be shuffled at will, but this French text ended up being little more than a curious exercise or parlor game while *Take It or Leave It* is a triumph of visual and verbal experimentation.

Kosinski's seeming conventionality is only one side of the coin. A book like *Steps* (1968) is filled with "disruptive" and fragmentary elements. It is a gathering together of what Robbe-Grillet would call *instantanés* and Beckett might call *textes pour rien*. Pronouns rarely have antecedents. Abstractions replace concrete language at every turn. The

generous blank spaces between sections make us think of the importance that Mallarmé ascribed to *la blancheur.* The unnamed, uniden-
tified "I" cries out at one point (in one of many italicized passages): *"If I
could become one of them, if I could only part with my language, my
manner, my belongings."*[20] This sounds like one of Beckett's disem-
bodied voices.

There is more fleshing out in Kosinski's other novels although the
blank spaces continue to arrest the eye in *The Devil Tree* (1973). The
boy's losing and regaining speech in *The Painted Bird* (1965) becomes,
perhaps, a metaphor for the Eden lost and then regained by the
generation which lived through the Holocaust and managed to survive
it. It could also be thought of, with some indulgence, as a metaphor for
the surfictionist who has abandoned traditional ways of writing and has
renewed himself through verbal and visual dislocations.

A novelist who can be as deceptively traditional as Kosinski yet
takes many of the experimental risks of Federman is William H. Gass. In
his first novel, *Omensetter's Luck* (1966), he seems to belong to a
language-intoxicated tradition in American literature which starts with
Melville, includes Faulkner, and ends up with Hawkes. There is a great
deal of writing in this novel, few blank spaces. Yet the traditional
elements of plot, character, and theme have been seriously tampered
with although they still exert a controlling presence. A comparison with
Light in August, which *Omensetter's Luck* occasionally resembles
(witness, for example, the similarities between the Reverend Jethro
Furber and the Reverend Hightower) reveals the extent that Gass has
passed beyond modernist practice and made accommodations to
surfictional demands. Gass' unpaginated *Willie Masters' Lonesome Wife*
(*TriQuarterly,* Supplement No. 2, 1968) is as rich and varied pictorially
as it is verbally: no two pages look quite alike; typefaces change with
startling regularity; photographs, designs, and doodles break up the text;
blue pages give way to green pages which give way to red pages which
finally give way to white glossy pages. The staples of traditional fiction
have been almost entirely eliminated. It is virtually impossible to
summarize, read aloud from, or even describe this text. Perhaps Gass
says it all in these four words: "imagination imagining itself imagine."

Kurt Vonnegut, Jr. has done his own art work for *Breakfast of
Champions* (1973). He has entered the frame of his novel with some help
from a literary alter ego, Philboyd Studge ("That's who I think I am
when I write what I am seemingly programmed to write"), and arranges
the unlikely narrative strategies which bring the science fiction writer,
Kilgore Trout, together with the Pontiac dealer, Dwayne Hoover. The

storyteller brings himself increasingly more into his story and creator and creatures finally come to confront one another on equal terms. Perhaps Philip Stevick describes Vonnegut's labors best when he speaks of recent fiction's "willingness to allow the compositional act a self-conscious prominence and to invest that act with love, a sense of game, invention for its own sake, joy."[21] "Love," "game," and "invention," certainly, are three words which belong in any advertising copy for *Breakfast of Champions*; one might be tempted, however, to substitute "sadness" for "joy," especially when one notices the tear dropping from Vonnegut's eye in the caricatured self-portrait which appears on an unnumbered page at the back of the book.

Ronald Sukenick's *Up* is also a novel of love, game, and invention. Ingredients of Jewish, artist, and academic fiction are all here, framed by surfictionist techniques. What seems unduly self-conscious in Roth's *My Life As a Man* appears to work in this fine example of what has been called a "self-reflective" novel. When Sukenick, the main character in his own novel, remarks at one point "Which leads me sometimes to consider whether any of this really happened and why it doesn't much matter since, if it didn't, I would have made it up,"[22] he seems to be speaking for himself, Federman, and those others who have recently started publishing with "Fiction Collective." These words would probably also have some bearing on Robert Coover's *The Universal Baseball Association, Inc. J. Henry Waugh, Prop.* which appeared the same year as *Up*. Instead of dislocating words and syntax, Coover seems to be engaging in an elaborate dislocation of sensibility. The baseball novels of Malamud, Philip Roth, and Mark Harris seem stillborn indulgences when placed next to *The Universal Baseball Association*.

The experiments of American fiction writers of the past decade seem endless. A reductive device, a variation on the lipogram, works very well in Walter Abish's *Alphabetical Africa* as the author moves up and down the alphabet adding on and then taking away so that the first and last (fifty-second) sections have words beginning only with the letter "a" while the twenty-sixth and twenty-seventh chapters use the entire resources of the alphabet. The narrating "I" is necessarily withheld until the ninth section. About this first-person the narrator remarks poignantly: "Eventually, I'm convinced every 'I' imparts its intense experience before it is erased and immobilized in a book. Ahhh . . . how fast it disappears."[23] The result is a prose work of rare poetic texture which even manages a certain amount of narrative and characterization.

Collections of short, sometimes elliptical, texts are very much in vogue. Some of the best of these are Barth's *Lost in the Funhouse: Fiction for Print, Tape, Live Voice* (1968), Coover's *Pricksongs and Descants*

(1969), Sukenick's *The Death of the Novel and Other Stories* (1969), and Gass' *In the Heart of the Heart of the Country* (1968). A collection of short pieces by various hands worth mentioning in this connection is *Statements: New Fiction from the Fiction Collective.*

One can go on endlessly discussing these experimenters who never cease to amaze with their inventions, dislocations, and disruptions. One has every reason to feel more comfortable about fiction now than critics did in 1950. The death of the novel does not seem as imminent as it did a quarter century ago.[24]

Notes

[1]Styron was for some years at work on a novel to be called *The Way of the Warrior* but announced in an interview with Ben Forkner and Gilbert Schricke, in the Fall, 1974, *Southern Review*, that he had temporarily put this aside in favor of a "book about Poland" (p. 929). Subsequently, in an interview with James L. W. West, III, which appeared in *Costerus*, 4 (1975), he offered a title for his novel-in-progress, *Sophie's Choice*. More discussion of this latter work appears later in my essay.

[2]Louis-Ferdinand Céline, *Journey to the End of the Night*, trans. John H.P. Marks (New York: New Directions, 1962), p. 109. Two sentences from this translation might conveniently serve as an epigraph for Hawkes' work as well as for that of other recent American experimenters: "When one's in this world, surely the best thing one can do, isn't it, is to get out of it? Whether one's mad or not, frightened or not" (p. 56).

[3]See my chapter "William Styron and the *Nouveau Roman*" in my *William Styron* (Bowling Green: Bowling Green Univ. Popular Press, 1974), pp. 19-36.

[4]I think this is the best word we have to describe certain recent experimental fiction writers. See Raymond Federman's superb collection, *Surfiction: Fiction Now . . . and Tomorrow* (Chicago: The Swallow Press, 1975), especially Federman's opening essay, "Surfiction—Four Propositions in Form of an Introduction," pp. 5-15.

[5]Ihab Hassan, *Contemporary American Literature 1945-1972: An Introduction* (New York: Frederick Ungar Publishing Company, 1973), p. 31.

[6]Norman Mailer, *Advertisements for Myself* (New York: Signet, 1960), p. 417.

[7]See Alter, "The Self-Conscious Moment: Reflections on the Aftermath of Modernism," *TriQuarterly*, 33 (1975), 209-30.

[8]See Philip Stevick, "Metaphors for the Novel," *TriQuarterly*, 30 (1974), especially pp. 137-38.

[9]It is interesting that John O. Lyons' *The College Novel in America* (Carbondale: Southern Illinois Univ. Press, 1962), which rather exhaustively covers the subject, does not mention *The End of the Road*.

[10]Morris Dickstein, "Fiction Hot and Kool: Dilemmas of the Experimental Writer," *TriQuarterly*, 33 (1975), 266.

[11]John Barth, *The Floating Opera* (New York: Bantam, 1972), p. 5. Subsequent references will be to this edition.

[12]Raymond Federman, *Take It or Leave It* (New York: Fiction Collective, 1976), unpaginated.

[13]Friedman edited a collection of short stories entitled *Black Humor* in 1965; his own story, "Black Angels," is reprinted in this volume.

[14]Georges Gary, " 'A Great Deal More': Une interview de Reynolds Price," *Ranam: Recherches Anglaises et Américaines*, 9 (1976), 145.

[15]See especially Frederick J. Hoffman's "The Sense of Place," in *South: Modern Southern Literature in Its Cultural Setting*, eds. Louis D. Rubin, Jr. and Robert D. Jacobs (Garden City: Doubleday, 1961), pp. 60-75.

[16]See my "Flannery O'Connor's Sacred Objects," in *The Added Dimension: The Art and Mind of Flannery O'Connor*, eds. Melvin J. Friedman and Lewis A. Lawson (New York: Fordham Univ. Press, 1966), pp. 196-206. Kathleen Feeley points out in her *Flannery O'Connor: Voice of the Peacock* (New Brunswick: Rutgers Univ. Press, 1972) that two of Eliade's books, *Patterns in Comparative Religion* and *The Sacred and the Profane*, were found in Flannery O'Connor's library.

[17]See chapter 5 of Josephine Hendin's *The World of Flannery O'Connor* (Bloomington: Indiana Univ. Press, 1970), pp. 131-57.

[18]See my "Towards an Aesthetic: Truman Capote's Other Voices," in *Truman Capote's "In Cold Blood": A Critical Handbook*, ed. Irving Malin (Belmont: Wadsworth Publishing Company, 1968), pp. 163-76.

[19]Jerome Klinkowitz, *Literary Disruptions: The Making of a Post-Contemporary American Fiction* (Urbana: Univ. of Illinois Press, 1975), p. x.

[20]Jerzy Kosinski, *Steps* (New York: Random House, 1968), p. 136.

[21]Philip Stevick, "Scheherazade Runs Out of Plots, Goes On Talking; the King, Puzzled, Listens: An Essay on New Fiction," *TriQuarterly*, 26 (1973), 362.

[22]Ronald Sukenick, *Up* (New York; Delta, 1970), p. 47.

[23]Walter Abish, *Alphabetical Africa* (New York: New Directions, 1974), p. 131.

[24]A great deal has been written about the surfictionists. See especially the issues of *TriQuarterly* which have the words "Ongoing American Fiction" on the cover. These issues contain first-rate fiction as well as valuable critical commentary. Aside from the *TriQuarterly* essays by Robert Alter, Philip Stevick, and Morris Dickstein mentioned in previous notes, one should see especially Albert J. Guerard's "Notes on the Rhetoric of Anti-Realist Fiction," *TriQuarterly*, 30 (1974), 3-50; Richard Pearce's "Enter the Frame," *TriQuarterly*, 30 (1974), 71-82; Edward W. Said's "Contemporary Fiction and Criticism," *TriQuarterly*, 33 (1975), 231-56; Robert Scholes' "The Fictional Criticism of the Future," *TriQuarterly*, 34 (1975), 233-47; and Gerald Graff's "The Myth of the Postmodernist Breakthrough," *TriQuarterly*, 26 (1973), 383-417. See also the essays by Myron Greenman, Robert S. Ryf, and Stanley Fogel in the Autumn, 1974 "Experimental Fiction" special number of *Modern Fiction Studies*. Other American journals which publish valuable criticism in this area are *Boundary 2: A Journal of Postmodern Literature* and *Diacritics*. Two new French journals, which published first issues in Paris in the spring of 1976, are both very much concerned with surfiction and postmodernism; they are: *Tréma* and *Revue Fançaise d'Etudes Américaines*.

A good number of books cover the area of American fiction which I have been concerned with in this essay. Along with Ihab Hassan's *Contemporary American*

Literature 1945-1972: An Introduction, the following seem to be among the most valuable: John W. Aldridge, *Time to Murder and Create: The Contemporary Novel in Crisis* (New York: McKay, 1966); Nona Balakian and Charles Simmons, eds. *The Creative Present: Notes on Contemporary American Fiction* (Garden City: Doubleday, 1963); Jonathan Baumbach, *The Landscape of Nightmare: Studies in the Contemporary American Novel* (New York: New York Univ. Press, 1965); Jerry H. Bryant, *The Open Decision: The Contemporary American Novel and Its Intellectual Background* (New York: The Free Press, 1970); Ihab Hassan, *Radical Innocence: The Contemporary American Novel* (Princeton: Princeton Univ. Press, 1961); Alfred Kazin, *Bright Book of Life: American Novelists and Storytellers from Hemingway to Mailer* (Boston: Little, Brown, 1973); Marcus Klein, *After Alienation: American Novels in Mid-Century* (Cleveland: World Publishing Company, 1964); Marcus Klein, ed. *The American Novel Since World War II* (Greenwich, Conn.: Fawcett, 1969); Blake Nevius, *The American Novel: Sinclair Lewis to the Present* (New York: Appleton-Century-Crofts, 1970); Raymond Olderman, *Beyond the Waste Land: A Study of the American Novel in the Nineteen-Sixties* (New Haven: Yale Univ. Press, 1972); Robert Scholes, *The Fabulators* (New York: Oxford Univ. Press, 1967); Max F. Schulz, *Radical Sophistication: Studies in Contemporary Jewish-American Novelists* (Athens: Ohio Univ. Press, 1969); Tony Tanner, *City of Words: American Fiction, 1950-1970* (London: Jonathan Cape, 1971); Helen A. Weinberg, *The New Novel in America: The Kafkan Mode in Contemporary Fiction* (Ithaca: Cornell Univ. Press, 1971).

FICTION IN THE SEVENTIES:
TEN DIGRESSIONS ON TEN DIGRESSIONS

Ronald Sukenick
University of Colorado

The history of American fiction since the fifties has been a mistake. From the vantage of the seventies, it would seem that the novel, in part along with the other arts, has been involved in a variety of fallacies the pursuit of which it can no longer afford to sustain. Every movement must have its heresies, and the movement of fiction through the seventies is no exception. However, instead of listing a series of Fallacies, I would like to discuss a number of Digressions. A Digression implies a wrong-headed though possibly interesting detour that may return one to the Path all the wiser. Let me begin with a few sweeping generalizations in full consciousness that sweeping generalizations are never the truth, but then, what is truth when it comes to fiction? I am assuming that Bellow and Malamud represent the fiction of the fifties, and it is still a very fine kind of fiction, at its best, as almost any kind of fiction is very fine at its best. The fiction of the sixties would be Barth, Barthelme, Pynchon, Brautigan and so on, that is, those innovators who are now well-known but not yet elder statesmen, who are considered, and in the strict sense are, "contemporary." Fiction writers who seem to represent something particular about the current decade, therefore, have been referred to as post-contemporary: George Chambers, Raymond Federman, Eugene Wildman, Jerry Bumpus, Ishmael Reed, Harry Matthews, Clarence Major, Steve Katz, Michael Brownstein, Jon Baumbach, Russell Banks, Robert Coover, among many others.

Fiction in the fifties was august and self-confident, not for any good reason, it just was. The novel was still the great symphonic form in the world of letters. There was the tradition of the "great novel." Fiction thought of itself as evolving periodically into imposing masterpieces that would justify the form. The important thing about *Ulysses* was not that it called into question the very fictive tradition it epitomized, but that it was a "great novel," one in a series. Only that could explain the awe in which it was held and the totality with which it was ignored by fiction in the fifties. Fiction at that time paid a great deal of lip service to Joyce, Kafka, Lawrence, Proust, Faulkner and literary modernism, but somehow all that had very little to do with us, with fiction in America, it can't happen here. Nevertheless, fiction was not completely comfortable with itself as it moved through the sixties. It began to manifest an uneasiness, an odd guilt, a certain confusion. Eminent novelists like Philip Roth and John Barth began to tell us that fiction was no longer possible, that it was at the end of its rope. What was so-called "black humor" again, it's hard to remember? In a recent article on the subject, subtitled "Fiction in the Sixties," Morris Dickstein reminds us,

> We must distinguish between verbal black humorists, such as Terry Southern, Bruce Jay Friedman, and even Philip Roth, whose basic unit is the sick joke or the stand-up monologue, and what I would call "structural" black humorists, such as Heller, Pynchon and Vonnegut. The former take apart the well-made novel and substitute nothing but the absurdist joke, the formless tirade, the cry in the dark; the latter tend toward overarticulated forms, insanely comprehensive plots. . . . Both kinds of black humorists are making an intense assertion of self—the former directly, the latter in vast structures of self-projection.[1]

Black humor, in both of its manifestations, indicated a loss of faith in the conventional forms of the novel, and an assertion of the identity, or at least the hand, of the novelist. The inevitable consequence was *The Parodic Digression.* These were novels by novelists who no longer believed in THE novel but felt compelled for one reason or another to write it. The literature of exhaustion, the death of the novel. One critic has labelled the novelists who became well-known in the late sixties as "regressive parodists," regressive because fiction at that time stubbornly refused to let go of its last superstition, that it is "about" something, that it is mimetic, that it can be validated on the grounds that it presents a superior vision of "reality," finer and deeper than that of history, journalism, or TV. If fiction couldn't do that, what then could it do? How could it compete with the daily newspaper? It couldn't, said Tom Wolfe. And for a while fiction believed him, in the guise of Norman Mailer and Truman Capote, among others.

The Journalistic Digression. Fiction is a kind of deep reportage. Thus novelists will be truest to their art if they become super-journalists and reporters using the techniques of fiction are in a position to usurp the novel. Fiction is not a kind of reportage. Those who believe this mistake one phase in the novel's development—realism—for the nature of fiction, though it must be said that this has been a chronic mistake even among those in the critical establishment favorable to fiction, who now reap what they have sown. The novel has always been connected with reportage but the two are not the same. *Moll Flanders* was supposed to be the inside dope on a prostitute and *Jonathan Wild* capitalized on "the true history" of that crook. In other words, fiction may pretend to be reportage, and vice versa, but they are two different things. One is of course also aware of all the phases in the development of the novel that have nothing to do with social realism, from Rabelais to *Finnegan's Wake*, from Choderlos de Laclos to late Henry James, Romance, allegory, psychological analysis, the novel of sensibility, Diderot, Sterne, Gothic, *Wuthering Heights*, the whole Modern novel, etc., etc. The point is that journalism is of necessity *after the fact*, it is a report about something that has happened; creative writing *is* the fact—before the act of writing there was no fact—that's why it's creative. *Wuthering Heights* is itself fact: a culture fact, an artifact. It is not about some other fact. *Kool Aid Acid Test* is about Ken Kesey; *Wuthering Heights* is about *Wuthering Heights*. "But it's also about the moors, a certain region in England, about Heathcliff, about the English family. . . ." Yes, that's right. It's about *Wuthering Heights*. Nevertheless, *The Journalistic Digression* represents a movement back into experience, from which the novel can isolate itself only at the cost of total suicide. By the 1950s, the conventions of the dominant realistic form in this country had become a formula and realistic fiction had lapsed into a dull formalism that began to incite widespread claustrophobia among its audience, which consequently began to desert it. The success of the "new journalism" in the sixties was a corollary of the novel's need to blast itself open to experience again.

The Hermetic Digression. Consider William H. Gass's clever way around the concept of imitation:

> Think, for instance, of a striding statue; imagine the purposeful inclination of the torso, the alert and penetrating gaze of the head and its eyes, the outstretched arm and pointing finger; everything would appear to direct us toward some goal in front of it. Yet our eye travels only to the finger's end, and not beyond. Though pointing, the finger bids us stay instead, and we journey slowly back along the tension of the arm. In our hearts we know what actually surrounds the statue. The same surrounds every other work of art: empty space and silence.[2]

In other words, fiction does not refer to a reality beyond itself. Okay. But given that art is not mimetic, it does not follow that it is hermetic. When we say that creative language is non-referential I take it we mean that it doesn't refer to other language, other concepts—it points toward the mute world beyond language, beyond history, and then itself falls silent. Art is an escape from language and abstraction—and verbal art is the most conclusive escape into our birthright in the world beyond language from which language above all separates us, and which, therefore, it has the power to restore. A statue out of Wallace Stevens might serve as a commentary on Gass's brilliant construction. Gass:

> But the writer must not let the reader out; the sculptor must not let the
> eye fall from the end of his statue's finger; the musician must not let
> the listener dream. Of course, he will; but let the blame be on himself.
> High tricks are possible; to run the eye rapidly along that outstretch-
> ed arm to the fingertip, only to draw it up before it falls away in
> space; to carry the reader to the very edge of every word so that it
> seems he must be compelled to react as though to truth as told in life,
> and then to return him like a philosopher liberated from the cave, to
> the clear and brilliant world of concept, to the realm of order,
> proportion, and dazzling construction.[3]

Stevens:

> One feels the passion of rhetoric begin to stir and even to grow
> furious; and one thinks that, after all, the noble style, in whatever it
> creates, merely perpetuates the noble style. In this statue, the
> apposition between the imagination and reality is too favorable to
> the imagination.[4]

The good of rhetoric is to connect us with the world, not separate us
from it. Art delivers us from abstraction and solipsism with a newly
vitalized (lively) sense of experience. It does not cage us in the crystal
perfection of art. When writing gets locked in the imagination it falls
under the dominion of the "bawds of euphony." Rhetoric. Literature.
This may account for the loneliness of Willie Master's wife. But while
hermeticism devitalizes the work, it at least focuses attention on the
validity of the artifact itself, from which *The Hermeneutic Digression*
tends to distract us.

The Hermeneutic Digression. There is an underlying dilemma of
interpretation that theorists seem to feel the need to confront, as here
Michel Foucault:

> Commentary's only role is to say *finally*, what has silently been
> articulated *deep down*. It must—and the paradox is ever-changing
> yet inescapable—say, for the first time, what has already been said,
> and repeat tirelessly what was, nevertheless, never said.[5]

I suppose one way out would be for criticism to itself become, as Harold
Bloom suggests, a kind of prose poetry— a kind of second-rate fiction
almost inevitably. It may be that the rushing wing of poetry will one day
be joined by the wagging tail of thought, but it would seem more likely
that poetry and fiction could incorporate theory (Valéry, Joyce, Stevens)
than the other way around. Perhaps one of the best things that can be
said for theory is that it's a good way to get rid of theory. When a
discipline becomes so detached it becomes detached from its object, or
even begins to displace it, you can be sure you are in for a certain amount
of grotesquerie. A journalist thinks that journalism is not reportage but a
kind of fiction, and a superior kind no less. Fine. Now where do I go to
get the news? A literary critic evolves the position that essay is the

essential art—and someone remarks that if he were a garbage collector he would think garbage collecting the central art. And why not? Today everything is art. The minimalists, "happenings" people, and pop artists have implied that life itself is art. The conceptualists tell us that ideas are art. Historians are beginning to tell us that history is art. And now professors claim that scholarship is art. But surely Harold Bloom's thesis of interpretation as misinterpretation and criticism as poetry is an elaborate joke. What Bloom is trying to tell us is that it's time for interpretation to do away with itself, thereby completing the cycle of a Digression and releasing us once more, much enriched no doubt, into the experience of the poem. In *The Anxiety of Influence*, he speaks of

> the mind's effort to overcome the impasse of Formalist criticism, the barren moralizing that Archetypal criticism has come to be, and the anti-humanistic plain dreariness of all those developments in European criticism that have yet to demonstrate that they can aid in reading any one poem by any poet whatsoever.[6]

The subversive absurdity of Bloom's thesis can only be a Pataphysical stratagem to return us from poetics to poetry and fiction.

The Conceptual Digression. The tenacity of fiction as imitation in our culture is not due merely to the sloth or ignorance of the publishing establishment, or even to its greed. We are a schizoid culture and have an enormous investment in our own neurosis. The idea of art as a mirror sustains a disconnected, emotionally dissociated attitude toward experience. Such art presents us with an image of our experience in a way that assures us it is not real: it is a reflection, only a picture, only a story. At last, a way of defining our experience in a form in which we do not have to take responsibility for it. The mode that must have been a means of meditation for Vermeer for us, as cliché, becomes a form of limited liability, a way of packaging our experience so that we can walk away from it. What we call realism saps our experience of its immediacy and authority, a process tremendously augmented by the electronic media and probably one reason for their great success. It is as if your fundamental image of yourself and your life were the one on the television screen, as if we were all actors playing roles. Those "primitives" who are said to feel that snapshots can steal your soul are correct. Finally it is the image on the screen that has all the reality, and experience becomes "fact" only, as they say, when you see it on the evening news. In the sixties we developed two ways out of this disastrous cultural schizophrenia, both essentially ways of getting rid of the mirror of art. One is that the mirror is an illusion, it doesn't exist, there's no difference between art and life: *The Experiential Digression.* The second is that the art work exists only in the realm of the mind and therefore is not a mirror but a window which requires no embodiment: *The Conceptual Digression*. Both are assaults on the idea of art as artifact. The degree of excess that developed in these two Digressions is an index to the urgency behind them. Art as a window implies that it is a means to reach some end other than itself. What? Can we seriously entertain ideas of transcendence? Those faery lands forlorn seen through the magic casement are forlorn precisely because they don't exist. If they did, perhaps a concept would be sufficient as a means of transporting us to them and the work of art as a sensuous artifact might be redundant. Possibly that ephemeralization so dear to the Post-Catholic Post-Moderns like McLuhan, Soleri, and William Irwin Thompson might then seem more appropriate. Conceptual Art dematerializes the art work and moves us toward mounting levels of abstraction. At the same time it moves us away from that union of sense and concept, matter and spirit, ego and world toward which our desire for wholeness of experience impels us and that occurs in a successfully embodied work of art. For that reason, ideas cheapen fiction when they dominate its form, as they do for example in those popular sci-fi-fantasy paintings by Escher, and that may be the trouble with so-called "speculative fiction," now being advanced by some eminent critics as the new wave. On the other hand as an analytic reflex, conceptual art is extremely useful for fiction. It destroys the idea of the novel as a consumer item and teaches us that fiction is an event in the field of experience that, like many other events, has the power to alter that field in significant ways. Conceptual art may also be a way of reclaiming the discursive for a tradition that has proceeded largely in terms of connotation throughout the Modern period. Furthermore, *The Conceptual Digression* in effect constitutes an attempt to confront and work through one side of our schizophrenic split between thought and experience. *The Experiential Digression* is an attempt to work through the other side.

The Experiential Digression. This involves the question of the frame. If art is continuous with experience there is no frame. Art is free, at last, to actually merge with life. Artists in the sixties were finding all sorts of ways of moving out of the frame. On one side happenings, on the other Segal's plaster casting of reality. Frank O'Hara, in a half-serious statement reprinted in a "New York School" anthology which the editors claim "in many ways speaks for us all," talks about writing a poem for a lover:

> While I was writing it I was realizing that if I wanted to I could use the
> telephone instead of writing the poem, and so Personism was born.
> It's a very exciting movement which will undoubtedly have lots of

> adherents. It puts the poem squarely between the poet and the
> person, Lucky Pierre style, and the poem is correspondingly
> gratified. The poem is at last between two persons instead of two
> pages. In all modesty, I confess that it may be the death of literature
> as we know it.[7]

The thrust of O'Hara's poetry, which was to claim the continuity of
poetry with experience as against its discontinuity in terms of technique,
abstraction, or content, was an enormous contribution. And I agree that
art must continually kill itself—but it always has to make sure it's art that
does the killing. The obvious step, for the literal minded, after O'Hara's
statement, is that the poem is unnecessary. Aha! art is life—just as we
thought, so who needs art? This leaves one open to *The Experiential
Digression*, the latest form of the ongoing American conspiracy against
art in favor of "real life," also known as "fact." Unless a line is drawn, the
horde of Factists blunder in waving their banner on which it is written:
"It really happened." Here is Tom Wolfe defending the new journalism
as against fiction:

> The reader knows *all this actually happened* [italics his]. The
> disclaimers have been erased. The screen is gone. The writer is one
> step closer to the absolute involvement of the reader that Henry
> James and James Joyce dreamed of and never achieved.[8]

This is what James and Joyce dreamed of? Too bad they didn't work for
the Hearst chain. This is the harvest of the doctrine of willing suspension
of disbelief: if art is illusion, then documentary is better because it's the
real thing. But on another level, the question of the frame has been a
troublesome one ever since action painting made a point of the
continuity of the act of composition with the rest of experience. The idea
that fiction has no special essence releases a lot of energy, but if it hasn't
then why not journalism? Why not journals? Why not graphics? Why not
comic books? Why not anything? With the loss of the frame, notes critic
Richard Pearce, the medium of fiction "asserts itself as an independent
and vital part of the subject," and citing Beckett as an example goes on to
say that the medium "comes to dominate the narrator, the characters,
and the story."[9] That is perhaps the most significant difference between
fiction in the sixties and fiction in the seventies. The latter has dropped
the sixties' sense of irony about the form, its guilty conscience about the
validity of the novel, its self-parody and self-consciousness. That self-
consciousness has become, in the seventies, a more acute consciousness
about the medium and its options.

The Concrete Digression. Of writers working innovatively with the
medium of fiction, among the most visible are those who are most
visually oriented. Concrete Poetry or, as I call it, Cement Poetry, with its

heavy handed sense of writing as a visual artifact, confounds issues by mistaking what the medium is. The discursive aspect of language can be ignored only at the risk of crossing the line between literature and graphics, and if it comes to that, I would rather look at Picasso. With the seventies' new consciousness of fiction as a medium, however, it becomes apparent that part of the medium is the look of print on the page. Page arrangement has become a factor in composition that many writers are working with, including Steve Katz, Peter Matthiesson, George Chambers, and Raymond Federman. Such writers have transformed the visual element of fiction from an implicit and inert compositional factor to an expressive one. The masterpiece of this current in seventies fiction is Federman's recent *Take It Or Leave It*,[10] which retains the communicative aspect of language by using it as a kind of melody as against the rhythm of radical page arrangement. It is the most successful attempt I know of to recognize and resolve the tension between the communicative and visual aspects of fiction.

The Oral Digression is complementary to *The Concrete Digression*, and proposes the spoken aspect of language as the essential literary element. The Oral Digression has had more influence on poetry than fiction, partly due to the inevitable preponderance of poetry on the reading circuit. The idea is abroad—propagated by such figures as Ginsberg, Snider, and some of the third world writers—that the ultimate context for poetry is the reading. Its influence has also been felt by fiction writers, and we are beginning to see such interesting mistakes as *Black Box*, the tape recorded magazine. The influence has been in some respects beneficial. Written language draws much vitality from spoken language, and the further it moves from the voice the greater the risk that it will go dead. That is why composition by tape recorder can be suggestive and energizing. But composition and finished artifact are two different things. Fiction, finally, involves print on a page, and that is not an incidental convenience of production and distribution, but an essential of the medium.

The Collagist Digression. It is now a commonplace that collage has been central to the modern and post-modern movements. Once the frame has been broken, there is no *a priori* form and works have to be patched together, or, at least, that is one way to go about it. Thus Donald Barthelme's much quoted comment that he only trusts fragments. The idea of collage has, in fact, become a cliché, and like all clichés, is misleading. While the broken frame leads to fragmentation, it is a fertile fragmentation that precedes the invention of new, if impermanent, form. To speak of fragments is to imply that finished and successful works remain fragmented, and this is not the case. We think in fragments and we compose in fragments, but the fictive art consists precisely in the use of the medium to compose out of fragments viable wholes. The medium in question is neither language in general, nor speech, but writing, which has its own reality and particular power. "Imagining," writes Jean Ricardou,

> and *imagining pen in hand* [italics his] are two entirely distinct activities. . . . Exercising the imagination while at the same time apprehending its movement—such is the privilege that writing seems to enjoy. The written fragment is not flight, mobility, disappearance, but rather inscription, a stable reference. With it, imagination changes status.[11]

Composition, in other words, is no longer controlled by the demands of the frame, nor is it left at a dynamic collocation of fragments whose form is indeterminate, but proceeds in and through the text to the creation of formal wholes which may be strange, surprising, and should be unpredictable, even to the author. Such fiction is akin to what George Chambers, in his novel *The Bonnyclabber*, calls "goingungoing" which involves a deferral of intention:

> The word means that one is and is not going where one is going. It allows one to feel surprise and thus pleasure, even amidst the ordinary operations of the everyday day. . . . Every step an adventure.[12]

This kind of fiction is not "about" anything except itself, that is, about the way we structure event through language, which is to say, finally, that it is about almost everything.

The Experimental Digression. I don't write experimental fiction. None of the writers I have mentioned in these remarks writes experimental fiction. If you want to know about experimental fiction, get in touch with Richard Kostelanetz. All good fiction today, in whatever form, is exploratory with regard to the medium and highly conscious of it—even realistic narrative, given the context of the seventies which it must take into account. Therefore Experimental Fiction is no longer a valid category, if it ever was. Aren't we really tired of the stale categories on the basis of which we mechanically conduct the same boring discourse about the future of the novel? Experimental versus conventional, new novel versus old novel, linear versus non-linear, commercial versus non-commercial, realism, surrealism, avant-gardism, modernism, post-moderism, the whole batch needs to be thrown overboard. Fiction writers today are writing from a point of view well anterior to the genres and subgenres of the novel. They begin by questioning the medium itself, and their work involves an exploration of the idea of fiction, not only in the novel, but in the culture at large. There is no such thing as fiction. Instead there is a continuing fictive discourse which continually redefines itself. There is certainly no such thing as THE novel. Instead there are as many novels as there are authentic novelists, and, ideally, there should be as many novels as there are novels of those novelists, since in an exploratory situation, every form should be idiosyncratic. Fiction itself proceeds by digression and cannot be predicted or defined. Each novel is a unique definition, a definition of itself. It follows that our criticism of fiction should make a progressive effort to defamiliarize the novel, to de-define fiction, as fiction simultaneously creates and decreates itself.

Notes

[1] Morris Dickstein, "Black Humor and History: Fiction in the Sixties," *Partisan Review*, 43, No. 2 (1976), 191.

[2] William H. Gass, *Fiction and the Figures of Life* (New York: Alfred A. Knopf, 1970), p. 49.

[3] Gass, p. 54.

[4] Wallace Stevens, *The Necessary Angel* (New York: Alfred A. Knopf, 1951), p. 8.

[5] Michel Foucault, "The Discourse on Language," in *The Archeology of Knowledge*, trans. A. M. Sheridan Smith (New York: Pantheon, 1972), p. 221.

[6] Harold Bloom, *The Anxiety of Influence* (New York: Oxford Univ. Press, 1973), pp. 12-13.

[7] Frank O'Hara, "Personism: A Manifesto," in Rod Padgett and David Shapiro, eds., *An Anthology of New York Poets* (New York: Vintage Books, 1970), p. xxxiv. (Reprinted from *Yugen*.)

[8] Tom Wolfe, "Why They Aren't Writing the Great American Novel Anymore," *Esquire*, 78 (Dec., 1972), 272.

[9] Richard Pearce, "Enter the Frame," in Raymond Federman, ed., *Surfiction: Fiction Now and Tomorrow* (Chicago: Swallow Press, 1975), p. 56.

[10] Raymond Federman, *Take It Or Leave It* (New York: Fiction Collective, 1976).

[11] Jean Ricardou, "Writing Between the Lines," in Federman, *Surfiction*, pp. 265-66.

[12] George Chambers, *The Bonnyclabber* (Princeton, N. J., and Western Springs, Ill.: Panache and December, 1972), p. 30.

BLACK FICTION: HISTORY AND MYTH

Darwin T. Turner
University of Iowa

Most Americans know a tale about a father who read adventure stories to his son. Night after night, the boy heard how a brave man outwrestled bears, killed alligators with a knife, and shot ferocious lions. One night, the boy finally asked, "Daddy, why doesn't the lion ever win?" The father answered, "Son, that lion will never win until he starts writing the stories himself." In the history of human civilization, however, the lions repeatedly have learned to write. As a consequence, nations and peoples have transformed their years of despair and degradation into legends and myths of exaltation. From the mists of the Anglo-Saxon past comes an Arthur, who gathered about him knights who personify the nobility, the bravery, and the character of an entire nation, even a race. Arthur and Camelot are the formalized ideals, recited as romance, glamorized into legend, and finally transformed into myth, to be modified and revived by poet laureates, dramatists, and novelists concerned with the mythic hero rather than the actual one.

Think of a time when most Englishmen were slaves in their own land, pawns in a despotic political-economic system headed by tyrannical Prince John, or so the story goes. Historians may insist that John was not a tyrant but a maligned victim of nobles who usurped his power. Historians may defend John, but generations of readers know that Englishmen were saved only by Robin Hood, who righted wrongs, robbed the rich to feed the poor, and restored Richard the Lion-Hearted to his rightful throne. When France was a fractured land, threatened by power-hungry nobles inside and an invincible English army outside, God sent a savior, Joan, who will return in spirit whenever France is in need. Like Arthur, Joan has transcended her personal history to become a myth celebrating the spirit of the nation and the people.

From such legends and myths, people derive inspiration, not to guide their personal daily lives, not even to improve their image in the eyes of others, but to celebrate their concept of their group, their nation, their race. Perhaps, some may say, we Americans live in an age too cynical to honor myths. Probing the most secret recesses of our nation's heroes, historians and reporters reveal the frailties that inform us that men are but men and women are not much better. But, even in this disillusioned era when credibility gaps seem to be the only truths, legends endure, and new romances have been created by the imaginative and the enterprising.

The American defeat at the Alamo is still retold as a tribute to the American frontiersman. Not so many years ago, American television, in the South at least, presented The Gray Ghost, Major Mosby, a Confederate guerilla who, impeccably dressed, exuding charm and nobility, repeatedly evaded, outwitted, and defeated numerically superior Union forces. Mosby is merely one of many figures populating that romantic, intensely propagandistic legend in which the chivalric Old South did not lose the war.

Scarcely a generation has passed since Margaret Mitchell, ignoring such actual heroes as the Robert E. Lees, the Stonewall Jacksons, and even the Mosbys, repopulated the South with dashing Rhett Butlers, beautiful Scarlet O'Haras, sensitive Ashley Wilkeses, and a horde of Blacks: devoted Mammies, comic Sambos, and savage Black Beasts. Despite his castigation of the Snopeses of his time, William Faulkner has perpetuated romances of the Old South and the myth that an Eden might have existed in the innocence of childhood in such a world. And in the 1970s the popular novel and film *The Outlaw* has attempted to glorify a Civil War Southerner's battle against the Union, "Indians," and forces of evil.

Needless to say, if people live only in dreams, they will die in delusion. They will replicate the arrow-armed "Indian" chiefs who prayed for ghost warriors to lead them to victory against the rifles of the "white eyes." While dreaming their romances, their legends, their myths, a people must work within reality for personal, immediate, sometimes limited goals. They must comprehend the actuality of their condition; they must understand that no "magics or elves / Or timely grandmothers" will improve the actuality. But a confident people must also have a transcendent vision of what might be, a vision drawn not only from their triumph but even from their despair.

Until the past decade, however, twentieth-century Afro-American novelists virtually ignored the possibility of using historical materials to achieve this vision or even to improve Afro-American images by reinterpreting the past. Such neglect is even more puzzling when one perceives how these two motives have dominated Afro-American writing. From the 1760s to the present day, essayists have defended Black people by refuting allegations against them. During the first half of the twentieth century, such well-known novelists as Charles Chesnutt, W. E. B. DuBois, James Weldon Johnson, Jessie Fauset, Rudolph Fisher,

Countee Cullen, and Ann Petry all sought to counteract derogatory images with more favorable fictive ones. Yet, among these novelists, only the academically trained historian W. E. B. DuBois sought to correct images of the past.

Inspirational romances and legends also constitute a significant tradition in Afro-American folk tales, drama, and poetry—but not in novels. Folk tales glory in High John de Conqueror, Shine, Stackolee, to name only a few. In such historical pageants as Langston Hughes's *Don't You Want to Be Free?* and Leroi Jones's *Slave Ship,* and in more traditional forms of drama, Afro-Americans have recounted the heroism of anonymous slaves and freedmen, as well as that of such well-known historical figures as Menelik, Toussaint l'Ouverture, Henri Christophe, Crispus Attucks, Frederick Douglass, and Nat Turner. Almost all well-known Afro-American poets who earned their reputations before 1960 have commemorated some aspect of the African or Afro-American past. The silence of Black novelists about history cannot be attributed to lack of material. This can be found in the research of historians Carter Woodson, Basil Davidson, and Chancellor Williams, or even in the biographies of the Afro-Americans whom William Wells Brown commemorated in *The Black Man: His Genius and His Achievement* (1858), published five years before the Emancipation Proclamation.

Consider the wealth of material in the narratives of fugitive slaves. What better material for a legend is there than William Wells Brown: fugitive slave, conductor on the Underground Railroad, and internationally prominent man of letters? Harriet Tubman, who repeatedly risked her life to lead slaves to freedom? Frederick Douglass, who discovered freedom in his vow never to let a man whip him again? Henry "Box" Brown, who fled from slavery in a sealed coffin? Ellen Craft, who daringly exploited her fair skin to pose as a Southern master when she and her darker husband fled North? Where can one find more exciting drama than the captures and breathtaking escapes of Henry Bibb? Nonetheless, Afro-American novelists in general have relinquished interpretation of the slave past to such white authors as Faulkner, Mitchell, Howard Fast, and William Styron.

The reasons for Afro-American reluctance can be hypothesized: One, educated by a system which inculcates the myth of Caucasian superiority and the inevitability of success for all but the lazy, the ignorant, and the immoral, many middle-class Black Americans have been ashamed that their ancestors remained slaves for two centuries. Moreover, until recently, Americans—Black and white alike—were taught that Africa had spawned only savages. Aspiring to champion his

people, Paul Laurence Dunbar wrote that he wanted to prove that they
were "more human than African." A second reason is that some Black
writers during the early years of the twentieth century consciously
proposed to forget the past. They believed that if they offered to ignore
the Afro-American hardships during slavery, Southern whites might
forget their own sufferings during the Civil War and Reconstruction;
then all Americans might unite in brotherhood. Third, undoubtedly
publishers have influenced the choice of subject-matter; for Black
novelists, more than dramatists and poets, have depended on the largest
publishing houses, which are owned by whites. The stories of such
censorship must be retold by the writers themselves. Certainly,
however, in a land so often divided about racial issues, publishers'
concepts of the interests of white readers frequently must have clashed
with the desires of Black novelists.

Although my comments until this moment may suggest that I need
write no more about Afro-Americans and historical novels, in this
Bicentennial year when many Americans are re-examining history, I
consider it appropriate and instructive to review decade by decade the
most significant historical novels by Afro-Americans of this century: Paul
Laurence Dunbar's *The Fanatics* (1901); Arna Bontemps' *Black Thunder*
(1936) and *Drums at Dusk* (1939); Zora Neale Hurston's *Moses, Man of
the Mountain* (1939); Frank Yerby's *The Foxes of Harrow* (1946), to
name only the first and best-known of many; W. E. B. DuBois' *The Black
Flame* (1957-1961); Margaret Walker's *Jubilee* (1967); Ernest Gaines'
The Autobiography of Miss Jane Pittman (1971); Frank Yerby's *The
Dahomean* (1971); and Ishmael Reed's *Mumbo-Jumbo* (1972).

Arbitrarily, I have defined "historical novel" loosely as any long
fictional story set in a time-frame at least one generation preceding the
author's birth. I have allowed one exception to this principle. The first
volume of W. E. B. DuBois' trilogy begins in 1876, eight years after
DuBois' birth. At the time when the volume was published, DuBois was
in his eighty-ninth year, and I am willing to expand my canon to include
as historical any novel which a trained historian writes about the early
years of a life almost one century long.

To compress this study into the prescribed limits, I propose to
survey the novelists' purposes, compare these with the intentions of
Afro-American novelists who were their contemporaries, and suggest
what values may accrue when Black lions tell the stories. If I move
beyond description and analysis into exhortation, please understand that
I am merely following Matthew Arnold's thesis that a critic may suggest

materials for artists. And if I seem to dwell on inspirational value more than on reinterpretation, perhaps I am merely suggesting that romances and popular novels may reveal values which might persuade Plato to retain some of their creators in his Republic.

When Paul Laurence Dunbar published *The Fanatics* (1901), Black Americans suffered what historian Rayford Logan has described as the nadir of Afro-American history. New to "the white man's burden" of colonizing territories of darker-skinned peoples, and desiring to effect reconciliation between North and South so as to expand economic opportunities, the Federal Government of the United States benignly neglected Afro-Americans. The nation averaged two hundred lynchings per year, and increasing numbers of the Southern states were enacting laws which for one-half century would effectively abrogate Blacks' rights to equal opportunity in voting, education, and public accommodations. The images of Afro-Americans in American literature were those popularized by Thomas Nelson Page and Joel Chandler Harris, who yearned for the good old darkies who lived only to care for their masters; by Thomas Dixon, who preached evangelically that the bestial Black race must be deported or exterminated before it corrupted Anglo-Saxons; and by musical "coon" shows which, though written by Blacks, catered to white audiences' enjoyment of lazy, amusing, ignorant, and amoral Black stereotypes.

Some Black novelists depicted the contemporary scene bitterly. Sutton Griggs, in *Imperium in Imperio* (1899), had suggestively considered the need for a separate state controlled by Blacks. In 1901, after years of attacking bigotry with restrained irony and pleas for recognition of Black virtue, Charles Chesnutt scathingly protested that instead of granting Afro-Americans opportunity to compete with white Americans the whites sought to destroy the Blacks.

In the same year, Dunbar, with no exhibition of the bitterness he had revealed a year earlier in *The Strength of Gideon and Other Stories*, sympathetically portrayed the manner in which whites of Southern Ohio were fanatically and foolishly divided by the Civil War. The antagonists are not motivated by any desire to liberate the slaves: Stephen Van Doren and Colonel Stewart defend the right of the South to govern itself; Bradford Waters favors supreme authority for the central government. Tom Waters fights for glory and excitement; Walter Stewart and Bob Van Doren believe that duty compels them to fight. And the women seem to have no political beliefs except to support the positions articulated by their male lovers. Before the war, these whites had tolerantly patronized the few Blacks who lived in their town. When the fighting intensifies and increasing numbers of southern Blacks flee into Ohio, the whites unanimously castigate the Blacks as animals responsible for all of the ills associated with the war. In one provocative chapter, "The Contrabands," Dunbar focused on the slaves who followed the Union troops into Ohio, where they expected to find freedom. Instead, they encountered violent opposition, not only from whites, but even from free northern Blacks, who feared that the influx would jeopardize their own insecure positions. Dunbar might have told this story well, for his parents had been part of the migrating "contrabands." Unfortunately, after the one chapter, Dunbar resumed his melodramatic saga of white confusion.

For more than a generation after Dunbar, Black novelists ignored historical fiction, even though Black history was emphasized in other avenues of Black life. During the World War I era, Black scholars, prompted partly by historians DuBois and Woodson, explored Black history. While white America reveled in the contemporaneity of Harlem in the 1920s, Alain Locke, a mentor of the Harlem Renaissance, urged Black artists to seek subject and style in their past; poets such as Countee Cullen and Langston Hughes evoked inspiration from the African heritage; and dramatists such as Willis Richardson delineated historical Black heroes. In contrast, the Renaissance novelists restricted their vision to the contemporary scene.

Although Hugh Gloster has identified John Paynton's *Fugitives of the Pearl* (1930) as the first genuine historical novel by an Afro-American,[1] the first of major consequence during the 1930s was *Black Thunder* (1936)[2] by Arna Bontemps, whose previous novel, *God Sends Sunday* (1931) had centered on a Black jockey. At a time when many Black Americans perceived their oppression to be mirrored by the unjust prosecution of the Scottsboro boys, accused of raping two white women, Bontemps, in *Black Thunder*, recalled Gabriel's abortive rebellion of 1800. In a preface to the 1968 reprinting of *Black Thunder*, Bontemps explained that he had written the book as "a possible metaphor of turbulence to come."[3] Thirty-year-old memories by authors cannot always be depended upon; nevertheless, a reader can perceive the intended emphasis upon liberty in the story of a Black hero who refused to be cowed by white forces.

Nineteen-year-old Gabriel has planned to capture Virginia with eleven hundred fellow slaves; on the night of the assault, however, a torrential rain, flooding the rivers which the assembling slaves must cross, reduces the army from eleven hundred to four hundred. Another two hundred desert because they fear that they are now too few to win or because they suspect that the "signs" have turned against them. Before the attack can be reorganized, two slaves betray the rebellion. In the bloody days following, while rebels and innocent victims are slaughtered by vigilantes and courts, Gabriel heroically evades capture until he surrenders in order to protect another man who has been mistaken for him. Gabriel dies proudly, knowing that he has never betrayed his fellows and that, for a time at least, he has been free.

This well-written novel is authenticated by Bontemps' extensive research, not only into records concerning Gabriel, but also into many slave narratives which provided him with a knowledge of African folk customs and a sensitivity to the conditions he had never experienced. Bontemps' artistic decisions, however, evidence the manner in which Black American writers have restricted their use of slave experiences. Despite his desire to delineate an heroic Black, Bontemps could not transcend the compulsion to validate the story, to prove that such circumstances and such a Black had existed. He fastidiously selected that historic rebellion which had the greatest chance for success and that leader most capable of winning. In making his choice, Bontemps rejected Nat Turner, because Nat was "too mystical," a condition which never seems to distract authors who retell the story of Joan of Arc. Furthermore, by limiting his story to the actual achievements of one leader, Bontemps relinquished his artistic prerogative to weave one story from many, or to "mediate on history," a right that William Styron cited a generation later to defend his exploitation of Nat Turner's story.[4]

The inspirational possibilities of *Black Thunder* are further weakened by Bontemps' narrative techniques and descriptive emphases. The novel begins with a picture of an aging house slave, Ben, dutifully winding a clock (regulating the time of the plantation) and hoping merely for a compliment that he is a good boy. A reader follows Ben's emotional progress from stage to stage. At first, too old to recall his youthful desire for freedom, he is momentarily inspired by the enthusiasm of other slaves. But the rain, the darkness of the night, and the fear of his own audacity in joining the plot, terrify him into rushing back to his plantation to fall at his master's feet and, sobbing, confess his sins. Finally, Ben, guilt-ridden, fears that suspicious slaves will take from him that life which he has betrayed his honor to preserve. Although his actions and speech may be melodramatic, Ben has a damnable aura of truth about him; consequently, he haunts the memory more vividly than the indomitable Gabriel, single-minded in his desire for freedom, or the admirable teen-aged Juba, single-minded in her love for Gabriel. Thus, a work that might have added a legend to Black history provides instead a metaphor for self-imposed servility.

When Bontemps wrote *Black Thunder*, America reverberated with rumors of revolution. The economic depression of the 1930s inspired Communists to hope that the moment had arrived. White authors attacked economic conditions. Near the end of the decade, new Black American writers, such as Richard Wright (*Uncle Tom's Children*, 1938) and William Attaway (*Blood on the Forge*, 1941), responded to the mood by describing contemporaneous political demonstrations and labor unrest. But, except for Bontemps and Zora Neale Hurston, no Afro-American novelists explored Black history for models of rebellion.

Bontemps' *Drums at Dusk* (1939) expands one recurrent image of *Black Thunder*. In the earlier novel, Bontemps had pictured Gabriel drawing inspiration from Toussaint l'Ouverture's successful revolution in Haiti. In *Drums at Dusk* (1939),[5] Bontemps fictionalized the earlier revolution. Interestingly, however, Bontemps, who gave Toussaint legendary status in *Black Thunder*, subordinated him in the later novel, which focuses on the whites of San Domingue, especially on Diron Desautels, a hot-blooded liberal member of *Les Amis des Noirs*. Continuously drumming at the consciousness of the whites in Haiti and of the readers in the United States, the Haitian slaves finally explode into a revolution guided by impetuous Baissou and wise Toussaint. Emphasizing the Black masses rather than a single leader, Bontemps perhaps adumbrated his new belief that the success of a revolution depends upon the masses, not the leaders. But, by comparing the Haitian Blacks with the white revolutionaries who overthrew the French monarchy and with newly-captured Africans who killed themselves rather than submit to Haitian slavery, Bontemps sets forth models of courage to be emulated by Afro-Americans.

In *Moses, Man of the Mountain*,[6] Zora Neale Hurston retreated even further into the past to comment on the problems and behavior of Blacks of her time. Like her contemporary John Erskine, who satirized such legendary figures as Galahad and Helen of Troy, Hurston mocked the Biblical story of Moses in a reversal of racial/ethnic identities which models the Egyptians nobles after white Southerners and the Chosen People after Black Americans. Although they had prayed for deliverance while in Egypt, the slaves soon weary of the rigors of their freedom in the wilderness: "I wish to God we had died whilst we was back in Egypt. There we was sitting down every day to a big pot of meat and bread. . . . We don't care if they did work us some."[7] Continuously grumbling about food, water, habitat, and anything else they can think of, they turn from Moses to such malicious and destructively envious leaders as the power-hungry Jethro and the envious Miriam, who, having inveigled herself into society by claiming that Moses is her brother, provokes mob hostility towards Zipporah, Moses' fair-skinned wife, when Miriam fails to receive the rewards she expects. Probably her best novel, *Moses, Man of the Mountain* provided Zora Neale Hurston a secure vehicle from which to satirize the behavior of Blacks and whites: if attacked for demeaning whites or Blacks, she could insist that, in the manner of Dunbar's preacher in "An Antebellum Sermon," she was merely "a-preachin' ancient . . . [not] talkin' 'bout to-day."

During the 1940s, encouraged by the temporary surge of liberalism that seems to follow America's wars, such Black novelists as Richard Wright, Chester Himes, and Ann Petry moved in "raceless" novels from protest about oppression of Blacks to portraiture of white protagonists. This was the path that Frank Yerby followed. After earning early acclaim for short fiction in the "protest" tradition, he became the first Afro-American to establish his literary reputation primarily on historical novels. Since *The Foxes of Harrow* (1946),[8] he has been perhaps the most popular historical novelist in the world; and some would say that translations and sales indicate that he is the most popular novelist, regardless of genre.

Yerby, however, did not win his audience by writing about Blacks. Until the 1960s, Yerby's protagonists in published novels were Caucasians who casually or morosely presume that success depends upon one's willingness to exploit the weak. Most often, his protagonists were outcasts, whose struggles to win and maintain a position in society enabled Yerby to adumbrate philosophical views about life and to attack myths about the past. As Yerby has said in a recent radio interview in Iowa City, readers are more willing to tolerate attacks on their great-grandparents than criticisms of their own behavior. Therefore, Yerby has gaily debunked the past, especially that of the American South:

> The South, he has pointed out, was founded by adventurers, outcasts and failures who migrated to America because they had nothing to lose; the actual aristocrats, having nothing to gain by emigration, remained on the continent. By exploiting people and the land, these immigrants amassed fortunes. Accustomed only to indolence and luxury, their children and grandchildren created the legends about aristocratic heritage.
>
> Second-generation Americans, Yerby has shown, did not resemble the idealized sterotypes of the myth. Educated in the North, they, like Etienne Fox, learned to drink, gamble, and wench while they were receiving "the gentleman's C." Returning to the South, they hunted and entertained; they read books infrequently and speculated philosophically even less frequently. Occasionally, they illogically assumed that they could defend their honor by shooting straight. Socially, their sisters towered above Fancy Williamson of the Carolina hills or Laurie Griffin of Mississippi

peasantry, but morally they were equal. While being raped by James Jarrett, Mary Knox of Georgian aristocracy realizes that she is enjoying herself. Impoverished Cecile Fox of Louisiana buys medical supplies with her body, her only barterable resource. Louisiana-born socialite Susan Drake, a married woman, shamelessly pursues the man she loves.

Yerby has charged that even the houses and towns have been idealized in the myth. Instead of being tastefully appointed, neo-Grecian mansions, houses of the early planters were rambling frame structures in yards littered with farm implements and livestock. Later houses were often architectural monstrosities (*Floodtide*, 1950). Supposedly the cultural mecca of the antebellum South, New Orleans was a pig-sty ravaged by disease and exploited by corrupt governments. . . .

Yerby has not spared Negroes. Depicting cringing slaves who fawn upon their masters and betray their fellows, he has argued that the American slaves rarely rebelled, because the traders wisely selected them predominantly from tribes made docile by centuries of bondage in Africa. In contrast, the slaves of Haiti, carelessly selected from proud and warlike tribes, overthrew their French masters. Furthermore, having been restricted to childlike existence devoid of formal education, dignity, or opportunity to assume responsibility for their welfare, American slaves, when freed suddenly, could not govern themselves. . . .[9]

The Foxes of Harrow presents Stephen Fox, an impoverished immigrant gambler who, starting with only a diamond stickpin, amasses a fortune, crashes into New Orleans society, marries a Creole whose family represents the height of that society, suffers emotional traumas (occasionally comparable to those of Gerald O'Hara or Rhett Butler of *Gone With the Wind*), loses his fortune during the Civil War and retires into a quieter life with the younger sister of his first wife. Even in his first novel, Yerby implanted more favorable images by describing such Blacks as Tante Caleen, a wise and psychologically shrewd conjurer; La Belle Sauvage, who kills herself rather than continue to live as a slave; and Inchcliff, who, by teaching himself to read, refutes Stephen Fox's racist (but kindly) conviction that Blacks cannot be educated. Unfortunately, many readers remember only the cowardly and ignorant Blacks.

During the 1950s, Afro-American literature turned inward as such Black writers as novelists Julian Mayfield and Paule Marshall, poets Gwendolyn Brooks, Robert Hayden, and Melvin Tolson, and dramatist-essayist James Baldwin, disdaining traditional protest, explored Black life without apparent self-consciousness. Afro-Americans, they suggested, were people, identical to other Americans in some ways, unique in others. But they were American people whose stories should be told without apology or explanation.

During the same decade, W. E. B. DuBois, then in his late eighties, began *The Black Flame*, a three-volume historical novel. In a postscript to *The Ordeal of Mansart*, the first volume, DuBois explained his motivation:

> I have used fiction to interpret those historical facts which otherwise would not be clear. Beyond this I have in some cases resorted to pure imagination in order to make unknown and unknowable history relate an ordered tale to the reader. In few cases I have made slight and unimportant changes in the exact sequence of historical events and in names and places. In no case have these changes altered, to my mind, the main historical background.
>
> It may well be asked, and as one who has done some historical research I join in the asking, why should one tamper with history at all in order to write truth? The answer of course is Never, if exact truth can otherwise be ascertained. But every historian is painfully aware how little the scientist today can know accurately the past; how dependence on documents and memory leaves us all with the tale of the past half told or less. The temptation then comes to pretend we know far more than we do and to set down as accurate history that which is not demonstrably true. To me it seems wiser and fairer to interpret historical truth by the use of creative imagination, provided the method is acknowledged and clear.
>
> When in this world we seek the truth about what men have thought and felt and done, we face insuperable difficulties. We seldom can see enough of human action at first hand to interpret it properly. We can never know current personal thought and emotion with sufficient understanding rightly to weigh its cause and effect. After action and feeling and reflection are long past, then from writing and memory we may secure some picture of the total truth, but it will be sorely imperfect, with much omitted, much forgotten, much distorted.
>
> This is the eternal paradox of history. There is but one way to meet this clouding of facts and that is by the use of imagination where documented material and personal experience are lacking. . . .[10]

No matter how literary scholars may evaluate its merits as a novel, *The Black Flame* is an impressive effort; and, like most of DuBois's other works, it is an important document in the literature of Black people. Focused primarily on Manual Mansart and his family, the trilogy re-examines the history of Afro-Americans from Manual's birth during a riot in South Carolina in October, 1876, until his death in 1954.

The dates, of course, communicate meaning to Blacks who know their racial history in the United States. One month after Manual was born, the House of Representatives, after the closest American Presidential election in history, selected Rutherford B. Hayes, who, by withdrawing Federal troops from the South, ended the efforts of the Federal Government to protect the citizenship rights of Afro-Americans in that region. Thus, a door was opened to violent physical repressions, abrogations of voting rights, and Jim Crow laws. In 1954, the Supreme Court declared segregation in public schools on the basis of race to be a denial of the constitutional rights of the children so discriminated against. At last, many Afro-Americans hoped, a new door had been knocked ajar; and, through the crack, they saw the equal opportunity that America promises to its citizens.

But DuBois repudiated such optimism. His work concludes in despair or madness: European nations are scheming to deceive Africans and Afro-Americans into supporting the Europeans' efforts to regain control of the world, and perceptive Black Americans are reviling their own impotence. At his death, Manual sees visions of two futures: in one, the world has been devastated by war; in the other, in a world of peace, oppressed peoples have become free. More sanguine and more patient than the author who created him, Manual rejoices in the vision of peace and freedom. But a perceptive reader must wonder which vision will be the actual future.

Let me admit freely the defects that traditional scholars can find in the trilogy. Clearly patterned after DuBois' dictum that "Art is Propaganda," *The Black Flame* examines Afro-American history since 1876 in order to enunciate the thesis that Capitalism, by provoking racial antagonisms, has tried to separate Black workers from white workers in order to maintain its control of the world, which it orders to worship Mammon. Furthermore, literary critics would say, although some characters are remembered vividly, often because of their poignant efforts to survive with self-respect, most characters are obviously designed as analogues for particular ideological or psychological concepts. (Notice the suggestiveness of the name, "Manual Man's Art.") Furthermore, even a staunch defender of DuBois must admit that, because he had a misguided purpose, was too old, or lacked artistic skill, DuBois failed to achieve maximum potential from his material. Consider, for example, how the following brief but potentially dramatic scene, rich in Afro-American folktale and folksong, might have been elevated into legend or myth. A white worker narrates the episode:

> ". . . by God, I know a man when I see him, and black Jim
> Henry was a man. . . ."

> "Jim Henry was a member of my local. And, of course, we let
> him work. But at the same time, he got the worst places on the job.

We saw to that. We worked in bad holes, in mud and water. He stood where we feared gas—you know—."

"One day we was all called to go down into a re-opened mine. Many whites refused outright, claiming it was dangerous and fearing gas. Others suddenly got 'sick' and went home. But Jim Henry's wife came right down to the mine and said, 'Be a man, Jim, go down—go down!' And this though the food was scarce at home, her clothes ragged, and she was worn by hard work and want. But there was the old fighting spirit in her eyes. He kissed her and went."

"Down into the darkness we entered the old forgotten diggings slowly and with fear. But Jim Henry walked ahead swinging his pick, until we came to the darkest, lowest level. Then some sniffed and muttered 'Gas!' Jim sniffed too. 'Taint no gas - just rot,' and he strode on. Most of us stopped and stood still. The boss swore at us, as Jim Henry rounded the far curve and went down into the hole. His voice rolled back singing: 'Dey ain't no hammer, ina dis mountain-' Then it stopped. We looked into the blackness and saw the air reddening. 'Fire!' we screamed. But the mist and fog killed our voices, and thick darkness settled over him."

"We began to crowd back, but Jim Henry went on down into the cold, muddy water. The fire still glowed ahead, flaring up and on. Then in the smoke wafting back he smelt it. He knew it was the death gas—soon, soon. There was no escape. We saw him straighten. He swung his pick on high and struck. Hell roared and then it was still. It was still as death."

"Course, I don't know what happened after that. But when they buried what was found of Jim Henry, some went down to the 'nigger' church for his funeral and they tell a tale. They say they heard a crazy preacher, and then they say Jim Henry's wife stood up and talked, which couldn't a been true for she dropped dead when they lifted him out of the mine. But they say she was there and that she was dim and gray and that she talked low and tight with sobs between, till she came to that song, my God that song:

'I've heard of a city called Heaven!' "[11]

Despite weaknesses apparent to those trained to be the mentors of Western literary scholarship, *The Black Flame* demonstrates an intention worth emulating. First, *The Black Flame* is a monumental effort to tell the story of Afro-Americans on the gigantic scale of Tolstoi's *War and Peace*. Second, several years before Black Arts writers propounded their first theories, DuBois drew from the heritage of Afro-American culture, as I have illustrated, by his uses of folksong and folktale. Third, *The Black Flame* presents American history from a Black perspective.

During the past decade, as Black Americans began to boast of their heritage and as publishers became—for a time, at least—more kindly disposed, increasing numbers of Blacks utilized historical fiction, some in traditional ways, others in ways significantly new for Black authors.

The list of writers could be expanded even further if I included those who have used historical material to provide a background essential to interpreting the action occurring in the present. For example, in *A Different Drummer* (1962) William Melvin Kelley delineated the protagonist's slave ancestors to explain the strength of character which enables the protagonist to burn his home, destroy his land, and leave the South forever. For the sake of brevity, however, I will restrict myself to four major historical novels published since 1966.

Margaret Walker's *Jubilee*[12] follows Black slaves, free Blacks, and freedmen in Georgia and Alabama from the 1840s into the 1870s. Focused on Vyry, modeled after Margaret Walker's great-grandmother, *Jubilee* relates in detail Vyry's experiences as a slave: her marriage to Randall Ware, a free Black; her childbearing and childloss; her hopes that Ware will buy freedom for her and for their children; her aborted attempt to escape and her punishment of seventy-five lashes. After the Civil War has ended, Vyry, resisting courtships, awaits Randall Ware's return. Finally, believing him dead, she marries Innis Brown, who has befriended her and her children. In Alabama, their new home, they repeatedly suffer from the hatred of whites until Vyry's services as a midwife win sympathy from some whites, who protect her. When Randall Ware eventually returns, Vyry decides to remain with Innis Brown.

In *How I Wrote Jubilee*, Margaret Walker has explained that she planned a book about the Black folk-people that would provide a deeper understanding of slavery, the Civil War, and Reconstruction and its aftermath from a Black perspective.[13] It is startling to realize that two-thirds of the twentieth century had passed before any Afro-American traced Black protagonists through those three critical periods of Afro-American history within a single novel. This effort alone denotes a new consciousness among Black writers.

Despite such new consciousness, *Jubilee* thematically echoes earlier Black writers. Just as Chesnutt and Dunbar once hoped that their revelations of the virtues and Americanness of Blacks would evoke compassion and justice from white Americans, so Margaret Walker hinges Vyry's survival on the hopes that endurance, good will, and good works will eventually be recognized and rewarded. Later, Margaret Walker felt compelled to explain that the success of Vyry and the failure of Randall should not be construed as her comments on twentieth-century Black strategies. Instead, she had merely described two nineteenth-century Blacks as they actually were:

> My great-grandmother was a definite product of plantation life
> and culture. She was shaped by the forces that dominated her life. In

the Big House and in the Quarters, she was raised according to Christian ethics, morality, and faith, and she could not react any other way. Her philosophy of life was a practical one, and she succeeded in getting the things she wanted and prayed for. She realized that hatred wasn't necessary and would have corroded her own spiritual well-being.

But Randall Ware was not of the plantation life and culture, and he could not be shaped by such forces. He belonged to an artisan class of free laborers and had neither the slave mentality of Innis nor the caste notions of Vyry. He was bitter because he was frustrated. He did not get what he wanted and he was conscious of how he had been cheated. He was forced to sell his land; he failed to get his political rights as a free citizen; he was shamed into a kind of cowardice at the cost of his life and manhood, and he was even denied the pleasure of seeing his children grow. He could not be expected to think or act in any way like Vyry or Innis. . . . I have not used him to place the words and ideas of the 1960's and a Black Nationalist in his head. He had that mind then.[14]

In the highly-respected novel *The Autobiography of Miss Jane Pittman* (1971),[15] Ernest Gaines, using a narrative technique reminiscent of the Federal Writers' interviews of former slaves during the 1930s, delineated the life of Miss Jane Pittman from slavery during childhood into the Freedom Marches of the 1960s. Like DuBois in *The Black Flame*, Gaines reviewed the history of America by focusing on a Black character. The effects, however, are significantly different. Unlike Mansart, a college president who meets influential people, Miss Jane remains among Black peasants who, servants and sharecroppers, wish for little more than a good life and independent ownership of a small piece of property. American history, viewed from Jane's perspective, is different; although she recalls such headline matters as world wars, she is more personally affected by the non-headline issues of the murder of a southern Black spokesman, her husband's fatal attempt to master a horse, Huey Long's contributions to the well-being of Black people, and the box scores of baseball games played by the Dodgers after Jackie Robinson has plunged through the color line.

Like Bontemps before him, Gaines sought inspiration from the past; therefore, the book serenades the Black desire for freedom, as it is reflected in Miss Jane, who, as a child, accepts a beating rather than continue to acknowledge the slave name given her by her owners. Refusing, even in childhood, to remain with her former owners after Emancipation, Jane sets out alone and afoot to travel from Louisiana to Ohio. Unable to travel as far as the borders of Louisiana, relatively secure and content in marriage, and favored on a plantation, Jane, like Bontemps's Ben, might have grown so old that she forgot her youthful

desire for freedom. Instead, following an instinct she cannot comprehend, Miss Jane, more than one century old, sacrifices security in
order to resume the walk to freedom. Since Miss Jane is average in
station, aspiration, and association, her quest for freedom cannot be
construed to represent merely the attitudes of Black leaders. Instead, it
represents the motive of the masses.

Almost thirty years ago, in an unpublished study of Black fiction, I
complained, "There has been no full-length romantic portrait of an Afro-
American legendary hero, though history does not lack men who might
be revealed. African princes, Hannibal, the greatest swordsman in
France, Crispus Attucks, many other Black heroes who gave their lives
for their adopted countries—from these could be drawn innumerable
romantic stories." Almost a generation later, in 1971, without knowing of
my proposal, a Black author responded. Although Hwesu, the
protagonist of Yerby's *The Dahomean,* is not modeled after a legendary
hero, he is himself an heroic figure worthy of legend.[16] Having examined
and glamorized protagonists from Europe, North America, and the
Middle East, while he debunked the myths of those cultures, Yerby, with
the same spirit, turned his attention at last to Africa to tell the story of the
son of an African leader who unwillingly earns a reputation for valor in
war (which he hates), reluctantly accepts the governorship of a territory
(which he governs well), but fails tragically when he and his family are
betrayed into slavery. The effect of *The Dahomean* is the same as that of
Yerby's novels about white cultures. One unconsciously imbibes Yerby's
criticism of the culture but remembers the protagonist vividly. Furthermore, unlike many of Yerby's American protagonists who are scoun-
drels, though charming, Hwesu—no less bold, intelligent and manly—is
a thoroughly decent man.

The innovative creation of a glamorous figure in Black historical
fiction was followed by a further innovation in Ishmael Reed's *Mumbo-
Jumbo.*[17] Evoking an historical myth to explain a more recent condition,
Reed in *Mumbo-Jumbo* insists that the Harlem Renaissance should be
attributed to the power of "Jes Grew," the survival of an African religion
whose teachings have been suppressed and concealed by Europeans for
more than two thousand years. Intermingled with the presentation of the
Harlem Renaissance, a twentieth-century phenomenon, is the myth of
Osiris, a young Egyptian prince skilled in the mysteries of agriculture
and in the arts of dance. Jealous of the popularity of Osiris (the Bull),
whose dances taught people to let nature speak through them, or to be
natural, Set, Osiris's half-brother, killed him. Despite the murder,
Osiris's dances spread into Greece (through Dionysus), and subsequent-

ly to Rome. As they spread, they were opposed by the Atonists, the followers of Set. This contest between the Atonists and the Osirians, according to Reed, has continued through the history of Western Europe. During the 1920s, therefore, the Atonists attacked and eventually seemed to curb the dances of Osiris. "Jes Grew" faded; and, burned by a Black nationalist, the book describing the dances of Osiris disappeared from the world. Reed continues optimistically:

> Jes Grew has no end and no beginning. It even precedes that little ball that exploded 100000000s of years ago and led to what we are now. Jes Grew may even have caused the ball to explode. We will miss it for a while but it will come back, and when it returns we will see that it never left. You see, life will never end; there is really no end to life, if anything goes it will be death. Jes Grew is life. They comfortably share a single horse like 2 knights. They will try to depress Jes Grew but it will only spring back and prosper. We will make our own future Text. A future generation of young artists will accomplish this![18]

Significantly, in a more recent novel, *The Last Days of Louisiana Red*, there is never a doubt about the eventual triumph of Papa La Bas, a practitioner of the true African religion.

One should not be surprised that Black novelists seem to have rediscovered the historical novel during the past decade or perhaps even to have discovered for the first time the varied ways the historical novel can be used. During a decade which emphasized Black pride and identity, increasing numbers of Black novelists told and retold the story of Black people. So, too, in the historical novel, Black authors, no longer merely offering rejoinders to slander, did not restrict themselves to self-consciously validated re-creations of Black history. Several created legends and myths without regard to those audiences—bemused, skeptical, and hostile—that seek nothing more from Black artists than a titillation of the senses expressed through presentation and explanation of the present or verification of the past. Perhaps Black novelists have finally perceived the significance of what Cervantes implied centuries ago: even though the Don Quixotes may perish, the stories of their visions and their dreams may inspire the Sancho Panzas to grow.[19]

Notes

[1]Hugh Gloster, *Negro Voices in American Fiction* (New York, 1965), p. 211.

[2]Arna Bontemps, *Black Thunder* (New York: Macmillan, 1936. Reprinted by Beacon Press, 1968).

[3]Bontemps, p. 100.

[4]I must digress into an ironic footnote. If Bontemps hoped that readers of the 1930s would gain from *Black Thunder* an insight into the mood of Blacks of their generation, even more white readers of the 1960s must have read Styron's novel with the hope of understanding the nature of Black rebels. Since Bontemps, thirty years earlier, had judged that Nat's excessive mysticism reduced him from the dimensions of a strong Black revolutionary leader, I wish I might have asked Bontemps how he evaluated the leadership qualifications of the Styronic Nat, into whom the white author fantasized homosexual yearnings, contempt for Black women, and lust for white women.

[5]Arna Bontemps, *Drums at Dusk* (New York: Macmillan, 1939).

[6]Zora Neale Hurston, *Moses, Man of the Mountain* (Philadelphia: Lippincott, 1939).

[7]Hurston, p. 29.

[8]Frank Yerby, *The Foxes of Harrow* (New York: Dial, 1946).

[9]Darwin T. Turner, "Yerby as Debunker," *Massachusetts Review*, 9 (1968), 569-77.

[10]W.E.B. DuBois, *The Ordeal of Mansart* [Book One of *The Black Flame*] (New York: Mainstream, 1957), pp. 315-16.

[11]DuBois, pp. 324-25.

[12]Margaret Walker, *Jubilee* (Boston: Houghton-Mifflin, 1966). The novel won a Houghton-Mifflin award.

[13]Margaret Walker, *How I Wrote Jubilee* (Chicago: Third World Press, 1972), p. 26.

[14]*How I Wrote Jubilee*, pp. 25-26.

[15]Ernest Gaines, *The Autobiography of Miss Jane Pittman* (New York: Dial, 1971).

[16]Frank Yerby, *The Dahomean* (New York: Dial, 1971).

[17]Ishmael Reed, *Mumbo-Jumbo* (New York: Doubleday, 1972).

[18]Reed, p. 233.

[19]This essay was prepared before the publication of Alex Haley's *Roots*, which satisfies many of my requests of Black authors.

THE OCCASIONAL NOVEL: AMERICAN FICTION AND THE MAN OF LETTERS

Daniel Aaron

Harvard University

All of us, I suppose, are familiar with a category of fiction, the one-shot or occasional novel written by men of letters—critics, poets, philosophers—which occupies an undefined space in the interstices of literary history. Sometimes these random forays into novel or short-story writing result in literary curiosities, valuable, perhaps, as social or autobiographical documents but otherwise of small distinction. But if the writer (whether he be a literary critic, theologian, or scientist) has a gift for language; and if the essayistic filler that usually makes up significant portions of occasional novels by non-novelists has substance as well as stylistic felicity; and if the author's mind is intelligently reflective in its own right; and if his scenes and descriptions have a modicum of reality and his characters are not merely animated ideas, then his novel may possess a dimension not ordinarily present in the work of proper novelists.

How are these "occasional novelists," as I shall call them (Samuel Johnson, W. H. Mallock, Newman, Swinburne, Henry Adams, Santayana, Edmund Wilson, and Lionel Trilling are a few examples), to be distinguished from out-and-out practitioners? Novel writing for them, as I have indicated, is a side business, not a central preoccupation. They are less likely to be caught up in the craft of fiction. This is especially true of a kind of amateur novelist I don't intend to deal with here: religious and political reformers, or journalists, unfrocked politicians, and demireps seeking to cash in on saleable experiences. But it can also be said of the intellectual or of the man of letters turned novelist (including those who are skilled analysts of fiction) that their novels in many cases are impatient and disrespectful, if not oblivious, to what to Henry James were adorable obstacles. Prose style is of more commanding importance in the occasional novel than plot, point of view, and characterization, as if the author hopes to achieve through verbal facility and ingratiating argument what he is incapable of attaining through narrative action. In his hands the novel becomes primarily something other than storytelling and literary entertainment. It can be an envelope for a set of principles, a surrogate memoir or history, a dramatized philosophy, an apologia, a device to make the esoteric exoteric. The same might be said, I realize, of novels written by proper novelists, but the occasional novel seems to me to be distinguished by certain hallmarks. I have mentioned some of them already, but let me now try to list them more systematically.

The occasional novel is likely to be schematic, unspontaneous, programmatic, self-conscious. Character and situation are kept subordinate to thematic purpose; intellect overrides imagination. In the occasional novel, the authorial voice is persistently loud and clear. The reader tends, finally, to be more impressed by the quality of the author's mind (often communicated through the insertion of reveries, dreams, musings) than he is by the charm or verisimilitude of the author's fictions. And whereas it is dangerous in bonafide novels to attribute to the author the ideas and sentiments of selected pontificators, it is less risky in the occasional novel. The hero, whether or not the author intends it, is usually the author or a good part of him. In the occasional novel, the author's intellectual apparatus is very much on display. The drama is concentrated on the level of ideas, the writing loaded with literary allusions, frequently erudite; and the characters engage in lengthy discussions on art, politics, and morals. The occasional novel is usually topical. It focuses on types that figure in a designated social setting in a period encompassing the author's lifetime. It tends to be personal, autobiographical, biographical with elements of the *roman à clef*. And because it assumes a readership that can identify and savor allusions to a shared intellectual experience, its appeal is necessarily restricted. Unless redeemed by literary graces or a suspenseful story line, it is always in danger of hardening into the documentary or the treatise. The occasional novel leans toward the moralistic and the didactic. The author is conveying a message of sorts. Even though he may present himself in the role of witty entertainer and at times is not above showing off, he is at bottom being serious.

Needless to say, no one novel illustrates to the letter the kind I have been trying to define and isolate, but there is a surprising similarity all the same to American occasional novels of the last century. The best of them were written by readers and critics of literature, no matter what their other backgrounds or abilities, and some of their authors may have begun their careers as aspiring writers and poets. But in most cases it is the quality of mind reflected in the occasional novel more than the author's technical skills that separate the handful of meritorious specimens from the ephemeral ones—above all the knack of making palatable serious and complex ideas and of communicating engagingly the excitement of intellectual play.

What preserves a novel like Henry Adams's *Democracy* (1880) from oblivion is not narrative suspense or subtlety of characterization. In fact, his characters are pretty uncomplicated despite his efforts to give them depth. Vulgarians and bounders are beheld and then carefully mounted for inspection; the characters he approves of simply mouth his observations on politics and society in the Gilded Age. But behind the wit and mental by-play accompanying the education of his heroine lies the history of a highly discerning man and his class. The novel (which deprived of its mental force and stylistic felicity could have faded into a mere period-piece composed of a fastidious snob) can be read as an extra chapter in the famous author's classic autobiography-cum-novel.

Henry Adams was a worldly man who masked his animus under a veil of comic irony. His younger contemporary, Paul Elmer More, was a learned critic and man of letters (unjustly neglected, in my opinion). But he was also the author of a forgotten and forgettable epistolary romance, *The Jessica Letters* (1904), written with an even more justly forgotten collaborator.[1] I mention this tepid and exasperating exercise to illustrate the point that intelligence and seriousness are not enough to salvage an occasional novel. The developing attachment between a prim New York editor, More himself, and a young Southern reviewer, becomes in More's words "a medium to vomit forth"[2] all his rage against sentimental and materialistic humanitarianism, with Jane Addams and the Rev. Lyman Abbott as the principal targets. Neither the dim presence of unfleshed characters in this self-conscious but not uninteresting interchange nor the drama of conflicting ideas justifies the fictional occasion.

Nor can liveliness and fun and melodramatic action guarantee literary permanence. Two novels come to mind written by once popular intellectuals and critics, both books out of print and rarely mentioned. Max Eastman's sole effort at novel writing, *Venture* (1927), is an unabashedly autobiographical and still readable *roman à clef* which, the author tells us, "compressed into two years immediately preceding America's entrance into the World War, certain historic events whose actual development occupied a period more than twice as long."[3] An "idea novel," to borrow Edmund Wilson's term, it manages to evoke the ambience of Greenwich Village bohemia and portrays many of the recognizable movers and shakers (sometimes but not always under their own names) who flourished in those ebullient times. By far the best sections are the conversations on social problems in which Eastman phrases his most trenchant aphorisms,[4] many of them muttered by an improbable Nietzschean tycoon. He later claimed that *Venture* was "perhaps, a little too 'clever' to be absorbing" and that critics therefore failed to grasp the seriousness of its theme: the hero's impulse "to experience to the full and recklessly the very *reality* of the world into which he was born" and his discovery of the class struggle.[5] But the novel's weaknesses are obvious. The passages on "love and life" border on the sappy, and the handling of the Paterson strike, the event that triggers the hero's conversion to revolution, is too much in the spirit of the "hard-hitting" melodrama.

If bizarre and scabrous incident could assure perpetual notoriety, James Gibbon Huneker's scandalous *Painted Veils* (1920) would still be on the publisher's lists. Near rape, naked waitresses, lesbianism, seductions, pregnancy out of wedlock, miscegenation, orgies, high-class prostitutes, and (for the times) lewd talk enliven this autobiographical novel set in the "New York, artistic and bohemian, of 1895-1905."[6] The novel divides its attention between the rise to fame of a self-centered and amoral opera singer (a composite of three celebrated divas) and a deracinated Parisian-born American critic of the Seven Arts (at once a decadent and idealized portrait of Huneker himself). Based upon real incidents and real people, many of them named, it is tinctured with Huneker's fantasies. Kenneth Burke caught its note exactly in his review when he described it as

> a remarkable essay in assimilation, as I suppose a novel by a critic
> should be. With marked Baudelarian morals, it also has bits after the
> St. James version, a generous application of psychoanalytic
> nomenclature, passages in the manner of our newest fragmentary
> writers, a few sentences of the thriller type, and most of all, frequent
> borrowings from James Huneker, the critic.[7]

Huneker had extra-literary reasons for writing *Painted Veils*. He had omitted any hints of his sexual life in his autobiography published shortly before, and he wanted to make some money. Money, however, was not the only motivation. Years before, according to his biographer, he had sketched an outline close in subject and theme to the novel, and the criticism of naturalistic fiction proclaimed by his alter-ego in *Painted Veils* suggests that Huneker had something more in mind than titillating readers of pornography. Huneker's spokesman calls for a psychological novel, neither "all empty incident" or "yet all barren analysis," presumably what *Painted Veils* was intended to be. Unfortunately, his one attempt to write a "social biography framed in harmonious happenings," a "searching characterization that not only paints your man without but also within," ends up, even conceding its touches of wit and brilliance, as self-parody and self-plagiarism. It uncomfortably approximates the kind of novel its author deplores: "cluttered-up with futile things" and resembling "a drawing room which you can't see because of the furniture or the bric-a-brac, so crowded is it with everything."[8] One might have expected as much from a work that, for all its long incubation, took forty-seven days to write.

The four novels which I shall consider in more detail, Edmund Wilson's *I Thought of Daisy* (1929), Kenneth Burke's *Towards a Better Life* (1932), George Santayana's *The Last Puritan* (1936), and Lionel Trilling's *The Middle of the Journey* (1947), are by no means unflawed performances, but they obviously were not dashed off. They illustrate characteristic and arresting features of the occasional novel but are more strikingly successful works of the imagination than the novels previously mentioned. Each is covertly autobiographical, each is a novel of ideas with distinct political and social overtones, each is given to a kind of aesthetic editorializing, and each is philosophical in spirit, psychological in method, and serious in import. All four authors can be classified as intellectuals and men of letters, one a professional philosopher and poet, the other three primarily literary critics who also experimented in various literary forms.

Edmund Wilson had published verse, a play, a few short stories, and a series of imaginary conversations before his first novel. Had he decided to devote himself to one genre, he might well have distinguished himself as a poet or playwright or novelist. But as Leon Edel observed, Wilson lacked the "single-mindedness"[9] of a Fitzgerald or a Dos Passos, and his questing mind impelled him to explore many kinds of literature and learning. An occasional poet of considerable power, he turned to verse when overmastered by emotion too personal for prose. He was scarcely less private in his plays and fiction, never quite able to detach himself from the experiences and events and problems that obsessed him or to survey them from an imaginative distance.

Wilson's notebooks and letters disclose the personal crises that lie behind the writing of *I Thought of Daisy* and account for both its acuity and (in spite of its carefully worked out design) its unresolved divisions. The events of the novel are telescoped into a few years of the mid-Twenties, but the experiences of an entire decade are drawn upon. The narrator's background and career are not unlike the author's. He is middle class, well educated, and intellectual. He comes out of the war eager to abandon his bourgeois heritage and susceptible to the ideas of stronger personalities. In each of the five sections which divide the novel, the narrator is exposed to attitudes and persuasions incarnated by one or more Greenwich Village types he encounters. But everything he thinks he is extracting from these associations is determined by his relation to two dominating figures: Rita Cavanagh, a thinly disguised Edna Millay, and Hugo Bammon, the narrator's old schoolmate and friend modeled in part after John Dos Passos. Before he can recover his equipoise, he must reconcile the polarities which they embody and carry to aberrant extremes—Rita's passion for art and her obsessive self-exploration that transcends social responsibility, and Hugo's commitment to a religion of social obligation that can unremorsefully dispense with culture and art.

Daisy, innocent, poignant, vulnerable, is the symbol for the America the narrator at the end of his spiritual journey can happily identify with. She represents, as Wilson told a correspondent, "ordinary human life undirected by special ideas."[10] By putting aside his snobberies and by coming to terms with what he can accept as sturdy and honorable in his own and his country's past, the narrator preserves himself from the "dreadful isolation," as he puts it, which so appalled him in Rita and Hugo. As they barricade themselves behind their "impregnable solitudes,"[11] he is breaking into the real world.

It is pertinent, I think, that Wilson found the writing and especially the re-writing of *Daisy* a grueling job and abated the drudgery of revision by working on chapters of *Axel's Castle*. The latter was animated by some of the same ideas on art and society he was getting at in the novel but "being criticism," Wilson confessed, he found it "easier to do, and in the nature of a relief, from Daisy."[12] All along he had seen the novel as a risk: "I mean [he wrote to Maxwell Perkins] from beginning to end, I have made characters, incidents, and situations subordinate to a set of ideas about life and literature, and unless the ideas are really put over, unless they are interesting enough to compensate the reader for what he is missing in action and emotion, for what he ordinarily gets in a novel, the whole performance will fail."[13] He had wanted it, he wrote to John Peale Bishop, "to be a pattern of ideas and all to take place, as to a great extent it does, on the plane of intelligence— and when I came to write the actual story, this had the effect of involving me in a certain amount of falsified psychology." Not even re-writing it took "this curse off it." He finished it with mixed feelings, calling it "my novel, such as it is."[14]

Wilson's strictures about *Daisy* are discerning, and his critics have not been slow to add their own. Because of its "reminiscent quality," commented Sherman Paul, it lacks dramatic immediacy: "one feels that this fiction is a species of memoir and that the narrator is working out in several equations the calculus of his life."[15] Probably it tried to incorporate too much. Wilson laid under contribution ten years of writing—verses, short stories, sketches, notebooks—to make his novel. He wanted "to get it into decent shape and get it off my hands, along with the interests, ideas and emotions mixed up with it."[16]

The upshot is a work that never quite comes off as a piece of fiction but which is nonetheless a noteworthy achievement. As social analysis, it is often brilliantly accurate. Intellectual set-pieces, like those moments of sustained reflection on Dostoevsky and Sophocles, on an America projected through newsreels, on demonology, on the redemptive past, are finely done. And Wilson's skill in integrating reverie and narration and allowing key characters to dominate particular sections (he acknowledged his debt to Proust) and his superb management of convoluted musical sentences give promise of the novelist he was distracted from becoming.

Kenneth Burke, to judge him by his one novel and by his critical statements expressed elsewhere, was never in danger of becoming a popular novelist. A critic and man of letters like Wilson, he also wrote his novel or anti-novel at the end of the Twenties, also put together a volume of criticism while he was composing it, also made it a vehicle for his aesthetic and social philosophy, also focused on the problem of Art and Life. Burke, however, was slower to qualify the artist's autonomy than Wilson and more resistant to "the mounting sociological emphasis in criticism."[17]

Towards a Better Life (1932) is very different from *I Thought of Daisy* in conception and style. It was written according to a set of rules implicitly and explicitly spelled out in Burke's *Counter-Statement*, a book of critical essays published one year before his novel, in which he rejected the dictum that novelists should be realistic and "life-like" and tell their stories in "a simple, running style."[18] What Burke admired in many novels, he discovered, were the very qualities which "threatened them as novels," a response that signified his "unfitness" to write in the conventional journalistic vein; but he saw no reason to discipline himself "in a field wherein one was so hopelessly outdistanced not only by lack of ability but even by lack of interest." For the kind of "fictive moralizing" he was interested in, plot was of no consequence. The "emotional predicaments" of his current figure could best be emphasized in an essayistic rather than a narrative form, his "lamentation, rejoicing, beseechment, admonition, sayings, and invective" in a declamatory style.[19]

Burke's novel is essentially the unfolding consciousness of one John Neal, a person of uncertain background, presumably a literary man, whose mental disintegration and increasing isolation constitute the action, such as it is. *Towards a Better Life* is at once a harangue, a sermon, a self-exploration, and an inquiry into varieties of social behavior with a vague narrative line or plot. Since Neal's revelations are unreliable, the stories of a false friend, of acquired and discarded women, of quarrels with acquaintances, and of an eventual retreat into silence are really correlatives for fundamental moral issues. Burke sees in his monologist "a kind of John the Baptist quality,"[20] and although he is a repellant personality, envious, cruel, selfish and boastful, his stabbing probes into the darker areas of human nature and his clairvoyant sense of his own and others' self-deceptions give him at times a prophetic character. If his story is a classic case of dissociation, Neal, like some of Hawthorne's brooding isolatoes, is gainer as well as loser. His twisted angle of vision enables him to detect the duplicities of the human heart. And it is not hard to believe that some of his pronouncements bear upon Burke's own thoughts on the bleak prospects of America, circa 1929-1931. They touch on competitive striving in personal relations and ignoble strategies for survival, on the nature of social hypocrisy and the conversion of moral imperatives into weapons, on the flimsiness of accepted pieties, on the way in which notions of success blur economic and cultural distinctions. Yet *Towards a Better Life* is never despairing. Its morbidity is tempered by the comic, and the protagonist's defeat is oddly affirmative, in that his extinction coincides with the moment when he is apparently transfigured by the prospect of communion he has done so much to undermine.

Burke's novel died aborning, despite some perceptive reviews, because he did not provide sufficient flesh for his conceptions and refused to satisfy his reader's "category of expectations."[21] The same criticism had been made of his first book, *White Oxen and Other Stories* (1924), by John Peale Bishop, who (although impressed by Burke's skeptical intelligence) objected to the author's refusal to "allow the material to make its own demands." And what Bishop said of *White Oxen* applied to Burke's novel: "he has recorded his sensibility without always having made use of it as an artist. He has given proof of the clarity of his mind, but in a way which is itself obscure."[22]

Towards a Better Life, above all a novel of ideas, does seem at times willfully obscure and devoid of props Burke might have employed to give it a narrative setting. It is also a language experiment of great eloquence and beauty as well as precision, written in a formal and rhetorical mode eminently suited to a drama of thought, if not of dramatic action, and devoid, in the language of Burke, "not only of the vices of journalism" but also its virtues.[23] It is a successful stylistic exercise and a work of art.

Burke's book came out in the traumatic year of 1932. He found, so he tells us, "the figure of its sales (or, more accurately non-sales) . . . also traumatic."[24] *The Last Puritan*, appearing four years later, made the Book of the Month Club. *Towards a Better Life* is cryptic, experimental, unconcessive; George Santayana's novel old fashioned, genial, and elegant. It deals with recognizable times and places and, where "discretion permitted,"[25] with real people; its tone is conversational, hardly declamatory, and without a trace of either lamentation or invective—and it is unambiguous. Santayana reiterates his theme throughout the novel and underscores it for commentators in his letters. Its success pleased but did not surprise him. "Though it may become a little philosophical in places," he wrote to a friend, "it is written fluently, intelligibly, in pleasant English, and the characters [as one critic said] are 'the very nicest people,' that is, rich and refined, or at least cultivated; and the public not familiar with such circles likes to enter them."[26]

Santayana disclaimed the name of novelist and called *The Last Puritan* "A Memoir in the Form of a Novel."[27] This was defensiveness on his part, not modesty, a way of taking advantage of the form (he declared novel-writing "the only living art")[28] without incurring the novelist's obligations. The philosopher-memorialist could express dangerous or hostile thoughts, sure to be "overlooked or timidly ignored by the critics,"[29] insert entertaining disquisitions, soliloquies, lectures, epistolary essays, epigrams. The omniscient author could freely rummage inside his characters and articulate their ideas and emotions with a clarity and penetration they themselves could never have mustered.[30] Of course this claim might be misinterpreted as a rationalization of a literary deficiency, but it was surely the correct stand for one "utterly bored and disgusted with the public world, the world of business, politics, family, and society" made only tolerable by "the glimmer of sport, humour, friendship falling over it."[31]

Had he tried to be "absolutely true to life," says the narrator of the novel, his audience would not have understood him.[32] Santayana refracted the world through his own eyes, but he demurred when charged with creating ghosts instead of characters. His characters might be masks for his spirit and speak his words. Still, his words reflected their sentiments. They were "fetched from an actual life, and only dressed, as an actor on the stage, for their social parts,"[33] and while they may have retained "a hidden and problematic side,"[34] they were very real to him.

How foolish it would have been, the narrator exclaims, if he had rejected the images provoked by their living models "when I have no other pigments at my disposal with which to paint mankind!"[35]

Be that as it may, *The Last Puritan* is a portrait of the author as much as it is a portrait of Oliver Alden and his entourage of friends and relations. All of his books, he once said—and he cited *The Last Puritan* in particular—betrayed directly or indirectly his tastes and preferences and his opinion of his subjects' virtues and vices.[36] Clearly Mario, Oliver's exotic cousin, is closer to Santayana's brand of Epicureanism and animal faith than his hero whose drearily privileged existence embodies everything Santayana found worthy and stifling about genteel culture in America: "its meagreness of soul and its thinness of temper and its paucity of talent."[37] He was not being coy when he intimated that he had written a "naughty" book[38] and feared it might be so regarded. His novel, for all of its smiles, is an exorcism of his American self, a shaking off of that part of the world where he had spent his formative years without ever accepting its values and aims or taking its culture very seriously. The idea of the book had been nagging at him for almost a half-century, so he must have felt a strong need to expel it, to dramatize his case, to clothe his arguments in the forms of men and women he had known on two continents.

Santayana's affectionately malicious dissection of the agonized Calvinist conscience occupies a modest and uncertain place in American literature. Perhaps the novel's distinction has less to do with the thoroughness and validity of its argument than it does with its urbanity, wit, and learning; its perceptive and poetic impressions of people and places. Santayana can be smug, his irony and feline sensibility tiresome, but he is never pompous or boring, and it would be churlish to demand more from *The Last Puritan* than it was meant to offer.

Lionel Trilling, the last of my occasional novelists, is no less mannered and no more experimental in his fictionizing than Santayana, but he does not wear the guise of the self-indulgent memorialist. He is writing a novel of ideas, too, but does so with assurance and with greater readiness to accept conventional modes of fiction. The moral and political judgments dramatized in *The Middle of the Journey* (1947) were enunciated at least as early as his studies of Arnold and E. M. Forster, and he had sharpened and expanded them in the essays he wrote during the 1940s aimed at what he considered to be "the pious social simplicities"[39] of so many American intellectuals. In fact his preface to these essays collected in *The Liberal Imagination* (1950) might well serve as a text for his novel. There he dwells upon the inseparable ties between literature and culture and the vulnerability of a philosophy of human nature and society which constricts emotion, relies excessively on mechanical reason, and pays insufficient recognition to life's unexpectedness, its terrors and complexities.

What turned out to be a novel began as a long short story, a form, Trilling notes, demanding a great deal of "thematic explicitness," in this instance, how the idea of death "is conceived by the enlightened consciousness of the modern age."[40] The hero, John Laskell, has nearly died of an illness, but his friends, the Crooms, with whom he is spending a troubled summer recuperating, neither can nor want to comprehend his brush with death. They are the exemplars of the liberal imagination, the progressive mind, sentimental and rigid, determinedly hopeful and unprepared for the unexpected or the dark side of things. Laskell loves them, but at the novel's end he must concede his estrangement, for he has passed through the stages of conversion: first sunk in materiality, then in love with easeful death, ready to abandon the world (the counter-sin), and finally rebirth or the resolution to be in yet out of the world. (Despite its Dantean title, *The Middle of the Journey* is Protestant in its theology even though Trilling espouses a secular humanism in making his case against the complementary heresies of man's absolute goodness and baseness.)

Had the setting not been the 1930s and had Trilling not introduced, at least indirectly, a real person, Whittaker Chambers, his novel might have been what he planned it to be, a *nouvelle* about death. The time, he notes, is crucial to the novel, and the entry of Chambers as Gifford Maxim links the theme of death with international communism and its guarantees of future bliss: mortality seems to the Crooms almost "reactionary," a "negation of the future and hope it holds for a society of reason and virtue."[41] With their trust in "the little people," they typify a Left mentality common in the Thirties which clung to the dream of the Enlightenment even when its ostensible agent, the USSR, was steeped in evil. Laskell's illness has led him to question the faith of the fellow-traveler and "to consent to the conditioned nature of human existence."[42] Maxim's political disaffection and his subsequent revelations of Stalinist iniquity and conviction of his own ineradicable guilt account for his brutal refutation of the liberal imagination. Each, by challenging the Crooms's stubbornly held pieties, threatens their peace of mind.

Trilling was referring to people like the Crooms when he wrote in the introduction to the recent reissue of *The Middle of the Journey* that his novel was "committed to history," to drawing out "some of the moral and intellectual implications of the powerful attraction to Communism felt by a considerable part of the American intellectual class during the

Thirties and Forties."[43] This was a subject Trilling ought to have been able to handle with authority, for New York City in the Thirties was the capital of the Left intelligentsia. Not only was he a first-hand observer of the ideological skirmishes; he was also personally acquainted with many of the participants, including Chambers, whose histrionic namesake in the novel prefigured the role the original would shortly be playing. Yet the novel, even supplemented by the informative if somewhat evasive introduction, offers a dim sense of the events that, given the involvements of his main characters, might have been expected to press upon their lives. The connection between bourgeois radicals like the Crooms and the Communist Party is very "tenuous" indeed; and allusions to contemporary figures and events that now and then crop up—references to hard times, to Hitler, to the Moscow Trials—do not sufficiently evoke the climate of the decade. The principals in his cast, for the most part, are recognizable types caught up in the ethical dilemmas that Communist allegiances induced, but they have no antecedants to speak of. What inner lives they possess are revealed by the omniscient author who is privy to their intellectual and emotional concerns and who can hardly refrain from commenting *sotto voce* as he implants, not always artfully, what he deems to be requisite information about them.

This is not said to play down his undoubted gifts. No less than Wilson or Burke, he displays, at moments, the novelist's eye for significant detail. He can observe, to give one example, "the practiced self-consciousness of a small town belle,"[44] or the look of a face "made intelligent by grief," intelligent, he adds meditatively, because grief by subordinating "all facts to one fact, is so like an act of intelligence" that sorrowing people for a time look wise.[45] Reviewers have rightly although (in my opinion) excessively praised his novel for its style, flashing insights, and psychological penetration and praised his skill in extracting interest and suspense from the clash of ideas. It might also be said that his studiously plotted novel in which motifs are recapitulated and symbols underlined shows Trilling's familiarity with the novelist's craft as well as catholic reading. Yet these virtues are not enough to make it, as some have claimed, a masterpiece, or even the novel of a "novelist," and we are all the gainers for his having resisted the temptation he once admitted to of giving up criticism for fiction.

Trilling's book, while hardly a powerful work of imagination and not wholly satisfactory either as a political novel or a period piece, nonetheless has its own distinction. It emits a kind of intelligence ordinarily absent in contemporary fiction; it bears out his contention that the "province of intellection" and the "province of poetry" engage in indispensable commerce, that intellectual content can add an aesthetic dimension to the novel.[46]

All of the occasional novels I have been discussing are distinguished to a greater or lesser degree by what Trilling would call their intellectual "cogency."[47] He found this ingredient abundantly present in modern European literature but conspicuously missing in most American imaginative writing of the same period. The novels by non-novelists, including his own, were written by men of letters responsive to the intellectual currents of their times, and although not equally successful in fusing thought with feeling, they relied upon ideas to give an emotional charge to their fiction. However they differed about art or politics or human nature, they were inheritors of a common culture and linked in their own ways to the same intellectual traditions. It was this inheritance and the quality of mind it produced that added substance to their novels and justified their impulse to present their ideas first spelled out in critical or philosophical works in a literary form which most of them were temperamentally or technically unequipped to manage.

Most genuine story-tellers, I suspect, are not inspired to write because they have a personal problem to solve or a message to deliver (despite the public pressure, especially in the United States, to inspire and edify). They start out with a situation or a character in mind and while by no means banishing ideas or "intellection" from their fiction, invent a series of actions which derive logically from that character or situation rather than from some pre-determined thesis. The occasional novels I have mentioned lack the openness and freedom of what I consider to be authentic novels not because they bulge with ideas or because they are didactic or topical—the same could be said of many novels—but because they are too contrived or too theoretical or too constricted by the force of inner needs. Wilson, Burke, Santayana, Trilling, in their own ways, are caught up in the pervasive theme of the 1920s and 1930s—the antipodal pulls of social involvement and artistic autonomy. They seem to find it impossible either to immerse themselves in a fictive world or to treat themselves as irreverently as they do the objects of their wit and satire.

If it be asked what their novels have added to the art of the novel or in what ways they have influenced the ideas of critics of the novel, it is probably fair to say, "Not much." Yet they have found a discriminating if limited audience. Their novels fall into the category of those "favorite-works-known-only-to-a-few" that every lover of books keeps in reserve for the occasion when he can exclaim to ignorant friends, "What, you haven't read *that!*"

And why is this so? Isn't it because their impulse to construct fictions around ideas or theses or personal problems meets with a response from those who share their intense interest—even delight—in mental exercise and intellectual confrontations that only a small number of novelists have incorporated into the tissue of their books? Granted that the occasional novelists have seldom managed to dramatize the life of the intellect as entertainingly as a Butler, a Dostoevsky, a Proust, a Musil, a Bellow. All the same, they can be formidable interlopers in the realm of the novel and contribute a valuable ingredient to an American fiction not remarkable for its treatment of ideas in ordinary human activity.

Notes

[1] *The Jessica Letters: An Editor's Romance* (New York: G. P. Putnam's Sons, 1904) was published anonymously by P. E More and Cora May Harris.

[2] Quoted in F.X. Duggan, *Paul Elmer More* (New York: Twayne, 1966), p. 69.

[3] "Note," *Venture* (New York, 1927), n.p.

[4] See Edmund Wilson, *Classics and Commercials* (New York: Farrar, Straus, 1950), p. 68.

[5] Max Eastman, *Love and Revolution: My Journey Through An Epoch* (New York: Random House, 1964), p. 500.

[6] Arnold T. Schwab, *James Gibbons Huneker* (Stanford: Stanford Univ. Press, 1963), p. 261.

[7] Schwab, p. 272.

[8] Huneker, *Painted Veils* (New York: Modern Library, 1920), pp. 145-46.

[9] Introduction to Edmund Wilson, *The Twenties* (New York: Farrar, Straus, Giroux, 1975), p. xxxvii.

[10] Edmund Wilson to Carey McWilliams, (October 18, 1929).

[11] Edmund Wilson, *I Thought of Daisy* (New York: Scribners, 1929), p. 264.

[12] Quoted by Edel in *The Twenties*, p. 246.

[13] Edmund Wilson to Maxwell Perkins (June 9, 1928).

[14] Edmund Wilson to John Peale Bishop (October 4, 1929).

[15] *Edmund Wilson* (Urbana: Univ. of Illinois Press, 1965), p. 55.

[16] Edmund Wilson to Carey McWilliams (October 18, 1929).

[17] Kenneth Burke, *Counter-Statement* (Los Altos: Hermes Publications, 1953), p. 213.

[18] *Counter-Statement*, p. 188.

[19]Kenneth Burke, "Introduction" to *Towards A Better Life: Being a Series of Epistles, or Declamations* (Berkeley: Univ. of California Press, 1966), pp. xii, xv.

[20]Towards a Better Life, p. xvii.

[21]*Counter-Statement*, pp. 211-12.

[22]"Gulliver on the Subway," in *Critical Responses to Kenneth Burke*, ed. W.H. Rueckert (Minneapolis: Univ. of Minnesota Press, 1969), pp. 7-8.

[23]*Counter-Statement*, p. x.

[24]*Towards a Better Life*, p. v.

[25]*The Last Puritan: A Memoir in the Form of a Novel* (New York: Scribners, 1936), p. 601.

[26]*The Letters of George Santayana*, ed. Daniel Cory (New York: Scribners, 1955), p. 309.

[27]*Letters*, p. 268.

[28]*Letters*, p. 207.

[29]*Letters*, p. 309.

[30]*The Last Puritan*, pp. 599-600.

[31]*Letters*, p. 208.

[32]*The Last Puritan*, p. 600.

[33]*Letters*, p. 304.

[34]*Letters*, p. 410.

[35]*The Last Puritan*, p. 601.

[36]*Letters*, p. 409.

[37]*Letters*, p. 193.

[38]*Letters*, p. 269.

[39]Lionel Trilling, preface to *E. M. Forster*, Second ed. (New York, 1964), p. 4.

[40]Lionel Trilling, "Introduction" to *The Middle of the Journey* (New York: Scribners, 1964), p. xi.

[41]*Journey*, p. xii.

[42]*Journey*, p. xxi.

[43]*Journey*, p. vii.

[44]*Journey*, p. 50.

[45]*Journey*, p. 289.

[46]Trilling, *The Liberal Imagination* (New York: Viking, 1950), p. 289.

[47]Trilling, *The Liberal Imagination*, p. 290.

THE AMERICAN PICTORIAL VISION: OBJECTS AND IDEAS IN HAWTHORNE, JAMES, AND HEMINGWAY

Viola Hopkins Winner

Near the beginning of Ernest Hemingway's *Islands in the Stream*, the painter-hero Thomas Hudson promises to make a picture for Bobby, the island barkeeper. Enthusiastically, Bobby starts to offer Hudson suggestions, becoming increasingly graphic and grandiose. All of the projected scenes are turbulent, violent, threatening, progressing from waterspouts, to hurricanes, to the sinking of the *Titanic*, and finally to a vision of the last judgment:

> "Don't shear off from it," Bobby said. "Don't be shocked by its magnitude. You got to have vision, Tom. We can paint the End of the World," he paused. "Full Size."
>
> "Hell," Thomas Hudson said.
>
> "No. Before hell. Hell is just opening. The Rollers are rolling in their church upon the ridge and all speaking in unknown tongues. There's a devil forking them up with his pitchfork and loading them into a cart. They're yelling and moaning and calling on Jehovah. Negroes are prostrated everywhere and morays and crawfish and spider crabs are moving around and over their bodies. There's a big sort of hatch open and devils are carrying Negroes and church people and rollers and everyone into it and they go out of sight. Water's rising all around the island and hammerheads and mackerel sharks and tiger sharks and shovelnose sharks are swimming round and round and feeding on those who try to swim away to keep from being forked down the big open hatch that has steam rising out of it."

After more of the same, Bobby concludes, "That would make a hell of a painting, Tom, if we can get all the movement and grandeur into it."[1]

The picture Hudson actually paints is of waterspouts, not Bobby's end-of-the-world vision. He prefers not to compete with the "old timers" Hieronymous Bosch and Pieter Brueghel, who had worked along Bobby's lines and would be, as Hudson says, "pretty hard to beat" (p. 21). Although Hudson later views tradition as helpful, here he feels the "anxiety of influence;"[2] unlike Nathaniel Hawthorne's Hilda, who, realizing her inadequacy before the Old Masters, gave up painting to become as a copyist their handmaiden, Hudson has persevered but he has succeeded by not trying for supernal meanings in the grand style. He paints only what he actually sees and knows: ". . . pictures of Uncle Edward. Pictures of Negroes in the water. Negroes on land. Negroes in boats. Turtle boats. Sponge boats. Squalls making up. Waterspouts. Schooners that got wrecked. Schooners building" (p. 17).

Hudson's avoidance of the monumental and the sublime is more than a sign that he, as a modern artist, feels the difficulty of competing with achievements of the past. There are metaphysical reasons for his self-imposed limits. The romantic vision of God in nature that inspired the appalling ambiguities of *Moby-Dick* as well as the awesome serenities of Lake Glimmerglass and Thomas Cole's *The Ox-Bow* has faded away; the orthodox God and the eschatology of Bosch and Brueghel are dead. The naive Bobby, without having seen the Old Masters, creates a vivid last judgment out of Bimini material: the Negro revivalist church, the rummies, the sharks and whales—sharply defined realistic detail in a framework of cosmic upheaval. For the sophisticated Hudson, however, there is only the realistic detail without the frame: God and nature are sundered; good and evil too complexly interfused to be allegorized; the only finality, death. Transcendence exists only in the object itself, as in the brief description of potato salad "covered with rough-ground black pepper" (p. 91), which has the luminosity and radiant clarity of a Dutch still life.

Hudson aims for the kind of truth in painting that Hemingway strove for in writing: he plans to paint the scene of David's epic struggle with the big fish "truer than a photograph" (p. 148). This conception of realism is less clichéd than it seems; "photograph" is comparable to "instant recording," Hemingway's phrase in *Death in the Afternoon* for newspaper writing. To make "very simple things . . . permanent, as, say, Goya tried to make them in *Los Desastres de la Guerra*," Hemingway wrote, the artist must both see and study things dispassionately.[3]

The bar painting embodies not only Hudson's artistic vision but his moral values; its position at the outset of the novel is thematically strategic and structural. In the first of three parts, we see Hudson at Bimini, the artist who by rigorous self-discipline has created order in a life threatened by ugly disintegration (represented by his writer friend, Roger) and marked by loneliness and loss. In his loving comradeship with his sons, Hudson finds joy and even a vicarious recovery of lost innocence in his oldest son's childhood memories of an Edenic Paris when Hudson himself was young. In the second part, after this interval of Paradise Regained in Bimini, comes hell. His two younger sons killed earlier in an automobile accident, Hudson has just received word that his remaining son Tom, an RAF pilot, has been shot down. In the third part, Hudson finds some solace and brotherhood as the captain of a cruiser tracking down a German submarine crew in Cuban waters. His courage unsinewed by the faith in the anti-Fascist cause that strengthened Robert Jordan, he pursues the Germans as sheer duty; the search is a disciplined activity, like his painting, which gives order and staves off emptiness and pain. The bar painting implicitly encompasses the ending, Hudson's limited, pragmatic heroism being foreshadowed in his artistic realism and rejection of sublimity.

Although Hudson works at his art only in the first part, the entire novel is presented through his painter's consciousness. Scenes are described as if they were pictures, or are associated with particular artists and works. Reflecting Hemingway's taste and art experience, Hudson alludes almost entirely to European painters, though his own work resembles Winslow Homer's Caribbean paintings. A Cuban scene recalls El Greco; a road into Havana, Hogarth's *Gin Lane*. Tom asleep is compared to a knight's tomb in Salisbury Cathedral. Men swimming resemble Cézanne's or Eakins' bathers. Hudson sees nature with a painter's eye for color and movement: for instance, "a pair of roseate spoon-bills" are described as "beautiful with the sharp rose of their color against the gray marl and their delicate, quick, forward-running movements" (p. 399).

These allusions and descriptive passages remind us that Hemingway's apprenticeship in writing included the study in Paris of the "Cézannes . . . [and] the Manets and the Monets and the other Impressionists that [he] had first come to know about in the Art Institute in Chicago."[4] Gertrude Stein's remark that Hemingway "looks like a modern and smells of the museums" may be taken both literally and figuratively, the latter being, I believe, her intention. She meant that at heart he was a traditionalist, not dedicated to making it new. Except for being snide about it, she was right. I have gone into detail about *Islands in the Stream* because it is squarely in the tradition of American literary pictorialism, employing most of its conventions and touching on its characteristic themes.

The precedents for using paintings or other art objects to frame action and intimate meaning are numerous. Most immediately, the bar painting recalls Tod Hackett's apocalyptic "Burning of Los Angeles" in Nathaniel West's *The Day of the Locust*. By devious routes, one could trace this use of painting to the Greeks, but this is a trek we need not make to define the American version of *ut pictora poesis*. By observing, as in my preceding discussion of Hemingway, how Hawthorne and

Henry James adapted and transformed pictorial conventions, we shall
uncover what is uniquely American in American pictorialism, of which
these are the basic conventions: works of graphic art are not merely
described as part of the mise-en-scene but are used to delineate
character and to develop themes; descriptions of people, places, or
nature reflect identifiable schools or works of art; art works provide
structural unity or have inspired a sense of spatial ordering within a
temporal form,[5] as for instance, the influence of Cézanne's paintings of
Mont Sainte Victoire on Hemingway's mountain iconography in *A
Farewell to Arms*. Typically, in pictorialist fiction, aesthetic values are at
odds with morality and Europe is identified with art and the past. From
Washington Allston's *Monaldi* to Bernard Malamud's *Pictures of
Fidelman: An Exhibition*, a remarkable number of works have exhibited
most or all of these characteristics; others are pictorialist in a more
limited way: Melville with his use of the whale painting in *Moby-Dick*,
Mark Twain with Emmeline Grangerford's drawings, Peter Taylor with
Bronzino's *Venus, Cupid, Folly and Time*.

As we all know, American writers in the Romance tradition are not
especially concerned about how the individual adjusts to circumstances,
that is, in the process of human development and in the social
personality. Rather, their interest lies in the moral meanings and
psychological effects of the individual's encounter with the social world.
The particular situation is used to explore a more general truth of human
nature or existence. To succeed as art, however, the particular situation
must be rendered palpably, convincingly, as if for its own sake. The
more abstractly oriented the writer, the more useful to him is the picture,
for it does double duty: it appeals to the mental eye and thus helps feed
the reader's ominivorous demand for graphic, vivid detail, and it
suggests its own invisible truths that the writer can exploit for his
purposes. Although there is the danger of a calculated, frozen, static
effect, art works are thus particularly rich as symbols.

For the novelist in a documentary or manners mode, the portrait is
only one of many things through which the personality reveals and
conceals itself, a fraction of the swarming materiality of daily life in
which meaning resides. The romance writer often singles out the
portrait, drawing on the painter's power to express psychological and
moral truths through a visible, tangible thing. Thus, Melville in *Pierre*
turned to portraits to multiply meanings, and in Hawthorne's *The House
of Seven Gables* the pervasive linking of pictures with people through
description and metaphor creates a unifying medium. The title itself,
like Washington Irving's *The Sketch Book* and James's *The Portrait of a
Lady*, alerts the reader to a spatial rather than a temporal ordering.

Spanning "better than two centuries," the narrative barely moves sequentially. Its structural pattern derives almost entirely from the house and its contents, the survival of the past in its objects and present occupants.

Of the four portraits linking the past with the present, Colonel Pyncheon's is the most heavily invested with allegorical meanings and structural purpose. A stern-faced "Puritanic-looking personage, in a scull-cap, with a laced band and a grizzly beard," the iron sword-hilt he is uplifting with one hand "being more successfully depicted by the artist than the Bible he holds in his other hand," the sword-hilt "stood out in far greater prominence than the sacred volume."[6] Unconsciously, "the painter's deep conception of his subject's inward traits had wrought itself into the essence of the picture, and is seen after the superficial coloring has been rubbed off by time!" (p. 59). The artist thus inadvertently exposes both the harshness of Puritanism and the evil of the man's soul. Analogously, just as the artist disguised his patron's characteristic expression for worldly reasons, Judge Pyncheon, the living embodiment of the painting, presents a benign front to the world, his inner nature concealed behind the mask of the smiling public benefactor.

As the past is alive in the present, the figure in the painting is fancifully described as living: he scowls at the breakfast preparations for Clifford and frowns when Mathew Maule bargains with Gervayse, even descending from his frame. He shivers in the cold desolate period of Phoebe's absence, is worshipped by the ghostly procession of his descendants, and is finally toppled from his position on the wall, becoming a picture again when the Judge's death and the betrothal of Phoebe and Holgrave break the spell. Dead in Colonel Pyncheon's chair, the Judge becomes a painting, a fly alighting on his face and creeping towards his open eyes, as it might on the ancestral portrait, but whereas the portrait has the life of art, the Judge is pure matter. The ironic contrast between the Judge, a mere thing in space, and his memorandum for the day, his spiritual essence, is pure visual melodrama. The scene is too elaborately embellished to harmonize with the understated artistry of the rest of the book, but in conception it not only balances the initial death scene of Colonel Pyncheon but completes the pictorial design.

Each of the other portraits functions similarly: Clifford, presented as both too fine for this world and as potentially an inhuman aesthete, is associated with the delicate, graceful minature by Edward Greene Malbone. Alice Pyncheon, betrayed by her Europeanized love of the

picturesque as well as by the American materialism of her father, had
been painted by a Venetian artist; the portrait is in the Duke of
Devonshire's collection at Chatsworth, prized for its artistic qualities,
not its subject. Holgrave's soul-revealing daguerreotype of Judge
Pyncheon confirms Hawthorne's preference for nature over art and for
American optimism, energy, and modernity over European
aestheticism and the past.[7]

The art themes and pictorial devices adumbrated in *The House of
Seven Gables* are at the core of *The Marble Faun*: the title, referring to
the character Donatello, who resembles a statue by Praxiteles and is
named after a Renaissance sculptor, indicates the shift from artless
America to the crumbling repository of the Pagan and Catholic past. In
the earlier work, the play of Hawthorne's imagination is deft and supple;
in the supposed "poetic or fairy precinct" of Italy, its tread is heavy and
willful. In Hilda's cry "The Old Masters will not set me free!"[8] one hears
the authors own voice. The past in Rome persists in alien objects that can
be neither dismissed nor imaginatively assimilated; they are counters in
an aesthetic allegory too labyrinthian to explore here.[9] The system of
references is admirably, ingeniously plotted; the ringing of changes on
key works (Guido's *Beatrice Cenci*[10] and *St. Michael*, Kenyon's
Cleopatra, Miriam's avenging Biblical women) is impressive and
innovative. No other novelist before Hawthorne so extensively and
variously used art works, real and imaginary, for thematic and
psychological purposes, and Hawthorne did so often with considerable
effectiveness and subtlety, especially to convey forbidden feelings and
buried wishes. The too frequent failure, however, to infuse allegory with
life and the lapses into the tone of the plaintive tourist who has seen one
madonna too many, betray the limitations of Hawthorne's visual
knowledge and sensitivity. His tendency was to look *through* the
painting to find spiritual meanings behind it, rather than *at* it, or to
attribute meanings where it is difficult objectively to find them. The
enigma of Beatrice Cenci's portrait is in the eyes of the beholder, one
concludes from looking at the picture itself dispassionately. Of course,
Hawthorne was scarcely alone in his literary approach to art and in his
identification of line with spirit and essence and color with matter and
accident, nor alone in worshipping such gods and goddesses of the
nineteenth-century pantheon of taste as Sodoma and Venus de Medici.
Moreover, taste has capricious tides: the Bolognese school is no longer as
"out" as when James judged Hawthorne to be an "exquisite provincial"
and posterity may consider our "minimal" art a nothingness. Still, the
fact remains that Hawthorne's European tour came too late to stir his
imagination deeply or to shape his ways of seeing; his allegorizing habit

of mind, transcendental aesthetic, and residual Puritan moralism were too deeply engrained. As a consequence, his pictorialism, especially when compared with James's or Hemingway's, lacks energy, radiance, and resonance.

Hawthorne's aesthetic values are ultimately religious and moral. Most Italian art is superficially beautiful, inwardly empty, insincere. Correspondingly, a "taste for pictorial arts is often no more than a polish upon the hard enamel of an artificial character" and the picturesque, a sign of decadence: "When life becomes fascinating either in the poet's imagination or the painter's eye" then "there is reason to suspect that a people are waning to decay and ruin" (p. 296). Art in a fallen world neither improves man morally nor consoles him when troubled. Only nature and religious faith can comfort and heal. Hilda experiences the sublimity of St. Peter's Cathedral as a "magnificent, comprehensive, majestic symbol of religious faith" (p. 350). Similarly, in his hour of trial during Hilda's disappearance, Kenyon finds no solace in work; his spirits rise when he leaves Rome for the countryside, but his discovery of the Venus in the excavations does not assuage his anxiety about Hilda, a sign, Hawthorne notes approvingly, that "He could hardly, we fear, be reckoned a consummate artist" (p. 424).

The picturesque becomes morally acceptable when associated with nature or fused with the religious sublime. Donald Ringe aptly summarizes the chief characteristics of Hudson River landscape painting which were literarily adapted by Cooper, Poe, Irving, as well as by Hawthorne: "the long perspective downward and reaching out to a framing range of hills, the mixture of the placid and the wild, the unified multiplicity of specific details, the accomplishments of men dwarfed by the infinite expanses of nature, even the ruins of a deserted fortress."[11] To this I would add that the viewer's eye typically is led to an opening in the sky, pure glittering light, signifying divinity. The scene that Kenyon sees below from Donatello's half-ruined tower corresponds closely to this pattern, the chiaroscuro of the picturesque merging with the infinity of the sublime. Kenyon is overwhelmed by religious reverence.

In the concluding scene in which Miriam ambiguously blesses the lovers, Hawthorne seems to be attempting a reconciliation of art and nature, past and present, through its setting—the Pantheon. It is a pagan temple in which the Christian altar is under the opening to the sky, God's eye. The two American artists nevertheless return to their homeland. Hawthorne's famous diatribe against Rome is more convincing than his conclusion that despite all he has said against it, Rome draws "us thitherward again, as if it were more familiar, more intimately our home, than even the spot where we were born. . . ." Rome as a "long-decaying corpse" carries more conviction (pp. 325-26).

Although *Roderick Hudson* is James's riposte to *The Marble Faun*, and owes more to its pictorialism than can be profitably summarized here, I turn to *The Ambassadors* instead. It claims our special attention as James's most pictorial novel in its sensuous surfaces and its remarkable range of pictorial techniques and analogies. It stands, moreover, between Hawthorne and Hemingway in its aesthetic ideas. Unlike Hilda who looks through substance and surface, which Hawthorne tends to view as inauthentic artifice, to the idea or essence that in effect exists in the mind of God, and, also, unlike Thomas Hudson who veers away from meanings except those inherent in truly representing the object itself, James's artists are equally responsive to the thing and to its meanings—historical, poetic, moral. The artist, both painter and novelist, James noted in "The Art of Fiction," strives to create "the illusion of life . . . to render the look of things," but notice the qualifying phrase that follows, "the look that catches the meaning."[12] James admired John Singer Sargent's paintings for their freshness of vision: ". . . they remind people that the faculty of taking a direct, independent, unborrowed impression, is not altogether lost" but an art that merely records impressions he considered a limited one: ". . . the highest result is achieved when to this element of quick perception a certain faculty of brooding reflection is added. I use this name for want of a better, and I mean the quality in the light of which the artist sees deep into his subject, undergoes it, becomes patient with it, and almost reverent, and in short enlarges and humanizes the technical problem."[13] Lambert Strether, like all of James's other heroes and heroines of consciousness, is blessed and burdened with "quick perception" and the "faculty of brooding reflection." He not only sees but reflects. As he responds to things in the present, his mind takes "fresh backward, fresh forward, fresh lateral flights."[14] The variety of social types in the London theatre leads him to the perception that in Woollett there are only two types, male and female. Strether's awakening, typically Jamesian, comes in Europe because American life is insufficiently rich—socially, historically, and visually, or so James believes—to stimulate the imagination. Similarly, the artist in "The Real Thing" fails when he uses the Monarchs for his fine illustrations not because of his moral or artistic inadequacy but because they appear too blandly typical to quicken his imagination. When Strether implores little Bilham not to make *his* mistake, but "to live," he says, "It doesn't so much matter what you do in particular, so long as you have your life" (p. 132). Little Bilham interprets this to mean "to see, while I've a chance, everything I can and *really* to see, for it must have been that only you meant" (p. 165). "Really to see," Strether realizes, is vastly more complicated than to theorize. On his arrival in Paris, ". . . the very air had the taste of something mixed with art, something that presents nature as a white-capped master chef" (p. 59). Paris hangs before him, "the vast bright Babylon, like some huge iridescent object, a jewel bright and hard, in which parts were not to be discriminated nor differences comfortably marked. It twinkled and trembled and melted together and what seemed all surface one moment seemed all depth the other" (p. 64). The conventional distinctions between the surface and the moral picturesque, nature and art, manners and morality of the New England mind seem as inapplicable to the seductive scene as the theory on which Strether set out to "rescue" Chad is to the appearance of Chad and his life.

Where does morality enter into James's aesthetic vision? Strether, looking about Gloriani's garden, remarks to little Bilham that everyone in Paris seems to run to the "visual sense."

> "There are moments when it strikes one that you haven't any other."

> "Any moral," little Bilham explained. . . . "But Miss Barrace has a moral distinction," he kindly continued as if for Strether's benefit no less than for her own (p. 126).

Little Bilham's remark seems casual, a conversational bridge, but the difference between "moral sense" (the faculty of making moral judgments) and "moral distinction" (a quality of mind and character) is essential to the novel. "Moral sense" is the "fine cold thought" of Woollett, a deductive rather than inductive approach to experience. Sarah Pocock is logically, not to say rigidly, consistent when, immune to Madame de Vionnet's "high rarity, her distinction of every sort," she pronounces her to be not "even an apology for a decent woman." Strether had hoped Sarah would have been affected "by her exquisite amiability—a real revelation" (p. 278), but nothing can be revealed to Sarah because she "knows" before she sees.

"*Really* to see," however, involves more than flexibility, neutrality, an empirical approach. As the passage quoted earlier describing the ideal artistic vision suggests, the artist who would be more than merely a brilliant technician must have the "imagination of loving," that is, a respect for otherness that is "almost reverent." It is exactly this imagination that Chad lacks. Dazzled by his transformation, Strether had thought him better than he was: Chad is finally only Chad, "the son of his father" (p. 341) in his shrewdness; like his mother, who never appears on stage but who makes herself felt—she is imaged as "some particularly large iceberg in a cool blue northern sea" (p. 298)—he has no imagination for others. He has marvelously improved in social grace and sensitivity but the secret of his "famous knowing how to live" is that "he habitually left things to others" (p. 312). As an artist of life, he has not humanized the technical problem. Appropriately, he has "encountered a revelation" in his study of advertising, to be his speciality in the family business if he returns (and he probably will). "It's an art like another, and infinite like all the arts" (p. 339), are almost his last words to Strether. It is also as an "art" the ultimate of form without content.

Strether's excursion into the country, climaxed by the recognition scene on the river, in Book Eleventh, is justly celebrated. The movement and feeling of vision, outer and inner, is given the richest and most sustained pictorial rendering in James's fiction, indeed in American fiction. The sensory detail, especially of touch, sound, taste, and texture, often synesthetic, is the objective correlative of the "immediate and sensible" and of the blend of nature and art that Strether has finally given himself up to wholeheartedly. There is the "taste of idleness" that doesn't need "more time to sweeten"; "he had nothing to do but turn off to some hillside where he might stretch himself and hear the poplars rustle. . . . He saw himself partaking at the close of the day, with the enhancements of a coarse white cloth and a sanded floor, of something fried and felicitous, washed down with authentic wine" (p. 302). This episode is also the culmination and poetic actualizing of previous clusters of imagery: the allusions to trains and time, as in Strether's impassioned plea to little Bilham in the fifth book, and to water and boats, as when Madame de Vionnet in her first encounter with Sarah in desperation "publicly drew [Strether] into her boat" (p. 219).

Strether takes the train to the outskirts of Paris for no purpose except to see the French countryside, "into which he had hitherto looked only through the little oblong-window of the picture-frame." He has hopes that he may see "something somewhere that would remind him of a certain small Lambinet that had charmed him, long years before, at a Boston dealer's and that he had quite absurdly never forgotten" (p. 301). Though low in price for a Lambinet, he had been too poor to buy it. Emile Lambinet, a student of Daubigny and Corot, was a minor nineteenth-century landscapist associated with the Barbizon school, the general quality of which is an unheroic, intimate, quiet, somewhat idealized treatment of nature: slow-moving rivers, luminous skies, tangled willows, light filtering through trees—these are the features of Lambinet's art. Popular in America in the 1860s, the Barbizon painters are outmoded, as Strether knows. His desire is not to find the painting but "to see the remembered mixture resolved back into its elements—to assist at the restoration to nature of the whole far-away hour." He gets off the train at the sign of the weather, air, light, colour, and his mood all favouring" and walks into the "oblong gilt frame." The past fuses with the present, nature reconstitutes art, it all "fell into a composition. . . . It was all there, in short—it was what he had wanted: it was Tremont Street, it was France, it was Lambinet. Moreover he was freely walking about in it" (pp. 301-02).

By "framing" the day in the country through a pictorial vision, James brilliantly exploited the inherent differences between temporal and spatial art forms and their common meeting ground in the symbol. Thematically, Strether is out of time, not only in having recovered the past through the landscape of Lambinet, but in his sense of emancipation from schedule and purpose, the moral imperative of a puritanical, utilitarian culture. His meditations on the recent past mingle with precise time notations— "some eighty minutes on the train," an hour of wandering, a half-hour nap, a returning train at 9:20—as a part of the "picture." This unfolding action, retrospective and sequential, both physical and mental movement, makes the picture device seem natural and easy, unforced. The intention being to portray Strether's feeling of the joy and beauty of life in the here and now, vindicating his moral revolution, the picture metaphor has the effect of stopping time and of placing before us as if for contemplation, his immersion and fullest realization of the "conditions" which in their difference from the "conditions" of Woollett, justify his conclusion that "in *these* places such things were, and that if it was in them one elected to move about one had to make one's account with what one lighted on" (p. 306), a conclusion soon to be tested by his meeting the lovers on the river.

When Strether reaches the village where he is to have dinner, the picture in which he has been moving changes from a Lambinet with its low-keyed idyllic vision to an Impressionist canvas with its pleasure themes, fresh, vibrant color, and concern only for things as seen in an instant rather than as distilled or generalized. The place itself, as described by James in his project for the novel—"a suburban village by the river, a place where people come out from Paris to boat, to dine, to dance, to make love, to do anything they like,"[15] was the kind of setting favored by Impressionist painters. The description of the scene in the text is virtually a "quotation" of a painting by Renoir or Monet of La Grenouillère, a popular bathing place near Bougival: "a small and primitive pavilion . . . at the garden's edge, almost overhung the water. . . . It consisted of little more than a platform, slightly raised, with a couple of benches and a table, a protecting rail and projecting roof; but it raked the full grey-blue stream. . . . Strether's confidence that had so gathered for him deepened with the lap of the water, the ripple of the surface, the rustle of the reeds on the opposite bank, the faint diffused coolness and the slight rock of a couple of boats attached to a rough landing place hard by." When a boat "drifted into sight," Madame de Vionnet's parasol is seen as making "so fine a pink point in the shining scene" (pp. 307-08). The shift from the Barbizon to the Impressionist mode corresponds with Strether's discovery that Madame de Vionnet and Chad are lovers; the idealized past gives way to the actualities of the present.

Strether's excursion into the country is the most fully and formally organized scene in the novel recalling specific Impressionist paintings and motifs. In its visual effects, the novel throughout reflects James's familiarity with the Impressionists, though he had serious reservations about their intentions and practice even in the late 1890s. Scenes in the theatres, public gardens, restaurants, café terraces, all may be related to works by Degas, Manet, Monet, Sargent, and others. As F.O. Matthiessen noted, Strether's luncheon with Madame de Vionnet on the Seine has the air of a Renoir.[16] The easy grace of her elbows on the table recalls the beauty of the informal poses of figures in a work such as his *The Luncheon Party of the Rowers*. The delicately precise notations of color in her clothes seem inspired by Whistler's finely shaded and muted color orchestrations. The description of her dress on the occasion of Chad's festivities for Sarah resembles, in its subtle shadings of color, Whistler's *Study in Gray and Green*.

More generally, the novel is permeated by the ethos of Impressionism—its optimism, its celebration through liberated color and light of ordinary people and earthly delights: eating, drinking, dancing, sitting in gardens, strolling down avenues. In no other James novel is food and drink, its texture and taste, so emphasized in detail and imagery. It is the only novel of his in which the hero munches toast, drinks pale bock, has a roll and coffee for breakfast, an *omlette aux tomates* and Chablis for lunch, and a *côtelette de veau à l'òseille* for dinner. Even Strether's image for fate and free will is culinary; consciousness is figured as a jelly poured into a mold, fluted or plain.

The correlations in style with Impressionism are more problematic because of differences in mediums. James's restricted point of view and emphasis on consciousness, as has often been observed, relates him to the Impressionist theory and practice of representing what the eye sees, not what the painter knows or thinks is there according to previous conventions. *The Ambassadors*, futhermore, may be said to consist of a series of multiple views, corresponding to the Impressionist practice of painting the same scene at different times and in different atmospheric conditions. Strether sees Chad in a succession of different lights; Mrs. Newsome and Sarah see him only as they have always conceived of him. James gives us still other viewpoints than Strether's of Chad: little Bilham hints that he liked Chad better as he was, before his transformation, and that he would best fulfill himself by going home. The crucial difference between James's Impressionism and that of the painter is due, however, not only to differences between the visual and verbal arts but to differing epistemological and ethical assumptions. The Impressionist vision excludes memories, literary and mythological associations, the past, numinous meanings: Strether's vision, and James's, comprehends these concerns of the whole being. Reality for James is a coalescence of the thing as seen and as imagined; Strether's responsiveness to associations and setting indicates a poetic faith in the continuity of human life.

Unity in Impressionist painting comes through color and light, not through line or volume or traditional perspective. The viewer has to create the final coherence; as John Rewald observed, "it is the eye of the beholder that establishes the cohesion of the countless signs scattered over the canvas, it is his eye that endows the painter's image with its ultimate gloss."[17] Similarly, the reader of a work of literary impressionism—and here I refer to all of James's writing in the late manner—must participate strenuously in the work, putting together the perceptions of characters and points of view. We are much more dependent on tone and nuance in our reading of "signs" in this kind of fiction than we are when mind and thing are separated and reality treated as more fixed and determinate.

Structurally, the novel is only partially Impressionistic. Its symmetry—its hour-glass form (E. M. Forster's figure for it)—is characteristic of linear, classical art, the antithesis of the painterly dissolution of form in Impressionism. James is especially American in his unreconciled dualities—linear-painterly, realism-idealism, tragedy-comedy.

At the end of *The Ambassadors*, having parted with Madame de Vionnet, the muse of his imagination, Strether is to return to that "native homeliness" that Kenyon and Hilda rejoice in regaining, but for him it will be an exile in limbo. The difference between James and Hemingway in their treatment of the European experience may be summed up by their images for Paris: "the vast bright Babylon," with all it implies of attraction and moral danger for the innocent, and "the moveable feast," suggesting celebration, innocent hedonism. Paris for Hemingway is youth, innocence, purity of sensation and of love. It is always there to come back to, actually and through memory. Hudson, as Hemingway said of himself, carries Paris with him. He cannot be exiled from Europe or an exile in it because he has assimilated it. Eakins and Cézanne are equals in his vision. "Home" is wherever he can make it. Art does not conflict with "life," or style with content, meanings, depth. Technique in art, in sports, in the professions, in almost whatever and in the unlikeliest settings, as exemplified by the making of a ham-and-egg sandwich in "The Battler" or of camp in "The Big Two-Hearted River," is a source of meaning and order in an otherwise irrational, absurd world.

Neither the misery nor the magnificence of the past that *had* to be confronted by nineteenth-century innocents abroad deeply touches the Hemingway hero. It exists as a reminder, however, that the old order survives marginally and as a symbol of loss. Jake Barnes and Bill Gorton look down from the bridge at Notre Dame, "squatting against the night sky." It is a dim, generalized presence on a dark island. " 'It's pretty grand,' Bill said."[18] The "great brown cathedral" in Pamplona is also solidly there, but not described in detail; what is precisely rendered is the feeling of the sun drying Jake's "forefinger and thumb of his right hand" (p. 97) after he leaves the church. " 'Some people have God,' [Jake] said. 'Quite a lot.' 'He never worked very well with me' " (p. 245), is Brett's answer; nor, it seems, very well for him. The relics of the past are on the periphery, suggesting traditional belief as well as modern man's exclusion from its sureties.

Only because of continuities and common tendencies has it been possible to point out the differences in the treatment of art objects and ideas in these three writers; from looking at *how* the pictorial vision is expressed in individual works, we must turn to the *what* again—the common denominator. In each of the works discussed, the protagonists are artists or artistic in sensibility; Europe as the symbol of art and of the past, or European aesthetic concepts such as the picturesque and the sublime, figures significantly. At the center of each, most broadly stated, is the conflict between human needs and art, or as Yeats expressed it, the choice between "perfection of the life, or of the work." In each, epistemological and philosophical questions are considered. In each, art works are used structurally and symbolically, as visual models or as devices to suggest space and overcome time.

There are various historical and social explanations for the greater significance of the pictorial in American fiction than in English, especially in the nineteenth century. Central to any consideration, however, is the tendency of American writers to see things not as ends in themselves but as carriers of ideas, of metaphysical meanings. In other words, the tendency towards romance rather than realism or manners, towards symbolic rather than imitative modes, towards states of mind rather than social personality. A concomitant is to find meaning in the spatial rather than in the temporal dimension, to aim for simultaneity or timeless states. The visual dominates the other senses in the American tradition, in realists as well as idealists. The American pictorial vision is visionary.

Notes

[1] Ernest Hemingway, *Islands in the Stream* (New York: Charles Scribner's Sons, 1970), pp. 19-20. Subsequent page citations are incorporated in my text.

[2] The context of the favorable view of tradition is a discussion between Roger and Hudson about the relative difficulties of painting and writing (pp. 77-78). Hemingway may have chosen a painter rather than a writer for his hero in order to distance himself from his character. If so, he failed, for he never sees through Hudson's emotional posturing. The autobiographical character of this book is both disturbing and moving. It reeks of self-justification and of self-pity. One feels that Hemingway, through the writing itself, was seeking tranquility, purpose, absolution. Thomas Hudson represents his ideal or better self: he works well, loves his sons, controls his drinking, has learned to live without marrying again. Roger represents his nightmare self: a popular writer who gets into sickening, disastrous fights and who fears that if he tries to write a serious book, it will turn into Hollywood trash. Roger's failure is partially rationalized in the distinction made between painting and writing—that "in painting the tradition and the line are clearer and there are more people helping you" and also that "It was luckier to be a painter because you have more things to work with. We have the advantage of working with our hands and the métier we have mastered is an actual tangible thing" (p. 103). The idea that tradition in painting is clearer may have something to it, especially if by writing is meant the novel rather than poetry, as the novel is such an open, fluid form. But the view that painting, because it is a material medium, is less demanding than writing is naive. Roger found painting fun and writing hell because he had never reached the point in painting where he had had to struggle with artistic problems. For the real painter, it is probably no more or less "fun" to practice his art than it is for the writer. Hemingway may have idealized painting because he aimed in prose for a purity of image uncontaminated by abstract thought realizable only in "an actual tangible thing."

[3] Ernest Hemingway, *Death in the Afternoon* (London: Jonathan Cape, 1932), pp. 10-11. Distrust of purely visual phenomena is characteristic of American painters. As Barbara Novak observes, in *American Painting of the Nineteenth Century: Realism, Idealism, and the American Experience* (New York: Praeger Publishers, 1969), p. 244, even American painters drawn to Impressionism "were still reluctant to trust appearances and sensations, tending to crystallize form and add a conceptual element that negated the perceptual purity of Impressionism." For a comprehensive survey of the influence of painting on

Hemingway, see Emily Stipes Watts, *Ernest Hemingway and the Arts* (Urbana: Univ. of Illinois Press, 1971). Reproductions of paintings Hemingway owned and admired are included.

[4]Ernest Hemingway, *A Moveable Feast* (New York: Charles Scribner's Sons, 1964), p. 13.

[5]My conception of pictorialism owes a great deal to Jean H. Hagstrum's *The Sister Arts: The Tradition of Literary Pictorialism and English Poetry From Dryden to Gray* (Chicago: Univ. of Chicago Press, 1958), p. 18, and to his more recent paper "Convention and Revolt in the Pictorialist Novel." There are relatively few books on the interrelations between the arts in America but increasingly numerous articles. The titles reveal the special interests of the following full-length studies: James T. Callow, *Kindred Spirits: Knickerbocker Writers and American Artists, 1807-1855* (Chapel Hill: Univ. of North Carolina Press, 1967); Donald A. Ringe, *The Pictorial Mode: Space and Time in the Art of Bryant, Irving & Cooper* (Lexington: Univ. Press of Kentucky, 1971); Clara Marburg Kirk, *W.D. Howells and Art in His Time* (New Brunswick: Rutgers Univ. Press, 1965); Ernst Scheyer, *The Circle of Henry Adams: Art & Artists* (Detroit: Wayne State Univ. Press, 1970), and my *Henry James and the Visual Arts* (Charlottesville: Univ. Press of Virginia, 1970). A useful critical anthology is John Conron, Ed., *The American Landscape* (New York: Oxford Univ. Press, 1974). Roger B. Stein in *Seascape and the American Imagination* (New York: Clarkson N. Potter, Inc., 1975) approaches his subject from the visual angle, this being the catalogue to the exhibition he organized under this title.

[6]Nathaniel Hawthorne, *The House of Seven Gables*, ed. Seymour L. Gross (New York: W.W. Norton & Company, 1967), p. 59.

[7]Alfred M. Marks in "Hawthrone's Daguerreotypist: Scientist, Artist, Reformer," in the Norton Edition cited above, pp. 330-47, gives an instructive account of the daguerreotype in Hawthorne's day and his use of the process in his novel.

[8]Nathaniel Hawthorne, *The Marble Faun: Or, The Romance of Monte Beni*, Centenary Edition, IV (Columbus: Ohio State Univ. Press, 1968), p. 334.

[9]Leo B. Levy has ably analyzed Hawthorne's treatment of visual concepts in several articles, most extensively on this novel in *"The Marble Faun:* Hawthorne's Landscape of the Fall," *AL,* 42 (1970), 139-56. Also critically important is Paul Brodtkorb, Jr.'s, "Art Allegory in *The Marble Faun," PMLA,* 77 (1962), 254-67.

[10]The nineteenth-century fascination with the Cenci legend and its application to Hawthorne is the subject of a chapter in Jeffrey Meyers, *Painting and the Novel* (New York: Harper & Row, 1975), pp. 6-18. For Melville in *Pierre,* Guido's *Beatrice Cenci* is a symbol of moral ambiguity. Edith Wharton's erotic fragment named after her tragic heroine "Beatrice Palmato" inevitably evokes Beatrice Cenci. For Hemingway in *Islands in the Stream,* a girl of the Cenci type has "the morals of a vacuum cleaner and the soul of a pari-mutuel machine, a good figure, and that lovely vicious face" (p. 100). The legend dies hard.

[11]Donald A. Ringe, "James Fenimore Cooper and Thomas Cole: An Analogous Technique," *AL,* 30 (1958), 32-33.

[12]Henry James, *The Art of Fiction and Other Essays*, ed. Morris Roberts (New York: Oxford Univ. Press, 1948), p. 12.

[13]Henry James, *The Ambassadors*, ed. S.P. Rosenbaum (New York: W.W. Norton & Company, 1964), p. 42.

[14]Henry James, *The Painter's Eye: Notes and Essays on the Pictorial Arts*, ed. John L. Sweeney (Cambridge: Harvard Univ. Press, 1956), pp. 227-28.

[15]Henry James, "Project of Novel," in Norton Edition, p. 397.

[16]F. O. Matthiessen, *"The Ambassadors,"* in Norton Edition, p. 433.

[17]John Rewald, "The Impressionist Brush," *The Metropolitan Museum of Art Bulletin*, 32 (1974), 55.

[18]Ernest Hemingway, *The Sun Also Rises* (New York: Charles Scribner's Sons, 1954), p. 77.

THE WRITER AS A CELEBRITY:
SOME ASPECTS OF AMERICAN LITERATURE
AS POPULAR CULTURE

John G. Cawelti

University of Chicago

In treating of American literature (by which I take it we mean primarily the canon of our "major authors") and its relationship to popular culture (those cultural forms, patterns, and processes most broadly characteristic of the American people), there are a number of problems worth extended treatment. For example, we might consider the interplay between the work of major authors and popular formulaic patterns like the detective story, the western, or the sentimental romance. Such a discussion would explore how popular formulas usually originate in some particularly successful work of a major writer which is imitated by others. In time, these imitations produce a standardized genre with conventions well known to writers and expected by an audience which has come to enjoy this particular kind of story. So the western orginated in the great success of Cooper's Leatherstocking Saga. Cooper's frontier hero and his plots of chase and pursuit through the wilderness became the basis of hundreds of novels and dime-novels in the nineteenth century and of innumerable films and television programs in the twentieth. In a similar way the detective story sprang from the Dupin stories of Edgar Allan Poe, while the sentimental romance originated with the novels of Samuel Richardson. We would see, in tracing the relation between popular formulas and serious fiction, how the most long-lasting formulas have undergone many transformations, frequently being revitalized by the influence of more original writers. In such a fashion, the western was given a new lease on life at the beginning of the twentieth century by Owen Wister, the detective story was transformed in the early 1930s by Dashiell Hammett and Raymond Chandler, and the sentimental romance was continually reshaped by the impact of major authors like the Bronte sisters. Our examination of this problem would also touch on the influence of established popular formulas and conventions of those writers we have come to think of as our major authors. We would want to study, with William Veeder, how Henry James exploited the stylistic and narrative conventions of popular romance in creating such major works as *The American* and *Portrait of a Lady,* or with Richard Slotkin, Edwin Fussell, and others, how the myth of the frontier was used by Hawthorne and Melville. Finally, we would want to look very carefully at that increasingly important tradition of American fiction which has employed a parodistic or ironic version of popular formulas as the formal basis for complex treatments of American cultural myths. Melville's *Pierre,* with its burlesque of sentimental romance, Twain's treatment of the western formula in *Roughing It* and the detective story in *Pudd'nhead Wilson,* and the contemporary novels of Thomas Pynchon, Thomas Berger, and Kurt Vonnegut, would be a few of the landmarks in that terrain.

Another quite different problem is the use of popular culture as a subject for serious fiction. Under this rubric we would need to trace the emergence of popular types and the vernacular as material for serious fiction. Fortunately much of this work has already been done for us by students of American humor like Walter Blair and of style like Richard Bridgman. These scholars have shown how experiments with the American language and a growing array of popular stereotypes like the Yankee pedlar, the Davy Crockett frontier roarer, the minstrel show Black, the spinster, etc., developed in the early nineteenth century and reached an initial literary culmination in the work of Mark Twain. The use of popular culture as a subject in the twentieth century has been less thoroughly examined and there is much that needs fuller treatment such as the role of Hollywood and other institutions of modern mass culture in fiction, the emergence of ethnicity as a subject, the role of sports as subject and symbol, and fictionalizations of popular movements like the counter-culture.

Still another approach to the relation between American literature and popular culture can be found by looking at the impact on writers of the ideology of a democratic popular culture. This ideology itself has undergone a considerable evolution from the conception of a new republican culture espoused by Jefferson and many of his contemporaries, through the transcendentalist vision of a democratic culture and Whitman's notion of the poet as democratic prophet, to the early twentieth century cultural analyses of critics like Van Wyck Brooks and philosophers like George Santayana who pointed to a destructive split between the genteel tradition of intellectual culture and the materialistic pragmatism of the masses. This highbrow—lowbrow analysis of American culture has had an important influence on writers and critics in the twentieth century, generating a rich literature of cultural controversy and analysis which has in turn served as a source of ideas for contemporary American writers and artists. It would be very useful to have a systematic account of the evolution of the popular culture ideology and an assessment of its impact on American literature.

Finally, there is the question of the popular reception of American literature and of the way in which the general public's response or lack of response to major American writers has shaped the development of our literature. In part, this is a question of the relationship between those works of literature which became best-sellers in their day, and those which we have later come to recognize as the canon of American literature. The study of best-sellers and of shifting popular tastes has been solidly grounded by the work of Frank Luther Mott, James D. Hart, Louis Wright, Russell Nye, Carl Bode, and other scholars, but there is another aspect to this problem which has not, to my knowledge, received much attention. In modern democratic societies, popular interest commonly manifests itself in the complex phenomenon of celebrity. Therefore, the writer's celebrity, or lack of it, plays an important part in his conception of his role and his relationship to his audience.

One of the primary mechanisms of popular culture, celebrity is popular interest in a person beyond or aside from his works or accomplishments. While the original source of public fascination may be the celebrity's creations, there is a tendency for public interest to fasten increasingly on the person, rather than, in the case of a writer or artist, on his works. Thus, it often happens that when the process of celebration is well under way, there are many members of the public who are familiar with, say, a writer or artist, without having read or seen a single one of his works. In turn, a writer's notoriety may lead members of the public who might not otherwise have done so to read his works. The enormous success of Ernest Hemingway's *The Old Man and the Sea*, published in *Life Magazine* and read almost immediately after its appearance by millions of people, testifies to the significance of Hemingway as a celebrity perhaps even more than to his reputation as a writer. Surely a considerable portion of those who read *The Old Man and the Sea* were reading a Hemingway fiction for the first time. No doubt many persons discovered Van Gogh's paintings after they had heard about him as the mad artist who cut off his ear.

Fame, the poet's spur, is intricately related to celebrity, though it is useful to draw some rough distinctions between them. Fame is the immortality of the poet in his work, the fact that he is known in and through his work to many generations. Because great artists have the fortunate power of injecting their imagination into language and visual form, thereby creating something which men can cherish forever, the quest for fame has always been a central motive of poets and artists. Celebrity is, one might say, a kind of immediate fame. It is largely in the present and its mark is being known as a person. The test of artistic fame is that one's words or images remain in the minds of men; the test of celebrity is being followed everywhere by a photographer. The dead poet may achieve a greater fame than the living man who wrote the poems; the dead celebrity is usually as important as last week's newspaper. Of course, there are exceptions to this. Many writers have achieved a lasting fame not so much through the permanent importance of their writings, but because of what their lives came to stand for: as instances we might cite Chatterton, Poe, and Wilde. In the former case, the writer's life has become far more important than any of his literary creations. The fame of Poe and Wilde is somewhat more complex in that many of their works are still widely read. However, it seems fair to say that their importance to literary history is as much a matter of their tragic and symbolic lives as of the greatness of their works. Here, fame has become a kind of extension of celebrity, something that occasionally happens when there is some basis on which the celebrity's person can pass over into fame or legend. In general, celebrity is transient and ephemeral. There is then a difference between fame and celebrity both in quality and in object. Celebrity is brief and intense; fame tends to be slower in growing and is relatively permanent. The object of celebrity is the person; the object of fame is some accomplishment, action, or creative work.

It would surely be a mistake to assume that celebrity is a problem utterly unique to modern times. The artist as person-performer and therefore, to some degree, as celebrity has been a factor since the dawn of literature. Certainly those wandering bards whose tradition led to the great epics of Homer had a kind of celebrity. One can easily imagine a village crowd gathered around one of Homer's grandfathers eagerly questioning him about his work, just as reporters cluster around one of today's literary celebrities. Yet there are certain characteristics of modern societies which give celebrity a particular importance for the artist. In a market society where the writer is dependent on the sales of his work, the temptation to let one's person become an advertisement for one's works is great. But there are other dimensions of modern mass cultures which thrust celebrity into the very heart of the creative process. Many writers, if not all, need to feel some contact with their audience. While it is possible for the writer, in complex modern societies, to have contact with individual members of his public and with the small coteries of his acquaintance, there is no way for him to have a complex relationship with the large and diverse public which constitutes, at least potentially, his audience. In a culture where so much communication is mediated by newspapers, radio, and television, the only way in which the general public can be present to a writer, and he, as person, to them, is through the mechanism of celebrity. The importance of celebrity as a means of contact between writer and audience is further intensified by the degree to which the writer aspires to address himself to the widest possible public. A writer in a culture which adheres to a democratic ideology is confronted with a difficult choice. He can reject celebrity and accept the limitation of addressing himself to an intellectual or cultural elite, but, in doing so, he must confront the ambiguous fate of an elitist creator in a democratic society. If he seeks to write for the mass of the people, he will almost invariably find himself caught up in the machinery of celebrity.

By contrast, in the first two decades of the nineteenth century writers seem less concerned with literary celebrity. Apparently, no established set of mechanisms for generating and purveying the writer as a person-performer existed. Instead, the relationship between the writer and his public followed the more traditional pattern of the community of taste and interest between an educated, aristocratic public and the writers it patronized and supported. In such a system the writer was known and respected primarily through his works and these were widely known in the limited circle to which he addressed himself. In addition, the writer had a strong sense of contact with his audience, not only because the audience knew and reacted to his work in personal exchanges, but also because he felt himself to be a member of the elite group which constituted his public. This pattern still prevailed at the time of Washington Irving, and must, in many ways, have shaped his elegant, educated style, the witty sophistication of his rhetoric, and the European flavor of his form and content.

However, in the first half of the nineteenth century many changes in the artistic situation came together to make the writer's celebrity an increasingly important issue. Increasing literacy, the greater cheapness of books and periodicals through new printing technologies, and the ideological emphasis of a democratic culture greatly increased the size and diversity of the writer's public, until, by mid-century, writers no longer felt themselves to be in any sense the spokesmen for a coherent, educated, and sophisticated elite. This generated a need for new forms of mediation between the writer and the large public. Furthermore, the wider circulation of books and periodicals led to the emergence of new attitudes on the part of publishers which made the catering to broader public tastes and interests an ever stronger economic imperative. The enormous success of writers like Scott, Cooper, and Dickens made it clear that a writer could appeal to the mass public without compromising his own artistic aspirations and interests. At the same time, the more successful he became with the general public, the more pressure there was on the writer to become a celebrity. Scott generally chose to stay out of the public eye and confine himself to his novels and poetry. Since he lived a very private life and did not travel to America, there was little chance for him to be known outside of his works. Cooper, however, was drawn into political commentary and even, to some extent, into politics. In prose writings like *Notions of the Americans* and *The American Democrat*, and in many of his later fictions such as the "Littlepage" series and *The Monikins*, we see him seeking to address his public—albeit not as successfully as in his Leatherstocking Tales—as a person with opinions on morals, politics, and society. Of course, most of these opinions ran sufficiently counter to the general trend of public attitudes that Cooper failed to become the kind of amazing celebrity that Dickens did as a consequence of his notorious American tour in the early 1840s. Dickens was one of the first to develop a primary form of modern celebrity: the writer as a spokesman of the common sense and basic goodness of the mass of the people, a role that has declined, but still exists in part in such present-day best-selling author-celebrities as Irving Wallace and Harold Robbins. Dickens had already become such a celebrity by the time he came to America so that his tour evoked an outpouring of broad public interest similar to that which greeted his countrymen, the Beatles, when they first came to America. The vast American outrage against Dickens' criticisms of America in the *American Notes* and *Martin Chuzzlewit* indicated the degree to which the public viewed Dickens as a symbolic person.

Another important model of the writer as celebrity to make its impact in this period was created around Lord Byron. The Byronic celebrity embodied a number of themes that would be of major importance in the later nineteenth and twentieth centuries. The components of the Byronic person-performer show in rather marvelous fashion that combination of high good fortune and transgression that we have seen as so characteristic of one important variety of celebrity. Of aristocratic lineage and enormous poetic gifts, Byron possessed those larger-than-life qualities which could become a dramatic object of public admiration. His youthful success as a poet served to enhance the celebrity potential of his birth and abilities, and, of course, he also possessed another characteristic that would be of importance in an age increasingly devoted to the pictoral and photographic representation of its public figures, great handsomeness of a sort highly appropriate to his role. Yet Byron's greatest celebrity developed as he became known for his rebellious political sentiments and actions and for his private life with its rich and complex erotic transgressions. Thus, Byron pioneered that basic celebrity image of the writer as political radical and moral rebel which would become one basic pattern of artistic celebrity in Europe and America.

Apparently, the Byronic image proved too radical for most nineteenth-century American writers, though its potential was evident in the posthumous celebrity accorded Edgar Allan Poe. A few minor figures, such as Fitz-James O'Brien, seemingly attempted to perform a version of the Byronic role, but without great success. The initial failure of the Byronic role as a celebrity model for Americans probably reflected a strong feeling on the part of both public and writers in the nineteenth century that American art should be moral and affirmative, the proper expression for a new democratic society. In Poe's case, as in Byron's, an early and tragic death perhaps enabled a public that cherished its moral principles to allow itself to be fascinated by the creative transgressor.

The problem of celebrity had become a serious difficulty for many writers by the 1840s and 1850s, to judge from the ruminations and perplexities of Hawthorne and Melville. Both achieved some minor celebrity as a result of the popularity of their earlier works, yet, in mid-career, both apparently endured the sense of having lost touch with the wider public and had to suffer the frustration of seeing writers they judged vastly inferior gain much wider celebrity. It is difficult to estimate the extent to which Hawthorne's disgust at the "damned mob of scribbling women" who had become the most celebrated novelists of the 1850s was a factor in the artistic difficulties he encountered in his later career. It would also be a vast oversimplification to claim that the failure to achieve a satisfying response from the larger public was solely responsible for Melville's gradual abandonment of the art of fiction. Yet, I am sure that a more careful examination of the careers of these two writers in relation to the roles and mechanism of celebrity available to them would show the failure of effective celebrity as an important factor in the shaping of their later careers.

By the end of the nineteenth century, the basic processes of literary celebrity had become well established: the personal tour with readings to audiences all over the country (Mark Twain, Artemus Ward, and other humorists were particularly successful at this), the interviews with reporters, the published accounts of "visits to the homes of great

authors" by cultural journalists like Elbert Hubbard, a proliferation of
reviewers and cultural gossip columnists, the tendency of writers to
establish themselves as public figures through regular columns, like
William Dean Howells, and other journalistic enterprises, such as those
by Stephen Crane, Frank Norris and Theodore Dreiser. These practices
would be intensified and further developed in the twentieth century
through the new media of broadcasting, which gave writers many more
opportunities to speak in their person to a broad public. In addition,
writers in the second half of the nineteenth century had tried out a
variety of new public roles: that of the poet-philosopher of democracy
and democratic culture along the lines of Emerson and Whitman; that of
the comic sage and commentator as developed by Ward, Nasby, Twain
and other later nineteenth-century satirists and comic writers; and that of
the genteel man of letters, a more traditional role elaborated after the
Civil War by men like Edmund C. Stedman, Richard Watson Gilder,
and William Dean Howells. The model of the democratic poet-prophet
had great attraction for critics and intellectuals and, in the early
twentieth century, was strongly advocated by Van Wyck Brooks and
other critics as the proper persona for American writers. It was never
very appealing to the public as a whole, however. Whitman had his
dedicated followers and disciples, but certainly did not become a poet
for the masses and a literary celebrity until, ironically, the twentieth
century had transformed him into an American classic. Emerson was
much more successful as a celebrity than Whitman in the nineteenth
century, but this was probably because Emerson's public figure also
embodied many elements of the traditional man of letters. This pattern
continued to be elaborated in the later nineteenth century. The idea of
the writer as spokesman for cultivated taste, responsible social and
political opinion, and uplifting sentiment continued to be the most
successful pattern for literary celebrity. In this period, Longfellow was
apparently the general public's favorite image of the poet, while that
group of men of letters anatomized by the writers and critics of the early
twentieth century as the genteel tradition, were, apart from the comic
performers, the nation's most important literary celebrities.

Yet, there were evidently severe limitations to the role of man of
letters. His audience was still a relatively small elite of educated readers,
subscribers to such cultivated periodicals as the *Atlantic, Harper's,* the
Nation, and the *North American Review.* The possibility of reaching a
wider public, such as the mass audience cultivated successfully by
Twain and by the popular writers of best-sellers like E. P. Roe, must
have tantalized Howells and James. Howells' move from Boston to New
York, from the center of genteel culture to the center of commercial

culture, and his increasing involvement in political and social causes in the 1880s and 1890s, was probably motivated in part by a desire to reach out from what he had come to feel as the restrictions of the genteel tradition to larger concerns and a broader public. The massive criticism which greeted Howells' courageous espousal of the Haymarket defendants certainly illustrated the degree to which the respectable public had cast the man of letters in a conservative or politically neutral role and resented his becoming a spokesman for unpopular or controversial causes. Yet his involvement in such controversial issues gained for Howells a broader national celebrity and helped create a model of the writer as social critic and reformer which many twentieth-century Americans would adopt.

Henry James's career suggests another set of insights into the ambiguities of literary celebrity. In his earlier novels and stories James had modelled his work sufficiently on prevailing popular conventions to become a highly successful young writer, while his work as critic and reviewer was beginning to establish a place for him within the ranks of leading men of letters. Like Howells, he set out in the 1880s to write the sort of panoramic social novel with contemporary political and social themes which seemed to reflect the new literary interests of the public. But he failed. *The Princess Casamassima* and *The Bostonians* did not succeed with the larger public and James's early potential as a literary celebrity faded. His response was ambiguous. On the one hand, he evidently accepted his separation from America and from the mass public and turned himself increasingly to the kind of complex psychological fiction for which his interests and artistry were most suitable. On the other hand, the lure of becoming a great public success still attracted him. Many of his tales of the 1880s deal with the ironic relationship between artistry and celebrity. In the early 1890s, apparently concluding that he could no longer write the kind of fiction which would appeal to the large public, he turned to the drama, hoping to reestablish connection with a larger audience through a different medium. He failed at this, too, of course, and by this time was evidently ready to cast aside the dream of celebrity and write his remaining masterpieces in a way that would please only himself and his small circle of readers. James's experience indicated both how important celebrity had become for the late nineteenth-century American writer, and how complex an impact the quest for celebrity could have even on the work of a creator so greatly gifted and artistically independent.

The twentieth century has brought with it a proliferation of the possibilities for artistic celebrity, as well as an intensification of its pressures. The development of film, radio, and television has made it possible for the writer to reach an even larger public than he could in the nineteenth century. Though book sales of more than a million are extraordinary, movies and television commonly have audiences of 20-40 million. A writer whose work is adapted into a popular film or television program can become an international celebrity overnight. One can think of many obscure writers suddenly catapulted into great celebrity by a highly successful film: Margaret Mitchell and *Gone with the Wind*, James Jones and *From Here to Eternity*, Mario Puzo and *The Godfather*. Even dead authors can become posthumous celebrities, as in the case of F. Scott Fitzgerald, where the *éclat* of a new film version of *The Great Gatsby* was accompanied by many new publications offering personal revelations about the author and his life. But the newer media have also proved to be a rather mixed blessing for writers. The collective nature of film and television production forces the writer into association with directors, actors, producers and technical people, making it nearly impossible for him to have any effective creative control over the final product. In addition, the organization of film and television production in America has tended to place the writer in a subsidiary position to the producer and the stars with the producer making the final artistic decisions and the audience likely to perceive the work primarily as the creation of its leading actors. The writer who becomes involved in film and television thus finds himself in a new and frustrating kind of anonymity. Some version of his work may be seen by millions of people, but he may be even less known to the public than a novelist whose actual readership is only in the thousands. For example, how many people recognize such names as Jules Furthman, Francis Marion, Nunnally Johnson, Robert Riskin, Sidney Buchman, Dudley Nichols, and Frank S. Nugent? Yet these were among the most successful screenwriters in the history of Hollywood and were at least partly responsible for large numbers of films.

Another important twentieth-century development in the processes of celebrity has been the increasing visibility of a celebrity society, a cultural elite which brings together certain members of the traditional aristocracy of wealth and high social position with certain individuals from the political, artistic, and mass communications spheres of society. The comings and goings of this celebrity elite, which used to be known as "cafe society" and is now referred to as "the jet set" or "the beautiful people," are extensively reported in newspapers and magazines. The group furnishes an inordinate proportion of the guests on major television talk shows and is the main object of gossip columns. Public interest in the lives and personalities of the celebrity elite intensifies fascination with the writers and artists who become associated with the group. Not only their own creative accomplishments, but their connection with the celebrity elite has made national figures of writers like Truman Capote and Gore Vidal, artists like Andy Warhol, and musicians like Leonard Bernstein.

But perhaps the most interesting twentieth-century development in the relationship between celebrity and literature has been the use by a number of major writers of their celebrity personas as an integral part of their art. One of the instances of this development is Ernest Hemingway; another is Norman Mailer. After his initial success as a writer had established his literary importance, Hemingway began in the early 1930s to create the celebrity figure of "Papa." Through his hunting exploits, his non-fiction reportage, his dramatic adventure, his position as a war correspondant in Spain and during World War II, and his association with members of the celebrity elite, Hemingway created a public persona which was in many ways a real-life version of some of the central characters of his novels. This figure had enormous appeal and influence and made Hemingway well known among a much wider public than those familiar with his novels. Indeed, the Hemingway persona of "Papa" was so attractive and compelling that it eventually began to eclipse those other sides of Hemingway which had also been a part of his greatest novels and stories. Certainly much of the later fiction, including *Across the River and into the Trees* and *Islands in the Stream*, are less humanly complex and powerful than the earlier masterpieces because the protagonist has become that larger-than-life stoic hero, that master of violence and scorner of death, who peers out at us from the pages of *Life Magazine*, instead of the tragically limited but artistically more powerful figures of Jake Barnes, Nick Adams, and Frederic Henry. It is tempting to say that in his later life, most of Hemingway's creative energy went into the creation of his celebrity persona, but that while brilliant as a public performance, this persona was insufficient to the demands of great fiction.

Mailer's case is somewhat different, for beginning with *Advertisements for Myself* he has quite consciously sought to make his personal celebrity directly into art and has found a form appropriate to this intention. Unlike Hemingway, who lived out to the end an ambiguous conflict between celebrity and art, Mailer has managed to integrate the two by making his public performances themselves into a kind of artistic exploration and then by writing about them in a quasi-journalistic form in which the protagonist as celebrity plays the central role. Mailer's open assimilation of his role as artist into his celebrity persona is certainly one solution to the problematic modern tension between the writer as artist and as celebrity, though probably not one that many novelists will choose or be able to adopt.

It is probably the case, however, that the intense pressures toward publicity of the twentieth century, and the emergence of writers for whom celebrity has become in different ways the center of their art, have made writers in general more conscious of the problem of celebrity and of its potentially deleterious effect on their work. A number of important contemporary writers, Saul Bellow, J. D. Salinger, and Thomas Pynchon prominent among them, have decisively rejected the role of celebrity and insisted on being known wholly through their works. Ironically, it turned out that the role of mysterious recluse adopted by Salinger and Pynchon had a great celebrity potential and very probably played a role in the large popularity of these writers. Bellow has been much more moderate in his seclusion, but by staying away from the literary and celebrity centers of New York and the West Coast, and by rejecting most of the many temptations offered him to appear on television, to make public appearances, or to comment on contemporary affairs outside of his fiction, he has stayed largely outside of the sphere of celebrity. It is perhaps significant that unlike so many American writers who have found themselves entrapped in the ambiguities of celebrity, Bellow's production and artistry have continued unabated well into his middle years.

Celebrity is so complex and in many ways so irrational that we may never fully understand it, but I will offer at least a few tentative speculations about the causes of the phenomenon. First, as compared to the length and complexity of a work, there is something immediately and more directly communicative about the image of a person. It may take hours to read a novel while one can receive a sense of a person in seconds. Reading a novel is a considerable task, but to watch a writer on a television talk show seems effortless. The personal image thus seems more intense and simpler in its impact than the printed page. The great importance of performance in almost all areas of popular culture bears out these observations. Most forms of popular culture involve some kind of person, an actor or star, mediating between the linguistic material and the audience. All the modern media of mass communications (movies, radio, television) are strongly oriented toward personalities and performance and the distinctive forms these media have developed in America such as the star vehicle, the talk show, the personally hosted news broadcast, etc., have intensified the personal quality to the degree that this seems to us nearly inherent in these media.

If we ask further why the performer-person is so important in popular culture we encounter two primary functions which I will generalize as the interpretive and the representative. As interpreter, the performer directs our attention and helps us to understand and respond to what he is saying by adding to his words the impact of tone of voice, look, and gesture. The news show host is a trusted authority who gives us the impression that we know and have the proper response to the truly significant events that are going on in the world. By extension, the writer as celebrity gives us an interpretation of his work by telling us about himself, his hopes, his background, or his literary intentions. Or by his own actions, he provides us with grounds for a more intense and immediate response to his work. Along these lines, many best sellers succeed because the book is based on historical incidents and persons we already recognize as important. The memoirs of important or notorious political leaders are often best-sellers and if these leaders have been involved in a celebrated scandal like Watergate, the resultant literary popularity is usually immense. Such possibilities are rare for the writer of fiction who does not ordinarily act in a public capacity, though several recent politicians, including John Erlichman, Spiro Agnew, and John Lindsay, have been persuaded to capitalize on their established celebrity by becoming authors of fictional thrillers. In these cases, the public's response to the literary work is intensified by the impression that these writers have a unique personal authority for the underlying reality of their stories. One of the most important aspects of interpretation has always been to establish what is "real" about a story and thereby to intensify our response to it. Here that function is carried out by the personal celebrity of the author.

Such considerations cannot be fully separated from the important representative functions of the person-performer. One such function is, if not simple, at least clear and obvious. The person-performer represents us; he stands in for us and plays the role we would play or would like to play at the event. The television talk show host interviews celebrities for us, asking the questions we would want to ask of them. The news commentator helps us to feel that we are present at significant events. The star of an adventure film or drama provides a center of identification, giving us the opportunity to share vicariously in the action. Celebrities are our stand-ins at important events, and the author, playing the role of celebrity, helps to guarantee and reinforce his position as our witness of contemporary reality. In addition, he represents the significance of his book and through his public comments we can share in some of the excitement accompanying its publication. Through the author's performance as a celebrity, we stand-in at the birth of an important literary work.

But there is also another representative function of the celebrity which goes beyond enabling our vicarious presence at significant moments. The celebrity also becomes a quasi-mythical figure in the sense that he symbolizes patterns of aspiration and value, positive and negative, and frequently both. Indeed, I might hazard the guess that many fascinating celebrities gain their position precisely to the degree that they embody conflicts of value and aspiration. This certainly seems to be the case with criminal celebrities, who comprise one of the most important categories of person-performer for modern democratic publics. The criminal seems to embody at once a fascination with forbidden and lawless deeds and a commitment to a society of laws and limits. Our interest in the criminal seems to be evoked in proportion to the significance of his crime and the apparent respectability of his background. Patty Hearst has been an ideal celebrity. Not only was she a young girl and a rich one at that, the heiress of all the ages, but her crimes symbolized a basic rejection of the society which had apparently offered her all a person could want. Such ambiguities are the essence of celebrity in its mythical function.

Not all celebrity is of this sort. There are simpler, less ambiguous figures—athletic victors, people of great wealth, men of power, etc.—but surely the most striking celebrities are those who manifest some kind of paradox or transgression: Howard Hughes, the reclusive millionaire; Marilyn Monroe, the baby-faced sex queen; Jackie Kennedy, the dark widow of the New Frontier; Henry Kissinger, the swinging diplomat. The reason for this may be that while the celebrity as mythical figure must embody some power or position or action that is larger than life, we are most deeply moved by those who also take upon themselves some of the tragedy and limitation of ordinary human beings, who live out for us our aspiration to immortal power and our sense of mortality. In sum, the true celebrity is a human creation of great power and complexity, which approximates in some ways the great mythical figures of ancient times.

Because of its complex significance, the role of celebrity is fraught with difficulties for the creative writer. The energy and emotional investment he gives to playing the role of person-performer inevitably detract from what he can give to his proper work. Should he fail to achieve a significant celebrity, the result can be greatly damaging to his ego and thus a threat to his very ability to create. If he succeeds, he faces the additional danger of being swallowed up into the myth of his celebrity, of becoming the simplified persona of his public legend. The complexity and importance of the phenomenon of literary celebrity and its influence on nineteenth and twentieth-century American writers suggest that a careful and thorough investigation of this problem would yield some important insights into the development of both individual writers and American literature as a whole.

A Conversation in Boston

James Nagel
Northeastern University

Throughout "American Fiction: A Bicentennial Symposium," in addition to the formal reading of papers, there was a continuing discussion generated by the essays and developed by members of the audience as well as the speakers. This dialogue took varying directions, theoretical, hermeneutic, historical, but always it touched on an assessment of the role of fiction in American cultural life in the context of the national Bicentennial celebration.

As the continuing dialogue grew and began to focus on central issues, it became evident that the brief exchanges following papers were not adequate to a full exploration of significant critical points, and we agreed to conclude the program with a period devoted exclusively to conversation among the speakers and interaction with members of the audience. When recorded on tape, the discussion periods of the Symposium ran for nearly six hours; as a result, what follows is a representative rather than exhaustive account. The official participants in the dialogue are all identified by their last names: these include Harrison T. Meserole, Milton R. Stern, Joseph Katz, Donald Pizer, Linda W. Wagner, Melvin J. Friedman, Ronald Sukenick, Darwin T. Turner, Daniel Aaron, Viola Hopkins Winner, John Cawelti, and the Director of the Symposium, James Nagel. Contributions by the audience are indicated as "Comment" or "Question."

As even this abbreviated record indicates, the responses to the papers were not simple encomiums to American fiction but rather a reflective discussion of its contributions to American life, its record as a field of analytical enquiry, and the extent to which it reflects the ethnic multiplicity and richness of American society. There was some concern with the origins of fiction in America and the extent to which the new status of nationality following the Revolutionary War had modified its components. There was a corresponding interest in the effects of the Civil War on fiction, on the participation of a new level of society in the nation's literature as readers of magazines and, increasingly, as writers, and on a new frankness in the novel, especially about erotic concerns. Another continuing topic was the intellectual justification of sustaining historical and critical categories which organize but simplify the complex pattern of literary development. Naturalism, Realism,

Impressionism, Modernism, Feminist Criticism, Black Fiction, Jewish literature, and Regional influence, especially Southern fiction, were all explored, as well as the aesthetic concerns of style and narrative voice. The participation of the reading public in creating mythic figures of American writers was given some analysis, in addition to the impact of the commercial interests of publishing houses on the type of literature which gets printed and continues to be available. No abbreviated account of this dialogue can fully represent the depth and richness it developed nor even suggest its sustained civility of tone, even when addressing controversial subjects, but it does seem entirely in keeping with the conception of "symposium" to attempt to represent something of the range and nature of this conversation.

Nagel: Perhaps in this concluding session of the Symposium there might be some value for all of us in attempting to clarify issues that have been raised in the papers, in asking further questions, and making some attempt, surely ultimately unsuccessful, to synthesize points of view and reconcile differing assumptions. Let me suggest as a structure that we begin by posing specific questions for individuals and conclude, perhaps, with some general questions about the growth and significance of American fiction.

Question: Professor Meserole, what was the first American novel?

Meserole: Well, there are several candidates. I suppose William Hill Brown's *The Power of Sympathy* is usually the one named. There are a couple of others earlier, but there is a question as to whether they are "novels."

Question: A great number of English novels were published and sold in the colonies and yet it took thirty or forty years before an American wrote a novel. Why is that?

Meserole: I think there are several reasons. First of all, it was much cheaper for publishers in America to publish an English novel since they didn't have to pay any royalties. By the way, they had to pay Rebecca Rush a hundred dollars for *Kelroy*, which was quite a sum in 1812. Of course, while there were no Americans writing novels when *Pamela* was published, this is not to say there was not the fictive instinct. Mary Rowlandson's "Captivity" narrative in the seventeenth century is full of fictive elements. There's an Indian who treats her well, she says: he even gives her a cold horse's hoof to gnaw on. And she writes imaginatively and observantly in her descriptive passages. There is "fictiveness" there. But no one was writing fiction in America until after mid-eighteenth century.

Question: I was just wondering why Early American scholars emphasize papers and journals but not the early attempts at fiction?

Meserole: First, there are so many good ones, and they represent major genres of the period. Second, they are available in modern editions that we can use in class. Recently I had to put together a reading list for a course in Early American Fiction, and it was hard to do. Consequently, one of the arguments in my essay is that we need to do some reassessment of early novels. *Kelroy* reads very well. Sure, there are odd things in it from a critical standpoint, but if you read widely in the period, and you know the kind of style you have to struggle with, to come upon Rebecca Rush is like waking to a bright spring morning; there is no gushing, no effulgence. She is witty: she has the greengrocer say "Dammit, I want my money!" in 1812, in an American novel. That's rare. There is only one place in this novel where she does the typical early-nineteenth-century trick of removing all the names and ending up with a letter and dashes. Mr. Walsingham's family is somehow related to the Duke of G____. Everything else is quite modern. And Mrs. Hammond is a genuine villain. I've been asking colleagues over the last couple of months whom they would name in American fiction as the consummate female villain, and I haven't gotten an answer.

Nagel: Professor Meserole is a valuable resource in our discussion for a number of reasons, one of which is that his scholarly interests span the period from the earliest Colonial American literature to the early fiction of the half-century or so following the American Revolutionary War. I would welcome some reflections as to what extent we can identify and describe a transition in American literature brought about by the new status of "nationality." Is there anything in early American fiction that distinguishes it generically or thematically from American literature preceding the Revolutionary War?

Meserole: One thing comes to mind immediately: beginning in about 1780, the cry began for a national literature: "Where are our

American novels?" "Who are our best American poets?"
"Why can't we read American poets?" And the answers
came in floods of bad poetry, worse fiction, and some
unbelievable plays.

Second, much criticism in early nineteenth-century
magazines uses as a touchstone: Is it American? If a story
contains an American setting, American hero, American
heroine, it is good. One of these early men was Theodore
Sedgwick Fay, who has the longest period of productivity of
any man in American literature: he published his first essay in
1823 in the *New-York Mirror* and his last book in 1889, and
from beginning to end they were terrible. Poe found that out
early: he tore apart a novel by Fay, calling it "the most
inestimable piece of balderdash with which the common
sense of the good people of America was ever so openly or so
villainously insulted." Whereupon Fay took umbrage and
wrote an essay called "The Successful Novel!!" in which Poe
is called "Bulldog." Poe demolished that one too, and then
wrote such a complete excoriation that Fay retired from the
arena. Criticism, much of the time, was puffery, and this,
too, distinguishes what was written after the Revolution
from what was written before.

Question: I wonder if you would say something about the definition
and sources of evil in early American literature? What
conventions are there in presenting a negative
characterization?

Meserole: In this novel, *Kelroy*, Mrs. Rush has put into Mrs. Hammond's mouth (appropriately, because she is a real "Tartar")
the rejection of someone's suitor by saying "I would rather
she marry a Turk or a Jew!" On the same subject, at the very
end of the novel, as a kind of light touch, Mrs. Rush
introduces a Frenchman, a rotund little fellow with a ready
lip who opens his heart to Emily, says Mrs. Hammond, "In
the way that most of his race does."

What makes them evil? I think one thing certainly: the
maintaining of invidious social distinctions makes them evil.
In this novel, particularly, those who do only the "proper"
thing at tea parties and sneer at the less fortunate are almost
always shown up by Dr. Blake, who runs around peering
into ladies' decolletages and spilling coffee on them. These
shallow social distinctions, being thoughtless, being unkind

to people, make them evil. And having knowledge of something mysterious, as with the elder Wieland, who disappears in a cloud of fire and smoke, can suggest evil because it hints of Satan's presence. Even Carwin's special talent ("biloquism") suggests evil, as does the fact that we don't know much about his background.

Question: Professor Stern, could you propose some distinctions for us between Romantic and contemporary fiction in terms of verisimilitude in the same way you might establish distinctions between the tale and the sketch? Perhaps you might use landscape as a point of reference.

Stern: I don't know that I can distinguish between the tale and the sketch entirely in terms of verisimilitude. I'm not sure I know what kind of critical language I can use which will allow me to distinguish between the landscape of contemporary fiction and the tale landscape of romantic fiction. In both cases you get a departure from what Don Pizer and Joe Katz would talk about when they're talking about Realism, but obviously the intentions are so very different. One cannot talk about the landscape with which Ralph Ellison takes you underground in the same sense that you could talk about the subterranean passage in the romantic tale, because clearly the intention there is a highly realistic intention, a very realistic intention. I came through the New Critical Mill and still bear some "internal differences where the meanings are," as Dickinson put it, so that I'm still afraid of talking about intention, and the proof of it for me is that we have not developed any kind of critical terminology which will really allow us to talk about this crucial difference that your question requires. One way to make the distinction your question points at is that the subliminated purposes of the "unreal landscape" of the romantic tale generally tended to be sexual; and I think the subliminated purposes of the "unreal landscape" in modern fiction tend to be political. Beyond that kind of beginning generalization, about which one could build all kinds of arguments, I don't have a language that allows me to really meet your point.

Question: Professor Katz, how do you explain the fact that Mencken, who was close to Realistic conventions, didn't understand them and didn't think highly of a writer like Dreiser?

Katz: Interestingly enough, about the time Mencken was writing the "Puritanism as a Literary Force" essay, he and Dreiser

were having a little set-to. *The Genius* had been banned and
Dreiser was running around trying to drum up signatures for
a petition, and he asked for Mencken's support. Mencken
finally wrote Dreiser an extremely blunt letter. I will have to
paraphrase it. He said "Dreiser, what do you expect? There
are lots of things that we say to each other that you can't put
in print."

Nagel: I'd like Professor Katz to comment on the extent to which
fiction in America after the Civil War was uniquely
representative of "United States" culture as opposed to
European culture and the extent to which "regional"
concerns began to become "national" concerns in the period
after the Civil War.

Katz: The Civil War was very important; it was, in many ways, an
illegal war. But decisions made as a result of it determined
that this would be a United States of America instead of a
group of individual states, loosely confederated. One result
was industrialism, which made possible greater communication and which open up isolated pockets of literary and
cultural experience in this country. During the period after
the Civil War there are writers drawn from the social classes
that traditionally did not supply literary people. There is a
"melting" that at first becomes an expression of local concern
but then infuses into the mainstream. I think this is the point
at which we begin to have a distinctly "American" literature.

Question: I'm interested in your explorations of eroticism during this
period but I'm wondering why you did not include Kate
Chopin in your remarks?

Katz: The reason for omitting her is an embarrassingly practical
one. At some point I realized I was covering a lot of ground
with a very small shovel and I felt that a group of things had
to go. I do find that she's within this stream but she was
simply omitted for practical reasons.

Aaron: Am I right in assuming that you feel sexual matters are
handled more emotionally and more interestingly by
Howells and by DeForest than by Dreiser?

Katz: Yes.

Aaron: I was interested in this question about Mencken because he
was pretty close to someone like Mark Twain; he had no
more sensitive feeling for sexual subjects than Mark Twain
did.

Katz: One of the interesting things to me is that beneath all the apparent placidity in the Realistic period, there's a hell of a lot going on. But the word "balance" is for me a key word here. You do it so long as you're not vulgar. Twain, in a scatalogical piece such as "1601," is not at all delicate or sensitive—he's not that kind of writer. He couldn't get away with it. On the other hand, nowhere is there in Crane's *Maggie: A Girl of the Streets* primary evidence that she is a prostitute, but, of course, she is. There's no way of escaping that recognition if we're in tune with the cultural conventions, and we, even now, are. So the broad kind of writer— Twain, Mencken, Dreiser, for example—I doubt could have written for a good publisher in 1890-1895. The timing was wrong.

Question: I'm wondering to what extent Crane is moving to actively create a system of pornographic literature?

Katz: To a very great extent he was depending on a knowledge of the conventions. Furthermore, it was not only a tradition of pornography but also a tradition of what I suppose is the equal but opposite of it, the moralistic tract. He takes this framework of the factory girl seduced, who falls, is cast out by her respectable family, has nothing at all to turn to and at the end there is the river.

Question: Do you think that Howells feels that the exploration of erotic subjects in literature is proper?

Katz: I know there are some stories, including a short story called "Editha," that seem to verge on sexual topics.

Nagel: Perhaps I can ask Professor Pizer for a clarification that might help relate his essay to the paper by Professor Katz. As I understand the early pages of your essay, the contention is that the restriction of Naturalistic themes to pessimistic determinism unnecessarily constricts and sharpens our interpretation of American Naturalism, and that other themes and other kinds of concepts ought to be admitted and examined as part of the Naturalistic stream. If we accept that contention, where are the distinctions between this expanded Naturalism and American Realism?

Pizer: Well, first let me clarify the direction of the early section of the essay. Actually, I'm not saying so much that we should not look at pessimistic determinism or any other philosophical angle traditionally taken in looking at Naturalism, but that we have been guilty in the past of adopting a very negative initial attitude, a predisposition to see any traces of this particular philosophy, or anything resembling it, as a detriment and as weakening the writer. So the thrust of the opening section was to suggest a need for a fresh view of the fictional qualities of this particular aspect of Naturalistic fiction. As far as the second part of your question is concerned, the very presence of this quality of pessimistic determinism is a distinguishing characteristic that one finds in Naturalism. I believe some years ago Sydney Krause edited a collection called *Essays on Determinism in American Literature* in which the essayists found it throughout American literature; but it is a more dominant element in the very end of the late nineteenth century.

Meserole: I'd like to ask whether you think the critic who objected so strongly to Naturalism objected to it because as a result of determinism there is no concept of free will, and there is, therefore, no possibility of creative art. Is it, then, a question of form or a question of aesthetics?

Pizer: I think both have been present in those critics who begin with a very derogatory attitude towards Naturalism. On the one hand determinism does deny to a certain extent the creative imagination, but on the other hand, the work before one—let's say *McTeague* or *An American Tragedy*—is a literary work which objectifies its author's creative imagination. The second is perhaps the more important difficulty among many critics of Naturalism, that is, if one denies the character choice—whether conscious or unconscious—one seems to limit the range of fiction and move it in the direction of a mechanistic pageant of events. What I'm suggesting is that this is not true, that the novelist can portray a thread of determinism in our lives along with other threads, but he can portray a thread of determinism with great power and sensitivity, and that we are at fault in *a priori* thinking that if this is present in the Naturalist frame of mind and in the fictional work itself, that it weakens and limits our interest in the writer and the work.

Aaron: I wonder how you feel about Lionel Trilling's comments against Dreiser in *The Liberal Imagination?*

Pizer: If you recall the essay, Trilling joins Dreiser and Parrington as two examples of minds supposedly devoted to the tradition of freedom in America, but themselves limited by being unreceptive to ideas, particularly ideas of the subtle kind; that they are closed minds devoted primarily to views about man which do not permit any kind of subtlety. Trilling's underlying motivation is, I think, political; that is, his objection to the acceptance by these and other figures of Marxist views of man. Trilling, in part, is fighting a literary battle within the context of the 1930s and the 1940s rather than viewing these figures in an independent way. Dreiser was the hero of the twenties and early thirties, and because of the political needs of that time—both literary politics and political politics—Dreiser was raised into a symbolic role, representing the ideal of freedom both in politics and in art. And I think Trilling is objecting to that out of a great shift of literary and political sympathies. So the essay is primarily interesting as itself illustrating a moment in American literary history rather than for any critical insight into Dreiser or Parrington.

Sukenick: To go back to Professor Meserole's question, isn't the act of creative composition a contradiction of pessimistic determinism?

Pizer: Yes, it is a contradiction in theory, but in reality we have the work there so we have to deal with that. We can, I think, indulge ourselves in being concerned with the philosophical problems that are seeming contradictions and paradoxes that arise out of the problem, but we still have the literary work there to confront.

Question: But isn't there a tension between Naturalism, as determinism, and the desire for stylistic beauty?

Pizer: There perhaps was an unresolved tension, and perhaps the lack of resolution appears in the awkwardness of prose. But I also think Dreiser just couldn't write English very well. There are many different approaches to Dreiser's prose style, and I don't think there is any one explanation of its weaknesses. But we have begun thinking of fiction in the last twenty or thirty years in terms other than the "bricks and mortar" of its prose and now also think of it in terms of its "rooms and house" as a whole. Despite the application of New Critical techniques to the reading of fiction, we do apprehend the novel in a somewhat different way than a lyric poem; we just don't read the prose that carefully or closely, and we are responding to larger units of aesthetic force than a syntactical solecism.

Question: Would you say Naturalism is a viable technique today?

Pizer: I think Naturalism is viable today if you have someone who is called a Naturalist and who writes a good novel which moves one. As far as particular novels are concerned, I think we do have continuing outbreaks of this disease which is American Naturalism, people like Mailer, Bellow, Styron. One finds compelling similarities between some of their interests, some of their techniques, and those of an earlier generation.

Question: Professor Friedman, you made the point, which has been made by other critics, that there are Jewish rhythms in *Herzog*. I was wondering if you would attempt some sort of informal demonstration of that.

Friedman: I think I'd have to have the text here in front of me. I've read *Herzog* five or six times and I continue to have that feeling. Sophie Portnoy's syntax, as perhaps another illustration of the same thing, twists and turns like a snake. Her language is barely syntactical in the classical sense. Her ruptured syntax has its own special "Jewish rhythm." Of course, Herzog himself is educated and he maintains his professional bearing with its precise speech—but some of the people who offer him advice use these "Jewish rhythms."

Aaron: Is there any audience that the post-modern writers have consciously been writing for? And how large is that audience?

Friedman: I think you have to distinguish among writers. It's obvious that Vonnegut is selling terribly well; he's a best seller. Obviously Ron Sukenick and Raymond Federman don't do as well, and that's why, of course, they've helped organize this Fiction Collective. Indeed, this is a way of maintaining integrity, of publishing for a limited audience. They don't have to put up with publishers and editors who want to rewrite their work, shorten it, change the visuality of the text. These are people who are not making a great deal of money but they've made a very strong commitment.

Sukenick: I think the answer to it is that the audience has to be created. I think that the audience will be created, partly through such gatherings as this, but as long as the books can be published, that will probably take care of itself. In fact, in a certain way I think it's a big advantage to have a small, even coterie-like, audience for a while because it allows the development of the individual writer without the interference of certain kinds of notoriety. That becomes a variable in the fact of composition which I think in some ways can be healthy and in some ways unhealthy. It's unhealthy for a young writer whose style is in the process of developing. But I think the primary question is really the rationale of this kind of writing, and I'd like to ask a question that might get onto another subject. What is the sense of Hawkes' rejection of the essential elements of conventional fiction?

Friedman: Well, I think that Hawkes has felt from the very beginning there was something that he was very unhappy about, that he was uneasy with, and he mentioned the four ingredients—plot, character, setting, and theme—which nineteenth-century novelists had thought were the essentials. I think nobody before Hawkes quite came out and said "this is devastating." If you read his first novel, there is a constant tension; he's looking for a narrative voice. He's trying to find a narrative position which he gets, finally, in *Second Skin*. I think he is worried up to that point. Afterwards, he's found his way. He does detour slightly in his latest novel, *Travesty*, with the dramatic monologue device, but I think with *Second Skin*, his best novel, he's found something that he'd been groping towards for some fifteen years.

Aaron: Isn't "place" very important in both novels?

Friedman: Well he changes "place" from novel to novel, which is interesting. He can write about Germany in *The Cannibal*, and he can write about England in *The Lime Twig*. He's constantly changing locale. I think Hawkes is telling us it doesn't matter. These circumstances work in a variety of places. I think he found his special sort of "place" with the "mythical" settings of *Second Skin* and *Blood Oranges*.

Sukenick: Can you read Price and Hawkes with the same values when they're really doing utterly different things?

Friedman: I find Price's novels overly long, perhaps too plotted. Hawkes never stops generating interest for me; I always find him exciting reading. Obviously Price and Hawkes are trying to do different things. Price agrees with Styron's *Esquire* statement that "there has to be a story"; Hawkes clearly does not.

Question: Isn't this curious that you have very good storytellers who
            are at the same time trying to break the pattern of all the
            elements of stories and this is an important element that
            creates something special in American modern anti-fiction.

Cawelti: One point that interests me is that when we first read Joyce
            and Faulkner we thought they were not telling stories. We
            discovered, after we had read them a while, that stories were
            not the same as plots, and that certain kinds of stories had to
            be told in certain ways. *The Sound and The Fury*, it seems to
            me, is a story—a fairly remarkable story—but it could not be
            told, as it turned out, in the chronological pattern. And that
            seems to me important to understand.

Nagel: Professor Winner, I was fascinated by your discussion of
            Literary Impressionism in Henry James. You mentioned
            several things: the restriction of the narrative to empirical
            data, the use of sensory imagery, synaesthesia, fragmentary,
            episodic units as the basis of fiction, and I'm wondering if
            you would comment on the extent to which you would feel
            comfortable in calling Hemingway's works Impressionistic.

Winner: I don't think I would; I think he was much closer to Cézanne
            because he really wanted something beyond what the eye
            perceives. He wanted to get into fiction another dimension:
            what is *known* to be there but without doing it in the way it
            had traditionally been done, to get away from all the literary
            associations of the past, which is what I think Cézanne was
            also trying to do. Cézanne was moving beyond Im-
            pressionism: Cézanne wasn't satisfied with just what the eye
            sees but wanted also to get "volume." I think that
            Hemingway is much closer to Cézanne, to Post-
            Impressionism, than to the Impressionistic theory and
            vision.

Nagel: So you would feel comfortable describing Hemingway as a
            "pictorialist" in the manner of Cézanne?

Winner: Yes.

Question: How did James feel about the Impressionists?

Winner: Well, James thought they were superficial; that by painting
            only what the eye sees, they excluded too much that is
            necessary for truly great art—reflection, association, moral
            and humane values. His initial response, in the 1870s, was
            negative. He understood their doctrines but didn't approve

of them. He was also put off by their technique—their visible brush strokes, their lack of "finish." Eventually, he became more sympathetic and even enthusiastic about individual painters such as Manet and Monet. His response to Whistler is typical of how he revised his earlier opinion of the Impressionists: at first, he thought his paintings were eccentric or merely decorative. Finally, he came to like Whistler very much, but not on technical grounds. He praised him for being a great "expressive" artist. In other words, James's aesthetic principles really hadn't changed but his eye had adjusted itself to what had initially seemed radically unconventional in Whistler's technique. Unfortunately, it is difficult to state with more precision what he thought about Impressionism in his late years because there is little evidence. He had written extensively on painting in reviews and essays in the 1870s and early 1880s, but after 1897 there really isn't much to go by, just a few scattered remarks.

Question: What artistic influences do you see in James's style?

Winner: His writings on art were most deeply influenced by Ruskin, but he also learned a great deal from Gautier, Stendhal, and Taine and other French writers.

Meserole: Professor Cawelti, there is another dimension of "celebrity" and "fame" in nineteenth-century American literature that you didn't mention: the various clubs. There was a Dickens Club, a Thackeray Club, a Browning Club, and others.

Cawelti: Yes, the clubs are interesting because they're just like the fan clubs, the Beatles Fan Club, and the Elvis Presley Fan Club. But there's a point at which what is the traditional form of relationship between writer and public gives way to this new form, and the new form becomes more and more intensified throughout the nineteenth century, particularly with the enormous proliferation of literary marketing and the technology for mass production of literary products.

Meserole: Well, it is somewhat different; with the Beatles Fan Club you can be sure that they have all heard the Beatles records, but there's no guarantee that in the early nineteenth-century Browning society, the Thackeray Society, the Dickens Society, the members read all of Thackeray, Browning, and Dickens. They talked about everything that had to do with Dickens, except the books.

Cawelti: That's really true of Beatle Fan Clubs, too. They gather
            material about the person more than about the works, and
            they're more interested in the intricacies of the details about
            who's married to whom than they are in the music. At least
            that's my impression.

Nagel: I'm interested in a clarification of the distinction between
            celebrity and fame. As I understood it, celebrity was a short-
            lived phenomenon, and yet in the example of Hemingway
            that you give, it is now the continuing celebrity that
            interferes, to some extent, with his fame.

Cawelti: Yes, but I suggested there was a third case, Jim, where
            celebrity comes to take on that representative mythical
            function, and that mythical function is rich enough that it can
            become the stuff of legend. Then I think something like
            celebrity is transposed into fame and becomes long-lasting.
            And I think that's what we may be seeing happening with a
            character like Hemingway. Certainly with Poe that happen-
            ed and his life became a legend.

Question: Don't some literary critics develop their own brand of
            celebrity?

Cawelti: There is an analogy between that and the popular music
            business in the disc jockey. The disk jockey presents, is the
            mediator between, the music and the audience and can very
            often become a celebrity in his own right. Dick Clark, for
            example, became a great celebrity during the rock period.
            That kind of mediation is analogous to the kind of critical
            notoriety that you suggest. But the whole problem you raise
            is that the system of mediation between readers and works
            is an area that we have not, as literary people, sufficiently
            explored and it is very complex and interesting. And
            celebrity is only one of a considerable variety of such
            mechanisms that I would, personally, like to understand
            better.

Question: Can a writer deliberately set out to become a celebrity?

Cawelti: Well, I think all one can say is that the creation of celebrity is
            largely *ex post facto:* it's very difficult to set down the rules
            for its creation ahead of time. One can make guesses about
            how it came about but celebrities get created in an
            extraordinary variety of ways, and about the only way you
            know the celebrity has been created is when people start

following him, and then once you have that you can begin to speculate about why it is. In T. E. Lawrence's case, of course, he was already a considerable celebrity before Lowell Thomas took over. And the public relations industry has attempted to bureaucratize the practice of celebrity and they have been, to some extent, successful. But the kind of celebrity we're talking about is a bigger thing than that, and I don't think that it can solely be manipulated.

Katz: Do you think it would be useful to make a distinction between celebrity and notoriety?

Cawelti: I think it could very well be an extremely useful distinction. When people recognize something as "notorious," they shy away from it. But it gets more complicated when you look at a case like Patricia Hearst, where there are clearly some people who treat her as a celebrity and others who treat her as notorious. I see these kids that go around with buttons of Patricia Hearst pictures; that's a form of celebration, not the fascination with notoriety. But it is, I think, a good distinction.

Comment: I'd like to add something to your thoughts about celebrity. Jacqueline Susann, who definitely sets out to write to make money, succeeded by selling all of her novels and making films of her novels and achieved a notoriety and I think also celebrity.

Cawelti: I don't know that I'd add anything to what you say; I have somewhat more respect for the function of this kind of writer than you do. That is, I think that it is a possibly responsible role for a writer to undertake to address a very large public and to try to bring to them a general decency of common sense about contemporary problems. I have a great deal of respect for Irving Wallace who is in that same category and who takes his responsibilities very seriously in this respect, and I would differentiate him from Susann and Harold Robbins, who have been equally successful in terms of sales.

Comment: But the quality of Wallace's writing is extremely good.

Cawelti: Well, I don't know about the quality of his writing, but the quality of his mind and intentions is certainly high.

Question: Professor Aaron, would you comment on the extent to which critical sophistication is an artistic advantage for an occasional novelist such as Edmund Wilson?

Aaron: Well, Wilson right from the start, from the time he could put pen to paper, was fascinated by fiction, fascinated by illusions and magic. He was writing stories and criticism of stories and was enormously interested in the theater even as a young boy. Even his early letters show a kind of feeling for structure and for planting interesting detail to bring the letter to a highly literary consciousness. And I think if he had devoted himself entirely to fiction, he could have become an extremely interesting writer. He always thought very well of his own fiction; he thought that *Memoirs of Hecate County* was his best work. He also thought of himself as a considerable playwright. For somebody like Wilson, for example, Shaw and Ibsen were tremendously important, because their ideas were not only integrated into their plays but they also had a life of their own. He saw the artist as a shaper and doer and maker, as an influence. In this respect his views coincided with the long American tradition of the writer and artist as lay preacher in a society that distrusted the intellect.

   The first really important reading for almost all of the writers that I've been talking about was European, not American. Some of them came to American literature quite late. The American writer Wilson was most interested in first was Henry James. He was writing some rather brilliant parodies when he was only seventeen. He also read the Transcendentalists, Emerson and Thoreau in particular, and you find him, even in the early twenties, when American literature was not considered of any importance, urging his friends to read Thoreau and Emerson.

Question: Professor Sukenick, where do you see the current trend going in about fifteen years?

Sukenick: I don't think I've thought that far ahead. I think it's unpredictable. I think it depends on a lot of cultural and sociological variables, which enter into the work, which I can't pretend to know about. I also think that it's dangerous to try to think about art as a historical progression with movements succeeding one another because then you are always looking for the next wave and its rationale. And finally the rationale, the criticism, becomes more important than the work. So I prefer to make statements that are dispensable, that you can throw away like kleenex. And the kind of suggestions I make in these digressions are like that. I hesitate to make any kind of prediction because in a way the very idea of my paper is that fiction is unpredictable as well as undefinable, except by itself.

Question: Doesn't that imply that writers themselves would make the best critics?

Sukenick: There was a time, I have heard, at Harvard, when they were thinking of hiring Nabokov, and somebody said, "Well, you don't need the elephant in the zoology class." But I would like to insist that there is a kind of writer's criticism that is extremely important and there are kinds of that criticism that straddle both academic and non-academic realms, Eliot's for example. I would say that that kind of criticism is largely unknown in the academic area. It's very important to writers, and at its best moments consistantly produces the best criticism on any terms. I would also like to argue that writers are becoming more conscious of what they are doing and more able to tell you what they are doing. I know that many writers still don't like to talk about what they are doing because they feel it spoils the mystery. But I suspect that may be a pose which perpetuates facile mysteries. There will always be a mystery, of course. But I do think that fiction writers and poets are capable of making their own case on an equal basis with academic criticism.

Nagel: You commented that there might be a healthy period for a writer in which he was not immensely popular in a commercial sense but during which there was a supportive coterie. I am wondering if the terminology developed by Professor Cawelti in his thinking about celebrity and fame would give you another set of terms in which to express those ideas. Was your fear one of the generation of celebrity and the possibility of its interfering with the creative process?

Sukenick: Well, it doesn't give me another set of terms, but it gives me some further thoughts. One of the problems is the problem of the audience, which makes the celebrity. That is, it is normal and red-blooded and American to want to sell a lot of copies of a lot of books and reach a large audience, and maybe it's a healthy and a good impulse, in fact, and not merely a greedy one, because we live in a country with an essentially populist, democratic rationale. On the other hand, it is not always possible to reach that kind of audience. Some writers can never be for everyone. Some writers are just for a select audience. One of the problems is the lack of stable, self-confident, reliable, and quickly perceptive critical establishment in this country. If you think about the reviewing mediums that are available, especially in fiction, the *New York Times Book Review* doesn't do that badly for what it is, but it's basically an organ allied to the commercial establishment. And there is nothing beyond that, except the kinds of things which academics write, concerning which there is a large gap between the production of a book and the appearance of something about it, so long that the book, and possibly the author, has died in the interim. I think that we need a good book reviewing medium and a good critical medium.

Question: Could you mention some recent writers who have also written significant criticism?

Sukenick: I will suggest two. One is Charles Olson, whose critical writing became enormously important in the sixties. And Jack Kerouac didn't write that much, but now it turns out that he was the center of the development of the "beat" generation" aesthetic. A specific example of the kind of critical, theoretical idea that creative writing develops occurred in the mid-fifties when Jack Spicer was talking about something called the "serial poem," a poem that doesn't end in one poem but is continued in another poem. It seems, from an academic, critical point of view, an insignificant idea, but in fact, because of the context of the poetry situation, it was a very important idea to poets because it did things like break down the idea of closure at the end of the poem, creating a more open poetry.

Question: Professor Turner, why haven't Black writers used Black history, especially the slave narrative, more extensively?

Turner: I am criticizing novelists more than other writers. Even though Black poets and dramatists have not used the slave experience as much as I think they could have, one can find in the poets and dramatists a use of the legends of the Black past. What I've suggested in my paper for this conference is not necessarily a direction for writers who aim towards a non-Black audience. The Black writers I envisage would not necessarily be writing to appeal to that white (or non-Black) audience. Instead, they would be writing for Black people. Thinking of a white American audience, many white writers have mythicized the American South and Southerners. I am perfectly willing to have someone else encourage them to continue. They want to inspire their own group, and I believe they have that right. So, when I'm talking about Black writers, I feel justified in wanting Black writers to glamorize or even exaggerate Black people of the past. I believe that this aspect of myth-making is more important than derogation of white historical figures. I admit that my feelings can be wounded when some of my heroes are distorted. I was wounded by Styron's distortion of Nat Turner in *The Confessions of Nat Turner*. I was fascinated that a columnist for a newspaper in Greensboro, North Carolina, didn't seem to know what the fuss was about when Blacks complained about Styron's characterization of Nat. But when *The Lion in Winter* portrayed Richard as a homosexual, that same writer had a fit on the literary page for about three consecutive weeks. Because I dislike distortions of my heroes, I wouldn't really encourage Black writers to slander white historical figures. And I can't really think of one Black novel in which there is a major white historical figure who is turned into a villain. The villains are fictional characters.

Question: Would you comment on the role of protest, of outrage, in Black poetry of the sixties?

Turner: It is significant that you ask about poetry. I think you don't find as much "outrage" in Black fiction of the sixties because much of it had been expressed in the forties. Even though James Baldwin was being called an "angry young man" during the sixties, Baldwin tried to say that he was not writing protest. In fact, if critics really look carefully at Baldwin's novels, even in the sixties Baldwin is preaching a sermon of love. Black outrage was limited primarily to poetry and drama because these were forms that were controlled by Blacks. Blacks could produce them without real concern about whether a white press would accept their views. You can find bitterness, you can find outrage in works of Black fiction during the sixties, but it's not of the degree that one associates with the militant, revolutionary Black Arts poetry.

Nagel: Professors Friedman and Turner have both written about
              various aspects of ethnic literature in America, as well as,
              especially in the case of Professor Friedman, about regional
              literature. Looking at the full sweep of American fiction that
              we have covered in these two days, I'm wondering if what
              we generalize as "American Fiction" is not really an
              amalgamation of various strains without a central core that
              represents a "standardized" American fiction. Since we are
              largely a nation of immigrants, are not American writers, to
              some extent, unavoidably writing out of their own ethnic
              and regional conditions?

Turner: Now you're almost touching off another speech, which
              would be longer than my prepared one. One of the problems
              of Black writers has been the fact that they have been pushed
              into a separate camp in such a way that their depictions of
              life have not been accepted as "universal." In contrast, the
              same kinds of experiences, if drawn from the lives of other
              ethnic groups, *have* been considered "universal." Last year
              in a seminar on fiction, I discussed *The Hit*, a novel by a
              Black writer, Julian Mayfield. It is the story of a middle-aged
              Black man who has decided that all of his life has been
              humdrum; he is now going to do something revolutionary.
              The most he can do in his experience is to win a fortune by
              gambling on the numbers. But he believes that one day he
              will hit the numbers; and on that day, he will finally ask the
              attractive middle-aged woman down the street to run away
              with him and start a new life in California. On the back cover
              of the paperback edition of Mayfield's book were excerpts
              from critical appraisals emphasizing that this was what life
              in Harlem was all about.

                    About the time of World War I, however, there
              appeared in New York a very popular German play called
              From Morn to Midnight, which was the story of a bank
              cashier in Germany who embezzled money with the hope
              that the woman down the street, who was also middle-aged,
              would run away with him. Critical appraisals called that
              play universal, but I find myself asking, "What's the
              difference between the frustrated Black American in New
              York and the frustrated German?" Critics' refusal to find
              "universality" in Black experience has affected some of the
              Black writers of the 1960s, who have said, "We're never
              going to break through this, therefore let's not try anymore.

As long as we're continuously trying to write for a white public that does not know us, as long as we're trying to educate them as to who we are, then we will never be able to fully develop as writers; we'll still remain at an elementary level. Therefore, whether we're going to be read or not, let's write our stories as we need to write them." I'd be the first to admit that some of the kinds of novels I'm asking for probably are going to be published only by vanity presses and read by relatively few people while the *Gone with the Winds* remain popular with white American readers year after year. But I don't want to take too long on this subject since it is directed to Dr. Friedman also.

Friedman: Well, I think we tend very largely for teaching purposes to categorize everything, and of course there are these overlaps. Ishmael Reed is Black but he is a kind of surfictionist: which category do you put him in? Ron Sukenick is a surfictionist and a Jewish writer who occasionally uses Jewish themes. Every region has to have its distinctive literature. I talked about Southern fiction, but of course there's southwestern and midwestern. I felt very keenly the need to speak about Black writers since 1950, but I assumed Darwin Turner would be doing that. And so I didn't say a word about a novel as important as *Invisible Man* which has not been mentioned yet, a very great novel, but I felt that this would somehow come up elsewhere. And maybe Ron Sukenick was getting at all this in his remarks about criticism. We do far too much of this categorization and placing of people and deciding that we have to use these categories.

Sukenick: I think one of the most important developments in these talks is Professor Stern's remarks about "denying;" the writer wants to deny American reality. I feel that, as a Jewish writer, my writing is not particularly strong in Jewish content. Let me illustrate by telling you something that a prominent Jewish writer once said to me. He said he felt English was not really his language and that he had an enormous amount of aggression toward the language. Which puts him somewhat in the position of Joyce, who wrote in English. I think it's possible that something which is very potent in American fiction is that there are many groups in the country which feel that the accepted American reality is not their reality, and therefore it "denies" them. And one response to it is to deny that reality but then to go ahead and try through fiction to re-invent that reality.

Question: Have we said enough about the important traditions of feminine writing in the nineteenth century? There must be forty or fifty women writers who were enormously successful.

Meserole: Who outsold every male novelist, whose novels ran into more editions, printings, issues, and reprintings, than any male novelist, and who made more money than any male novelist.

Wagner: I was all set to speak to this after Professor Turner and then the subject shifted. I did mention Gertrude Stein rather prominently, saying that we need to resurrect her, and I mentioned Edith Wharton, but my approach is usually craft-oriented and I'm afraid that most of the novelists we think of as modernists were really not picking up on what was happening. But I think if we're going to look at contemporary writers, we have to be very much aware of the pockets we get into. Joyce Carol Oates has certainly been mining the Realism-Naturalism vein, although I don't think she's where most American women novelists are right now. But that doesn't mean she can't have her own little pocket that she fills very well. This suggests some kind of critical impasse that we're all in and I'm as guilty of it as the next person and when you work hard to get women in, you feel somehow as though you have critically flipped over into that category, which the Academy does not much admire, of feminist criticism.

Turner: May I ask a question about that last comment, because it's related to an idea that I have about Black writers? You mentioned that, in a chronological study of craft, you find some of the women writers not as advanced artistically as the men. Is there a possibility that this limitation is the result of the isolation of female writers; that is that they did not have the opportunity to identify and associate with some of the individuals who were engaged in exploratory "avant-garde" writing? Certainly, if one looks at Black writers, one sees only two or three in the twentieth century who have had close association with white avant-garde writers in America. Has this been the situation with women also?

Wagner: It is not just isolation, it is also being able to learn from other women writers that have preceded you. If the people you're working with are largely male, then you're fighting for your own intellectual honesty; I suppose all the way along you're at odds with the very people who probably should be supporting you, and Virginia Woolf's observation was that it will probably be a hundred years before we have *great* women poets.

Friedman: Well, something just came to mind. Jerome Rothenberg has invented a word, "ethnopoetics," which somehow combines a great deal of what we've been saying. His own poetry, of course, is a marvelous expression of it. He's lived with Indian tribes. His poetry responds to a certain ethnicity which is a very strange mixture: his New York Jewish background and his living with American Indians, and so on. There is a strange and vital kind of blending of things in Rothenberg's work. And Rothenberg deserves to be better known and more widely read than he is. He's becoming a major figure.

Meserole: I would remind you that the first major woman poet in English was Anne Bradstreet. She was a genuine artist. She was a woman who thought deeply and warmly and carefully and wrote wry commentary about her "rambling brat" taken to England and published in rags without her knowing it. I always get a little uneasy when criticism begins to take directions I feel tentative about, and one of the things I feel very uneasy with in working with earlier periods, colonial American particularly, is ethnic distinction. I think a great deal of effort has gone into trying to exhume the writings of every Black man and every Black woman in American literature, and I'm glad it has. In the process we have given very careful concern to Phillis Wheatley, for example, whose design for writing, whose reasons for writing, were so distinct from any modern woman that we have to set her apart. And yet every technique, every force, has gone to place her in a line of Black women writers or Black male writers from the beginning of America's history to the present, and I feel uneasy with that. I would like to raise the point that particularly in the early period we have to be as much concerned with the audience for what was written as for the writer who wrote it. As John Cawelti shows in a very fine recent book, formulas for writing were imposed upon writers or they didn't get published. You write according to

the formula or forget it. It seems to me those things have to
be taken into account in criticism: they may be non-literary,
but they must be reckoned with.

Turner: I want to point out that just as Anne Bradstreet should be
recognized, Phillis Wheatley, a Black slave, was the second
woman in America to have a volume of poetry published.
But I don't think there should be any uneasiness about setting
forth a line of writers of any group. Certainly Phillis
Wheatley is markedly different from many of the female
Black and white American writers of the twentieth century.
But consider what is conventionally done in literary
scholarship: by selecting almost any arbitrary pattern, one
can identify a group—Romantics, New England writers,
Southern writers, and so forth. Yet, when certain groups—
such as Black writers—are identified, an uneasiness
develops. Now I will grant that there are some Black writers
of the 1960s and 1970s who have tried to impose their own
definitions and to say that Phillis Wheatley should be *out*
because a line of communication including her is not
ideologically correct. But if one says, as I do, that Afro-
American Literature is literature by anyone of African
ancestry who has resided in the United States long enough to
be influenced by the culture, then Phillis Wheatley is in the
line; and the line is not only Black, it is also American. But this
fact is seldom considered by some of the anthologists who
omit Afro-American authors even though those authors are
very American in their writing. One last comment: Gwendolyn Brooks, in her early volumes of poetry, was following
the practice of writing about people she knew best; these
were Black people. But, if you read some of the poems
without knowing that she is a Black woman, it would be very
difficult to detect that they are about problems any different
from those faced by many people who are poor, problems
faced by women whose boyfriends, sons, and husbands are
going off to war. Yet a major American poet-critic once said
that Gwendolyn Brooks obviously wrote about Black
people, and that, as long as she wrote about Black people,
she was writing about a minor subject and would remain a
minor poet. Incidentally, there's no absence of female
writers in Black literature. I do recognize that many teachers
and scholars focus excessively on such males as Ralph
Ellison, Richard Wright, and James Baldwin, but

anytime one traces Black American literary history, one finds Black women writers prominent in every genre and in every generation—from Lucy Terry and Phillis Wheatley in the eighteenth century to the present.

Nagel: Professor Winner, I think you should follow up.

Winner: Well, it seems to me that some women writers have been neglected because of a bias in criticism, Edith Wharton, for example. She was not neglected in her own time, she sold very well and was critically recognized. But it seems to me that here is a major writer who hasn't really been given her due until fairly recently. Similarly Sarah Orne Jewett and Willa Cather. There are a lot of American women writers who aren't taught in courses because they don't fit into the patterns that are popular in teaching. Insofar as women writers have tended to write more about society with a small "s" rather than a captial "S," that is, more in the domestic, manners vein than men writers, and to be more conservative, they tend to be viewed as minor, as less important than writers who are more overtly conceptual and broader in their social interests. As an example of determinism, Dreiser is much more likely to be cited or used than Wharton, though Lily Bart is as much a "wisp on the tide" as Sister Carrie.

Nagel: I'm not sure what it means to be neglected. My wife and I spent a good deal of the summer looking at some seven hundred items on Sarah Orne Jewett, which strikes me as being a fairly substantial list. At least it did when we read through it. I think perhaps there is not enough recognition and understanding of what is actually there. The matter of what is in print is, of course, a serious issue because it determines what can be taught. Jewett's *A Country Doctor* should be in paperback. Louisa May Alcott's novel *Work* is out of print and yet should be taught. We could quickly assemble a lengthy list of works that we would like to teach that are simply not available.

Comment: This is a major problem that we have. Professor Cawelti was talking about the general reading public, and yet there is a special class, in the colleges, of reading public that has grown since World War II, while the general reading public has shrunk and gone to television.

Katz: A practical comment on the commercial test, on the quality
            paperback and the classroom anthology. I have a prediction,
            and I would bet a lot on it, that you will find that fewer and
            fewer quality paperbacks will be produced. What I'm
            saying is the quality paperback and the college paper text
            are both doomed. They're dying out. There are two reasons
            for this that I see. One is the age of photocopy. All of the
            people who are depending on royalties are being financially
            hurt and, therefore, the outlets diminish. Equally important,
            and perhaps much more interesting, is that there was a time
            when the survey course, the undergraduate entry level
            courses, were regimented. The publisher could count on
            hitting it very big or very, very small, so he would publish a
            series which included *Main-Travelled Roads* and *The Wept
            of Wish-ton-Wish* and he knew that if the series hit he could
            count on ten thousand copies, and so publishers were risk
            oriented at that time. But mention *Kelroy* to a publisher
            today and it clears the room, and it has nothing at all to do
            with the merits of the novel. We have put ourselves in a
            situation in which what we're talking about is the un-
            availability of certain writers. Ernest Hemingway and F.
            Scott Fitzgerald some day will be the only people available
            in paperbacks.

Nagel: I think it is important to note that in the period that Joe's
            paper covered, the post-Civil War period in America, the
            major writers carrying on New England regionalism were
            women: Rose Terry Cooke, Mary Wilkins Freeman, and
            Sarah Orne Jewett represented, in one sense, a kind of
            conservative norm for New England regionalism. And yet
            very few of their works are still in print.

Sukenick: I think one place where ethical responsibility is most
            important as a special and institutional factor is in the
            publishing industry. One should not underestimate the
            influence of the New York publishing establishment in
            forming and encouraging the kinds of novels that are
            predominent in a given area and for supressing other kinds.
            The New York publishers have become enormously profit-
            oriented: they deal in units, in sales units, that are so large
            that it is not even worth publishing a book that can make a
            modest profit, so an enormous number of things get cut out.
            The kind of novel that tends to get accepted, for example, by

ethnic writers, by Black writers, tends to be the kind of "subject matter novel" that has to do basically with sociology rather than the art of fiction. The kind of novel that tends to get accepted and pushed by the publishers are those which will be saleable in areas where money is made, in movies and subsidiary rights. A novel that's going to sell to the movies requires plot and character, and therefore that kind of novel still predominates. There may be an audience for many other kinds of novels, small, modest, but reasonable audiences, but the publishers don't let the books speak to those audiences.

Aaron: I think it was pointed out as early as about 1905 that stories in magazines were carefully selected to buttress the things that were being advertised.

Katz: I don't want to be misunderstood; I was talking about Mary E. Wilkins Freeman, Edith Wharton, rather than novelists of this generation. I was talking, in other words, about the "quality paperback" which is addressed to a limited audience, in large part to teachers who will use the books in undergraduate courses, not to trade publishing today. But I agree with you about the conglomerates taking over and cutting short an awful lot that could be developing. One of the factors is that we have a smaller novel reading audience and larger manufacturing costs, and I gather that trade publishers publishing a novel feel lucky to break even and depend on subsidiary rights sales for profits.

Sukenick: That's the line the publishers take but I don't believe it. For example, judging by the way books sell in the millions these days, it seems that there's a larger novel reading audience. Television, which is usually perceived as interfering with that audience, may, in fact, build up the audience.

Meserole: Part of the problem involves the novel that is written today and is expected to have a life of only six months or a year. The publisher has few storage costs; he has relatively small distributional costs; his advertising budget is decided ahead of time. What we're after, I think, in having novels in print for teaching, is not a life of six months or a year; we want them in print three or four years, or more. So we have a problem in keeping them in print—more than just getting them into print.

Nagel: It is customary and, I think, appropriate to conclude
           festivities of this sort with an expression of gratitude to the
           people who have contributed. It would be a very long list in
           this case. Obviously our speakers have sacrificed a good deal
           of their valuable time and energy to not only travel here but
           to work on their papers. To them, of course, we are all
           deeply grateful. But a number of my colleagues have also
           contributed in important ways to the success of this
           Symposium. While I have been at the front enjoying the
           papers and comments, Wally Coyle has been at the back
           making sure that we were able to proceed on schedule and
           without technical complications. Guy Rotella and Candy
           Brook not only handled registration but worked to ensure
           that these two days would be as comfortable for all of us as
           possible. Many of our graduate students worked behind the
           scenes on the small details that we tend to take for granted.
           The members of our audience were remarkably faithful in
           attending more than a dozen hours of papers and discussions
           and they have made important additions with their com-
           ments and questions. On behalf of the Northeastern Univer-
           sity community, I want to express our appreciation to all of
           you. Thank you.

INDEX

Aaron, Daniel, vi, 127-141, 180, 182, 185, 190, 201
Abish, Walter, 95
Adams, Henry, 127, 129
Adams, John Quincy, 27
Aderman, Ralph, 2
Adkins, Nelson F., 2
Afro-American Literature, 109-126, 192-199
Alcott, Louisa May, 199
Allan, Harry T., viii
Allibone, Samuel, 5
Allston, Washington, 146
Alter, Robert, 82
"American Fiction: A Bicentennial Symposium," i, viii, 175
Anderson, Sherwood, 65-67, 69, 70-71, 74
Archibold, William, 92
Arnold, Matthew, 112, 136
Attaway, William, 116
Attucks, Crispus, 111
Austin, William, 4
Austen, Jane, 45

Baldwin, James, 118, 193, 198
Balzac, Honoré de, 54
Banks, Russell, 99
Barth, John, 67, 72, 79, 84, 93, 99-100; *Chimera*, 84; *The End of the Road*, 84-85; *The Floating Opera*, 84-85; *Lost in the Funhouse: Fiction for Print, Tape, Live Voice*, 95; *The Sot-Weed Factor*, 84
Barthelme, Donald, 72, 79, 99, 106
Bateson, F.W., ii
Baumbach, Jon, 99
Beckett, Samuel, 84, 93-94; *Watt*, 91
Belknap, Jeremy, 12
Bellow, Saul, v, 52, 67, 81, 87-88, 99, 140, 172; *Dangling Man*, 81-82; *Herzog*, 87, 184; *Humboldt's Gift*, 81; *Seize the Day*, 81, *The Victim*, 82
Berger, Thomas, 162
Bergson, Henri, 67, 69
Bishop, John Peale, 132; *White Oxen and Other Stories*, 134

Blair, Walter, 162
Blechman, Burt, 87
Bloom, Harold, 102-103
Bode, Carl, 163
Bontemps, Arna, 123; *Black Thunder*, 112, 114-116; *Drums at Dusk*, 112, 116; *God Sends Sunday*, 114
Boyeson, H. H., 35
Brackenridge, Hugh Henry, 5, 10; *Modern Chivalry*, 4
Bradstreet, Anne, 197-198
Brautigan, Richard, 99
Bridgman, Richard, 162
Broner, E.M., 72
Brontë, Emily, 101
Brontë [Sisters], 161
Brook, Van Wyck, 162, 168
Brooks, Cleanth, 65
Brooks, Gwendolyn, 118, 198
Brown, Charles Brockden, 1, 3, 5; *Arthur Mervyn*, 4; *Edgar Huntly*, 4; "A Lesson on Concealment," 2; "Memoirs of Mary Selwyn," 2; *Wieland*, 4, 8
Brown, William Hill, 4, 176
Brown, William Wells, 111
Browstein, Michael, 99
Bryher, Winifred, 68
Buck, Pearl, 69
Burke, Edmund, 7
Burke, Kenneth, 130, 133, 138-39; *Counter-Statement*, 133; *Towards a Better Life*, 131, 133-135
Butor, Michael, 80-81, 91-92
Byron, George Gordon [Lord], 166-167
Bumpus, Jerry, 99

Cady, Edwin H., iii, 37, 40
Camus, Albert, 81, 84
Capote, Truman, 89, 92-93, 100, 171
Carter, Everett, 36, 40, 49
Cather, Willa, 65, 70-71, 199; *O Pioneers!* 71
Cawelti, John G., 8, 161-174, 186-189
Cézanne, Paul, 186

Index

Freeman, Mary E. Wilkins, 200-201
Freneau, Philip, 2; *Father Bombo's Pilgrimage*, 4
Fussell, Edwin, 162
Friedman, Bruce J., 72, 87, 100; *About Harry Towns*, 87; *The Dick*, 87; *A Mother's Kisses*, 88; *Stern*, 87
Friedman, Melvin J., iv, 79-98, 184-185, 195, 197
Frohlich, William A., viii
Fuchs, Daniel, 85, 89; *Williamsburg Trilogy*, 85

Gaines, Ernest, 112, 123
Garland, Hamlin, 200
Gass, William H., 79, 93, 101; *In the Heart of the Heart of the Country*, 95; *Omensetter's Luck*, 94; *Willie Master's Lonesome Wife*, 94
Gilder, Richard Watson, 168
Ginsburg, Allen, 106
Gloster, Hugh, 114
Godey's Lady's Book, 14, 15
Grass, Gunther, 84
Grau, Shirley Ann, 90
Greene, Theodore, 14
Griggs, Sutton, 113

Haley, Alex, vi
Halleck, Fitz-Greene, 2
Hammett, Dashiell, 161
Harris, Joel Chandler, 113
Harris, Mark, 84, 86, 95
Hart, James D., 163
Hassan, Ihab, 81-82
Hawkes, John, 68, 72, 79-82, 87, 89, 93-94, 185; *The Beetle-Leg*, 80; *The Blood Oranges*, 80; *The Cannibal*, 79-80; *Death, Sleep and the Traveler*, 80; *The Innocent Party: Four Short Plays*, 80; *The Lime Twig*, 80; *Second Skin*, 80
Hawthorne, Nathaniel, 4, 13, 18, 22-26, 28, 40-42, 53, 134, 143, 145, 148-150, 162, 167; "The Artist of the Beautiful," 29; "The Birth-Mark," 20; *The Blithedale Romance*, 17, 41; "The Celestial Railroad," 20; "The Custom House," 17; "Drowne's Wooden Image," 20; *The House of the Seven Gables*, 41, 146, 148; *The Marble Faun*, 17, 30-31, 148, 150; "Rappaccini's Daughter," 20; "Roger Malvin's

Burial," 20; *The Scarlet Letter*, 15, 30-31; "Sights from a Steeple," 40-41; *Twice-Told Tales*, 15, 41
Hayden, Robert 118
Hearst, Patricia, 174, 189
Heller, Joseph, 68, 72, 100
Hemingway, Ernest, 52, 65-73, 144-145, 149-150, 155-156, 171, 186, 200; *Across the River and into the Trees*, 171; "The Battler," 156; "The Big Two-Hearted River," 156; *Death in the Afternoon*, 144; *A Farewell to Arms*, 146; *Islands in the Stream*, 143-145, 171; *The Old Man and the Sea*, 163
Himes, Chester, 117
Hitchcock, Enos, 5, 12
Hoffman, Charles Fenno, 15
Holmes, Oliver Wendell, 4
Howe, Irving, 67, 75-76
Howells, William Dean, 35-41, 49, 67, 168, 180-181; *Criticism and Fiction*, 43
Hubbard, Elbert, 168
Hughes, Langston, 111, 114
Hulme, T. E., 23-24, 67
Huneker, James Gibbon, 130
Hurston, Zora Neale, 112, 116-117
Hyman, Stanley Edgar, 83, 87

Imagism, 66-67, 69
Imlay, Gilbert, 12
Impressionism, 67, 73, 154-155, 186
Irving, Washington, 4, 149, 165; "The Art of Book-Making," 3; *The Sketch Book*, 146; "Stout Gentlemen," 3

James, Henry, 18, 30, 41, 53, 66, 68-69, 82-83, 101, 105, 127, 146, 149, 150-156, 161, 169, 186-187, 190; *The Ambassadors*, 150-156; *The American*, 162; "The Art of Fiction," 150; *The Bostonians*, 169; *The Portrait of a Lady*, 86, 146-147, 162; *The Princess Casamassima*, 169; "The Real Thing," 150; *Roderick Hudson*, 150; *The Wings of the Dove*, 83
James, William, 41, 67, 69, 73
Jarrell, Randall, 83
Jefferson, Thomas, 162
Jewett, Sarah Orne, 199, 200
Johnson, Edward, 20-21
Johnson, James Weldon, 110

205

Index

Index